Spanish

Phrase Book & Dictionary

Kate - 231 977
Pedro - 231/24   Rin 83

Proolongación pu los Incas #
1721

Tfno - 234385

Carola de Yábar
Kate - 241 668
Magistras II G-15

Other languages in the *Collins Phrase Book & Dictionary* series:

FRENCH

GERMAN

GREEK

ITALIAN

JAPANESE

PORTUGUESE

These titles are also published in a Language pack containing
60-minute CD/cassette and phrase book

HarperCollins*Publishers*
Westerhill Road,
Bishopbriggs, Glasgow G64 2QT

www.collins.co.uk

First published 2004

Reprint 10 9 8 7 6 5 4 3 2 1 0

© HarperCollins*Publishers* 2004

ISBN 0 00-716527-7

Typeset by Davidson Pre-Press Graphics Ltd, Glasgow

Printed in Italy by Amadeus SpA

Introduction

Your *Collins Phrase Book & Dictionary* is a handy, quick-reference guide that will help you make the most of your stay abroad. Its clear layout will save you valuable time when you need that crucial word or phrase. There are four main sections in this book:

Everyday Spain – photoguide

Packed full of photos, this section allows you to see all the practical visual information that will help with using cash machines, driving on motorways, reading signs, etc.

Phrases

Practical topics are arranged thematically with an opening section Key talk containing vital phrases that should stand you in good stead in most situations.

Phrases are short, useful and each one has a pronunciation guide so that there is no problem saying them.

Eating out

This section contains phrases for ordering food and drink (and special requirements) plus a photoguide showing different eating places, menus and practical information to help choose the best options. The menu reader allows you to work out what to choose.

Dictionary

The practical 5000-word English-Spanish and Spanish-English Dictionary means that you won't be stuck for words.

And finally, there is a short Grammar section explaining how the language works.

So, just flick through the pages to find the information you need. Why not start with a look at Pronouncing Spanish on page 6. From there on the going is easy with your *Collins Phrase Book & Dictionary*.

Useful websites

Currency Converters
www.x-rates.com

Foreign Office Advice
www.fco.gov.uk/travel/
  countryadvice.asp

Passport Office
www.ukpa.gov.uk

Health advice
www.thetraveldoctor.com
www.doh.gov.uk/traveladvice

Pets
www.defra.gov.uk/animalh/
  quarantine/index.htm

Transport
www.renfe.es
  (National rail network)
www.raileurope.com
  *(Info on Train travel and
  passes)*
www.iberia.es *(National airline)*
www.metromadrid.es
  (Madrid metro)
www.metrobilbao.net
www.tmb.net
  (Barcelona)

Driving
www.aseta.es
  (Spanish motorways)
www.dgt.es

Sightseeing
www.tourspain.es *(National
  Tourist Office site: links to
  national parks, what's on, etc.)*
www.revistaiberica.com
www.okspain.org
  (To Spain from the US)
www.goski.com *(Skiing info
  for Pyrenees and Andalucia)*

Internet Cafés
www.netcafes.com

Culture & Activities
www.surinenglish.com
  *(Costa del Sol news in
  English)*
www.gomadrid.com
  (What's on in Madrid)
www.cyberspain.com
www.webmadrid.com
  (Information on the capital)

Hotels
www.hostels.com/es.html
  (Hostel accommodation)
www.parador.es *(Paradors)*

Contents

Pronouncing Spanish

We've tried to make the pronunciation under the phrases as clear as possible. We've broken the words up to make them easy to read, but don't pause between syllables. The syllable to be stressed is shown in **heavy type**. Spanish isn't really hard to pronounce and once you learn a few basic rules, it shouldn't be too long before you can read straight from the Spanish.

Most letters are pronounced as in English: **b**, **ch**, **d**, **f**, **k**, **l**, **m**, **n**, **p**, **s**, **t**, **y** and (usually) **w** and **x**.

As for the vowels, **a** is always as in **tap** (never as in **tape**); **e** is always as in **pet** (never as in **Pete**); **i** is always 'ee'; **o** is always as in **hop** (never as in **hope**); **u** is always 'oo' rather than the English sound **hut**. They keep their sound even in combination with other letters, so 'au' (eg **autobus** ow-to-boos) is like English 'ow', not like English **automatic**.

The letter **h** is always silent, and **r** is always rolled (even more strongly when double **r**). Spanish **v** and **b** are pronounced exactly the same, something like English **b**, while **q** is like English **k**.

The letter **c** before **e** or **i** and the letter **z** are pronounced like the **th** in **thin**. The letter **g** before **e** or **i** and the letter **j** have the guttural sound you hear in the Scottish word **loch** and which we show as **kh**.

Basic rules to remember are:

Spanish		sounds like	example	pronunciation
ll		million	**calle**	*ka-lye*
ñ		onion	**mañana**	*man-ya-na*
c		cat	**comer**	*ko-mer*
c	(before e/i)	think	**hacer**	*a-ther*
g		got	**gafas**	*ga-fas*
g	(before e/i)	loch	**hijo**	*ee-kho*
z		think	**zapatos**	*tha-pa-tos*
j		loch	**hijo**	*ee-kho*
q		kick	**quiero**	*kyer-o*

OPEN

Most shops close for lunch, approx. 1.30–4.30pm and stay open till about 8.30pm.

CLOSED

CERRADO

PAY HERE

The word *caja* actually means till or cash box.

ENTRANCE

Look out for the words *entrada libre* which mean free entry (for museums, etc).

FORBIDDEN

The word for forbidden is *prohibido*.

EXIT

Salida is also used for exit on motorways.

TIMETABLE

horario

The word for hour is *hora* (the 'h' isn't sounded.)

PUSH

PULL

TIRAR

YOU

The polite word for 'you' is *Usted* (abbreviated to *Vd.*).

Usted está aquí means 'you are here.'

OUT OF ORDER

If something is working, you will see the words *en servicio*.

OUT OF ORDER

no funciona

INFORMATION
You will notice in Mallorca that the Spanish is slightly different. This is Mallorquín.

ICE FOR SALE
hielo = ice

Symbol for the euro. Spain is in the euro zone.

 Prices are generally written with a comma. This is the price per kilo (*kg*).

 **PRICES**

Cash machines are known as *cajero automático* and are widely available. You can carry out the transaction in English and it saves time queuing in banks to change money. Check your bank's handling fee before you go on holiday.

Most banks can be identified by the word *Banco* or *Caja*. The big banks in Spain include *BBVA*, *Banco de Santander*, *Caixa de Cataluña* and *Caja España*. Banks are generally open in the morning until about 2 pm.

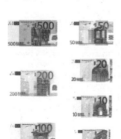

The euro is the currency of Spain. It breaks down into 100 euro cents. Notes: 5, 10, 20, 50, 100, 200, 500. Coins: 2 euro, 1 euro, 50 cent, 20 cent, 10 cent, 5 cent, 2 cent, 1 cent.

Although coins are officially *cents*, Spanish people call them *céntimos* (*then-tee-mos*), a more familiar Spanish term. Euro is pronounced *eoo-ro*.

Euro notes are the same throughout Europe. The backs of coins carry different designs from each of the member European countries.

Some cash dispensers are accessed by swiping your card in the door. Either the green light will flash for you to enter (*acceso libre*) or the red light will flash to indicate out of service (*fuera de servicio*).

Importe exacto = coins
No devuelve cambio = no change given.

monedas   COINS

Cash machines operate as at home.
Borrar = clear
Cancelar = cancel
Anotación = proceed

ONLY CARDS (for paying toll)

Tipping in Spain is usually about 5-10% of the bill. This is to cover service which is generally not included.

recibo   RECEIPT

billetes   BANKNOTES

Tobacconists are known as *estancos,* state-licensed shops which sell tobacco products, stamps, bus tickets, postcards and basic stationery. Look out for the maroon sign with the yellow script and the leaf logo. If you want stamps it is much easier to buy them here. Post offices are not as easy to come across.

Friends and acquaintances usually greet each other with a kiss on each cheek if one of the people is female. Greetings between men involve a simple shake of the hand. Even if you are introduced to someone for the first time, the same rules apply.

POLICE The *Policía local/municipal* deals with local bylaws and parking. The emergency no. is 092. The *Guardia Civil* deals with traffic accidents and driving offences.

SE VENDE 270544

se vende = for sale

se alquila = for rent

KEEP TICKET UNTIL EXIT

CONSERVE SU ENTRADA HASTA LA SALIDA

The word for a transport ticket is *billete* or *tique* (for bus) and *entrada* for entry ticket to museum, cinema, etc.

TOURIST INFORMATION

OFICINA DE TURISMO

The tourist office can help with accommodation, local attractions and transport, etc. There will usually be one English-speaker in the office.

Accommodation is divided into several different categories: hotels, *pensiones* and *hostales*. There is not much difference between the latter two. They are usually owned by a live-in proprietor, like very large guest-houses, and do not provide meals.

Most tourist beaches have a lifeguard and flag system. They are cleaned regularly and have shower (but not changing) facilities.

AGOTADO **SOLD OUT**

Museo MUSEUM

Most museums close one day a week, normally Mon. In this sign the museum is closed Tue (*Martes Cerrado*). *Domingos* = Sundays.

HORARIO
De 10:00 a 21:00.
Domingos de 10:00 a 14:30
Martes Cerrado

There are 3 dates worth mentioning when admission in some museums is free. These are: May 18th (International Museum Day), October 12th (Spanish National Holiday), and December 6th (Constitution Day). You can sometimes also get a discount with an International Student Card.

Playa = beach
Hamacas = sunshades

This sign indicates restricted swimming areas.

The word for post office is Correos. Signs and postboxes are yellow.

 SWIMMING POOL

You must wear a swimming cap at all indoor pools.

GENTS

LADIES

ENGAGED

VACANT

LIBRE

NOT DRINKING WATER
The word for water is *agua* (*ag-wa*).

When sending normal letters or cards, find a yellow postbox. If you have a choice, use the slot marked *EXTRANJERO* (Overseas).

Red boxes are for a faster service (*urgente*) for which you pay a higher rate.

TOILETS Look out for the words *Servicios* and *Aseos*, both mean toilets.

SERVICIOS

Spanish people are very conscious about recycling. Most homes have 2 or 3 different rubbish bins: one for organic material, one for inorganic material and one for paper. The containers in the street are labelled: blue for paper, yellow for containers and inorganic material, grey for organic material and green for glass.

Don't be fooled by the letters on the taps. *C* is for *caliente* which means hot and *F* is for *frío* which means cold.

Timetables

LOS DÍAS	THE DAYS
lunes *loo-nes*	Monday
martes *mar-tes*	Tuesday
miércoles *myer-ko-les*	Wednesday
jueves *khweb-es*	Thursday
viernes *byer-nes*	Friday
sábado *sa-ba-do*	Saturday
domingo *dom-een-go*	Sunday

In Spanish, neither months nor days start with a capital letter as they do in English.

LOS MESES	THE MONTHS
enero *en-er-o*	January
febrero *feb-rer-o*	February
marzo *mar-tho*	March
abril *av-reel*	April
mayo *ma-yo*	May
junio *khoon-yo*	June
julio *khool-yo*	July
agosto *a-gos-to*	August
septiembre *sep-tyem-bre*	September
octubre *ok-too-bre*	October
noviembre *nob-yem-bre*	November
diciembre *deeth-yem-bre*	December

departures   arrivals   frequency

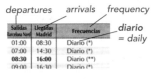

diario = daily

Salidas Barcelona Nord	Llegadas Madrid	Frecuencias
01:00	08:30	Diario (*)
07:00	14:30	Diario (*)
08:30	**16:00**	Diario (**)
09:00	16:30	Diario (*)

OPENING HOURS

Horario de Apertura

Lunes a Viernes: — Mon to Fri
de 8:30 a 20:30 h.

Sábados: — Saturdays
de 9:30 a 14:00 h.

Domingos y Festivo : — Sun and holidays closed
CERRADO

TIMETABLE
Horarios = times

FECHA   DATE

mañana   MORNING

tarde   AFTERNOON

READING TIMETABLES

LLEGADAS
ARRIVALS

RETRASADO

DELAYED

(1) No circula los domingos. —— no service on Sundays
(2) Tren Lince. Circula los viernes.—— Lince train. Runs on Fridays

SALIDAS
DEPARTURES

(1) Para en Calatayud

Para en Calatayud
stops at Calatayud

TRAIN TIMETABLE KEY

Aranjuez	Ciempoz	Valdem	Pinto	Getafe Industrial	Sol
16.00	16.10	**16.15**	16.20	**16.25**	16.
16.30	16.40	16.45	16.50	16.55	16.
17.00	17.10	17.15	17.20	17.25	17.
17.30	17.40	17.45	17.50	17.55	17.

a.: Laborables excepto sábados.
d.: Sábados y festivos.
x.: Efectúa parada en Seseña 5 min. después de Aranjuez.
(1): No circula del 01/08/00 al 01/09/00 ambos inclusive.
(2): Circula diario del 01/08/00 al 01/09/00 ambos inclusive.

a.: *Weekdays (**laborables**) except Saturdays (**sábados**)*
d.: *Saturdays (**sábados**) and holidays (**festivos**)*
x.: *Stops at Seseña 5 minutes after (**después de**) Aranjuez*
(1): *No service (**no circula**) from 01/08/00 to 01/09/00 both (**ambos**) inclusive*
(2): *Daily (**diario**) service from 01/08/00 to 01/09/00 inclusive*

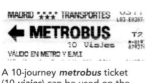

A 10-journey *metrobus* ticket (10 *viajes*) can be used on the metro and buses. When you use it on the bus, you must validate it in the machine beside the driver.

A 10-journey bus ticket is known as a *bono-bus*. It must be validated in the machine next to the driver in the direction of the arrow. These tickets can be used by a group of you, provided it is validated for each person.

paseo and *calle* both mean street.

BASEMENT **HERE**

TOURIST INFORMATION
Notice the slightly different spelling in this Majorcan sign.

plaza (*pla-tha*) = square.
Plaza Mayor means main square

abbreviation for *plaza (pza)* on bus

TOWN CENTRE
Notice the circular pictogram for town centre. This is becoming more common in Europe for meaning centre.

you are on the top floor
VD. = Usted = you
planta = floor
alta = top

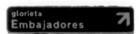

glorieta = roundabout

Playa = beach

Sign on leaving town

market

police station

A & E

town hall.
Notice the spelling on the Majorcan sign

TAXIS
Prices are usually displayed at the taxi stand. Taxis are generally white. If a taxi is free it shows a green light and the word *libre*. If it has passengers it usually shows a red light with the word *ocupado*.

Bus stops with the number of service and stops en route. You should flag down the buses at the stop as they don't always stop automatically.

COACH STANDS

BUS STATION

Tickets for underground and bus on sale here.

The national rail network is called RENFE.

PLATFORM

TRAIN TRAVEL

station

metro

high-speed train

ticket office

long distance
regional

info point

Type of ticket:
sencillo = single
ida y vuelta
(*regreso*) = return

Automatic ticket machines are becoming increasingly common.

City centre (note the circular sign). If you don't see your destination signposted, follow the *todas direcciones* (all routes). To get to the town centre, follow *centro ciudad*.

GUARDED PARKING

FULL

SPACES

LIBRE

In cities and towns note the colour-coding on road signs

white: *major route from a town*

yellow: *places of interest to visitors – the port*

green: *street names*

major route signposted from a town; to the Autovía

NO PARKING
ambos lados = both sides
reservado minusválido = disabled parking

SPANISH SPEED LIMITS
In built-up areas the limit is 50 kph. On ordinary roads 90 kph and on dual carriageways (*autovías*) and motorways (*autopistas*) 120 kph.

PAY & DISPLAY

Indicates that parking must be paid for. Times are Mon-Fri, 9am to 2pm and from 5 to 9pm. On Saturdays from 9am to 2pm.

Spanish motorways are signposted in blue. The speed limit is 120 kph. Motorway info website is **www.aseta.es**. Some motorways *(autopistas)* are free and some carry toll charges (which can be expensive). Look out for the sign **peaje** (toll).

Payment is due on completion of each sector covered. You do not receive tickets.

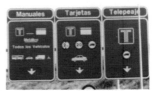

At the toll stop you have a choice of payment: either cash (*Manuales*) for all vehicles (*metálico* means cash), card (*Tarjetas*) or prepaid (*Telepeaje*). *Sólo tarjetas* = cards only

EXIT/JUNCTION 214. The word for exit is **salida**.

AREA DE SERVICIO
Services are available on taking the 162 exit.

PETROL
Colour-coded pumps: black for diesel (*gasóleo*), green for unleaded (*sin plomo*) and red for leaded (*super*). 95-octane petrol is usually fine for most cars, unless they have powerful engines or are towing a caravan.

Garage for repairs. This one offers 24-hour pick-up truck and tyre service for cars.

lavado manual = handwash
cambio de aceite = oil change

ALIMENTACIÓN
General grocer's. Small shops' opening hours are 10am to 2pm and 5pm to 8.30pm.

SALES
Sales usually take place in Jan/Feb and again in Jul/Aug.

SUPERMERCADO

Large supermarkets are found on the outskirts of towns. These include *Pryca*, *Eroski* and *Alcampo*. Locker and present-wrapping areas are usually available. You must leave bags in a locker at the entrance or with an attendant who will give you a token to return as you leave.

 **PAY HERE**

QUICK CHECKOUT
Maximum 10 items

Supermarket trolleys generally take euro coins to release.

OPENING HOURS
Supermarkets and dept. stores stay open all day.

- *summer opening hours*
- *Mon to Sat*
- *open*
- *from 10 in the morning*
- *to 10 at night*
- *Sun and hols closed all day*

MARKET
Larger towns will have a daily market and smaller ones a weekly market.

FARMACIA **PHARMACY** Sells medical items for which you often don't need a doctor's prescription. It's a good place to seek advice for minor ailments and suggested non-prescription medicines (including some antibiotics). Each town has a 'duty chemist'. Every chemist will list the duty chemist rota (*Farmacia de Guardia*) in the window or posted nearby. You can also find this list in local newspapers, including English language ones.

BREAD (*pan*)
When asking for bread, ask for *una barra* (similar to French stick) or the

number of rolls (*bollos*) you want. For a more rounded country loaf, ask for *un pan*.

ORGANIC
Bio generally indicates organic produce.

GLUTEN-FREE
Singlu indicates gluten-free products. In this case gluten-free flour (*harina*) for bread and pastry.

Sin azúcar means without sugar.

CARNICERIA M. SALTO
ESPECIALIDAD EN TERNERA • CERDO • CORDERO

BUTCHER Specialising in veal (*ternera*), pork (*cerdo*) and lamb (*cordero*)

Desnatado means fat free.

You can ask for cheese or ham by the number of slices (*lonchas*) rather than by weight.

Jamón serrano is cured ham; cooked ham is known as *jamón de York*.

MILK (*leche*)
Milk is almost always UHT (long-life). To get the type you want, go by the wording, not the carton colour, as these may vary. Here, blue is for whole milk (*leche entera*), green is semi-skimmed (*semidesnatada*) and pink is skimmed (*desnatada*).

TO TAKE AWAY

para llevar

 **POSTBOXES**

POST OFFICE

Two posting boxes, one for national mail, the other for overseas (*extranjero*).

Addressing an envelope:
Avda./ = abbrev. for *avenida* street
esc. = abbrev. for *escalera* floor
izqda = abbrev. for *izquierda* left
dcha = abbrev. for *derecha* right
3º 2 = 3rd floor, door number 2
postcode and town

Larger cities usually have a phone centre (*locutorio*) where you phone from a booth and pay afterwards (by credit card or cash).

There is no shortage of payphones. If you see it lit up on the display *solo llamadas gratuitas* it means free calls only, i.e. emergency numbers or the operator.

Many places offer deals where you buy a number of hours in advance (e.g. 5, 11, 16), which works out cheaper. However, check how many days you have to use up your hours – some offers are not as good as they look.

Phonecards (*tarjetas telefónicas*) come in denominations of 6 and 12 euros.

 The word for 'at' is *arroba* (ar-ro-ba).

www dot is **WWW.**
tres uve dobles punto
(*tres oo-be dob-les poon-to*).

- Spanish has two forms of address, formal and informal. You should use the informal **tú** only when you know someone well; otherwise use **usted**.
- **Hola** is more informal than **buenos días** or **buenas tardes**.
- The easiest way to ask for something is to name it and add please, **por favor**.

yes	no	that's fine
sí	**no**	**¡vale!**
see	*no*	*ba-le*

please	thank you (very much)	don't mention it
por favor	**(muchas) gracias**	**de nada**
*por fa-**bor***	*(**moo**-chas) **grath**-yas*	*de **na**-da*

hello	goodbye	good night
hola	**adiós**	**buenas noches**
o-la	*a-dyos*	***bwe**-nas **no**-ches*

good morning (until lunch)	good afternoon/evening (until dusk)
buenos días	**buenas tardes**
***bwe**-nos **dee**-as*	***bwe**-nas **tar**-des*

excuse me! (to catch attention)	sorry!	what?
¡oiga por favor!	**¡perdón!**	**¿cómo dice?**
oy**-ga por fa-**bor	*per-**don***	***ko**-mo **dee**-the*

a...	a coffee	2 coffees
un... ('el' words)	**un café**	**dos cafés**
oon...	*oon ka-**fe***	*dos ka-**fes***

a...	a beer	2 beers
una... ('la' words)	**una cerveza**	**dos cervezas**
oo-na...	*oo-na ther-**be**-tha*	*dos ther-**be**-thas*

a coffee and two beers, please
un café y dos cervezas, por favor
*oon ka-**fe** ee dos ther-**be**-thas por fa-**bor***

Key Talk

● *Spanish doesn't often use the words for 'I', 'you', 'he', etc., so to ask a question you simply change the intonation of a statement and put a question mark in your voice:* **¿tiene una habitación?** *(Do you have a room?)*
● *To get someone's attention, you can use* **por favor, señor/señora.**

I'd like...	we'd like...
quería...	queríamos...
ke-__ree__-a...	*ke-__ree__-a-mos...*

I'd like an ice cream	**we'd like to visit Toledo**
quería un helado	queríamos visitar Toledo
ke-__ree__-a oon e-__la__-do	*ke-__ree__-a-mos bee-see-__tar__ to-__le__-do*

do you have...?
¿tiene...?
__tyen__-e...

do you have any milk?	**do you have stamps?**
¿tiene leche?	¿tiene sellos?
__tyen__-e __le__-che	*__tyen__-e __sel__-yos*

do you have a map?	**do you have cheese?**
¿tiene un mapa?	¿tiene queso?
__tyen__-e oon __ma__-pa	*__tyen__-e __ke__-so*

how much is it?	how much does ... cost?
¿cuánto es?	¿cuánto cuesta...?
__kwan__-to es	*__kwan__-to __kwes__-ta...*

how much is the cheese?	**how much is the ticket?**
¿cuánto cuesta el queso?	¿cuánto cuesta el billete?
__kwan__-to __kwes__-ta el __ke__-so	*__kwan__-to __kwes__-ta el beel-__ye__-te*

how much is a kilo?	**how much is each one?**
¿cuánto cuesta el kilo?	¿cuánto cuesta cada uno?
__kwan__-to __kwes__-ta el __kee__-lo	*__kwan__-to __kwes__-ta __ca__-da __oo__-no*

- You often hear the expression **claro**, meaning 'of course' or 'yes'.
- **Hasta luego** (as-ta **lwe**-go) means 'see you later'.
- If you want to apologise for bumping into someone (and perhaps causing them to spill their drink), you say ¡**perdón!** **lo siento** (per-**don** lo **syen**-to), 'excuse me! I'm sorry'.
- Ladies = **señoras**, gents = **caballeros**.

where is...?
¿dónde está...?
don-de es-**ta**...

where are...?
¿dónde están...?
don-de es-**tan**...

where is the station?
¿dónde está la estación?
don-de es-**ta** la es-tath-**yon**

where are the toilets?
¿dónde están los aseos?
don-de es-**tan** los a-**se**-os

is there/are there...?
¿hay...?
aee...

there is no...
no hay...
no aee...

is there a restaurant?
¿hay un restaurante?
aee oon rest-ow-**ran**-te

where is there a chemist?
¿dónde hay una farmacia?
don-de aee **oo**-na far-**math**-ya

are there children?
¿hay niños?
aee **neen**-yos

is there a swimming pool?
¿hay piscina?
aee pees-**thee**-na

there is no hot water
no hay agua caliente
no aee **ag**-wa kal-**yen**-te

there are no towels
no hay toallas
no aee to-**al**-yas

I need...
necesito...
ne-the-**see**-to...

I need a taxi
necesito un taxi
ne-the-**see**-to oon **tak**-see

I need to send a fax
necesito mandar un fax
ne-the-**see**-to man-**dar** oon faks

Key Talk

- 1º = **primero** = first; 2º = **segundo** = second, etc. **Primera** (which goes with feminine words) is abbreviated to 1ª
- C/ = **calle** = street.
- s/n (or S/N) = **sin número** = no number (this is used in addresses because some places don't have a number. For example: **Calle de España s/n**).

can I...?
¿**puedo**...?
pwe-do...

can we...?
¿**podemos**...?
po-de-mos...

can I pay?
¿**puedo pagar**?
pwe-do pa-gar

can we go in?
¿**podemos entrar**?
po-de-mos en-trar

where can I...?
¿**dónde puedo**...?
don-de pwe-do...

where can I buy bread?
¿**dónde puedo comprar pan**?
don-de pwe-do kom-prar pan

when?
¿**cuándo**?
kwan-do

at what time...?
¿**a qué hora**...?
a ke o-ra...

when is breakfast?
¿**a qué hora es el desayuno**?
a ke o-ra es el de-sa-yoo-no

when is dinner?
¿**a qué hora es la cena**?
a ke o-ra es la the-na

when does it open/close?
¿**cuándo abren/cierran**?
kwan-do a-bren/thyer-ran

when does it begin/finish?
¿**cuándo empieza/termina**?
kwan-do em-pye-tha/ter-mee-na

yesterday
ayer
a-yer

today
hoy
oy

tomorrow
mañana
man-ya-na

this morning
esta mañana
es-ta man-ya-na

this afternoon
esta tarde
es-ta tar-de

tonight
esta noche
es-ta no-che

is it open?
¿**está abierto**?
es-ta ab-yer-to

is it closed?
¿**está cerrado**?
es-ta ther-ra-do

- Mr is **Señor** (sen-**yor**), abbreviated to **Sr.**
- Mrs or Ms is **Señora** (sen-**yo**-ra), abbreviated to **Sra.**
- Miss is **Señorita** (sen-yo-**ree**-ta), abbreviated to **Srta.**
- If you are trying to get past, perhaps in a busy street, or off a crowded bus, you can use **¿me permite?** (me per-**mee**-te).

Sr. y Sra
Avda. / F

how are you?
¿cómo está?
ko-mo es-ta

fine, thanks. And you?
muy bien, gracias. ¿Y usted?
mooy byen gra-thyas ee oos-ted

my name is...
me llamo...
me lya-mo...

what is your name?
¿cómo se llama?
ko-mo se lya-ma

I don't understand
no entiendo
no en-tyen-do

do you speak English?
¿habla inglés?
a-bla een-gles

do you understand?
¿entiende?
en-tyen-de

I don't speak Spanish
no hablo español
no a-blo es-pan-yol

this is my husband/wife
le presento a mi marido/mujer
le pre-sen-to a mee ma-ree-do/moo-kher

pleased to meet you
encantado(a)
en-kan-ta-do(a)

I've enjoyed myself very much
lo he pasado muy bien
lo e pa-sa-do mooy byen

the meal was delicious
la comida estaba deliciosa
la ko-mee-da es-ta-ba de-leeth-yo-sa

we'd like to come back
nos gustaría volver
nos goos-ta-ree-a bol-ber

Money – changing

● Spain is in the eurozone. Euro is pronounced **eoo**-ro and cent, known as **céntimo**, is pronounced **then**-tee-mo.
● Check bank opening times as most close around 2pm. Look for the words **Banco** and **Caja** (**Caixa** in Catalan).
● **Oficinas de cambio** (bureaux de change) stay open longer than banks but charge more commission.

where can I change money?
¿dónde se puede cambiar dinero?
don-de se **pwe**-de kam-**byar** dee-**ne**-ro

where is the bank?
¿dónde está el banco?
don-de es-**ta** el **ban**-ko

where is the bureau de change?
¿dónde está la oficina de cambio?
don-de es-**ta** la o-fee-**thee**-na de **kam**-byo

when does the bank open?
¿cuándo abre el banco?
kwan-do **a**-bre el **ban**-ko

when does the bank close?
¿cuándo cierra el banco?
kwan-do **thyer**-ra el **ban**-ko

I want to cash these traveller's cheques
quiero cambiar estos cheques de viaje
kyer-o kam-**byar es**-tos **che**-kes de **bya**-khe

what is the rate...?
¿a cómo está el cambio...?
a **ko**-mo es-**ta** el **kam**-byo...

for pounds
de libras
de **lee**-bras

for dollars
de dólares
de do-**la**-res

I want to change £50
quiero cambiar 50 libras
kyer-o kam-**byar** theen-**kwen**-ta **lee**-bras

where is there a cash dispenser?
¿dónde hay un cajero?
don-de aee oon ka-**khe**-ro

I'd like small notes
quería billetes pequeños
ke-**ree**-ya beel-**ye**-tes pe-**ken**-yos

spending – Money

● Major credit cards are widely accepted. Usually the card is passed through a reader, but sometimes you have to enter your PIN on a keypad.

● Cash machines are widespread and you'll be able to use English instructions. **Fuera de servicio** means 'out of service'.

● Take your bank's phone number in case of problems.

how much is it?
¿cuánto es?
kwan-to es

how much will it be?
¿cuánto me costará?
kwan-to me kos-ta-*ra*

I want to pay
quiero pagar
kyer-o pa-*gar*

we want to pay separately
queremos pagar por separado
ke-*re*-mos pa-*gar* por se-pa-*ra*-do

can I pay by credit card?
¿puedo pagar con tarjeta de crédito?
pwe-do pa-*gar* kon tar-*khe*-ta de *kre*-dee-to

do you accept traveller's cheques?
¿aceptan cheques de viaje?
a-*thep*-tan *che*-kes de *bya*-khe

how much is it...?	**per person**	**per night**	**per kilo**
¿cuánto es...?	por persona	por noche	por kilo
kwan-to es...	por per-*so*-na	por *no*-che	por *kee*-lo

are VAT and service included?
¿incluye el IVA y el servicio?
een-*kloo*-ye el *ee*-ba ee el ser-*beeth*-yo

can I have a receipt?
¿puede darme un recibo?
pwe-de *dar*-me oon re-*thee*-bo

do I pay a deposit?
¿tengo que pagar un depósito?
ten-go ke pa-*gar* oon de-*po*-see-to

I've nothing smaller
no tengo cambio
no *ten*-go *kam*-byo

keep the change
quédese con la vuelta
ke-de-se kon la *bwel*-ta

Airport

- The word for airport is **aeropuerto**.
- Most signs will be in Spanish and English.
- The word for 'flight' is **vuelo**. The word for 'delay' is **retraso**.
- Check out airports of southern Spain on **www.andalucia.com/travel/airports/home.htm**.

to the airport, please
al aeropuerto, por favor
*al aee-ro-**pwer**-to por fa-**bor***

how do I get into town?
¿cómo se va al centro?
*ko-mo se ba al **then**-tro*

where do I get the bus to the town centre?
¿dónde se coge el autobús para el centro?
***don**-de se **ko**-khe el ow-to-**boos** pa-ra el **then**-tro*

how much is it...?
¿cuánto es...?
***kwan**-to es...*

to the town centre
al centro
*al **then**-tro*

to the airport
al aeropuerto
*al aee-ro-**pwer**-to*

where do I check in for...?
¿dónde se factura para...?
***don**-de se fak-**too**-ra pa-ra...*

which gate is it for the flight to...?
¿cuál es la puerta del vuelo para...?
*kwal es la **pwer**-ta del **bwe**-lo pa-ra...*

boarding will take place at gate number...
el embarque se efectuará por la puerta número...
*el em-**bar**-ke se e-fek-twa-**ra** por la **pwer**-ta **noo**-me-ro...*

last call for passengers on flight...
última llamada para los pasajeros del vuelo...
***ool**-tee-ma lya-**ma**-da pa-ra los pa-sa-**khe**-ros del **bwe**-lo...*

your flight is delayed
su vuelo sale con retraso
*soo **bwe**-lo **sa**-le kon re-**tra**-so*

Customs & Passports

- EU citizens with nothing to declare can use the blue customs channels, which are subject to spot checks.
- There's no restriction by quantity or value on goods purchased by travellers in another EU country, provided they are for their own personal use (this covers gifts). For further information, check **www.hmce.gov.uk**.

I have nothing to declare
no tengo nada que declarar
*no **ten**-go **na**-da ke de-kla-**rar***

here is... | **my passport** | **my green card**
aquí está... | mi pasaporte | mi carta verde
*a-**kee** es-**ta**...* | *mee pa-sa-**por**-te* | *mee **kar**-ta **ber**-de*

do I have to pay duty on this?
¿tengo que pagar derechos de aduana por esto?
***ten**-go ke pa-**gar** de-**re**-chos de a-doo-**a**-na por **es**-to*

it's for my own personal use
es para uso personal
*es **pa**-ra **oo**-so per-so-**nal***

here is the receipt
aquí tiene el tique
*a-**kee tyen**-e el tee-**ke***

the children are on this passport
los niños están en este pasaporte
*los **neen**-yos es-**tan** en **es**-te pa-sa-**por**-te*

I'm... | **English** (m/f) | **Australian** (m/f)
soy... | inglés(esa) | australiano(a)
soy... | *een-**gles**(**gle**-sa)* | *ow-stra-**lya**-no(a)*

I bought it/them in Spain
lo/los compré en España
*lo/los kom-**pre** en es-**pan**-ya*

Asking the Way - questions

- You can ask the way with **¿el museo, por favor?**
  Nothing more complicated is required.
- You can get maps free from the local Tourist Information
  Office, and street maps of the neighbourhood are displayed
  outside all Madrid's Metro stations.
- You can also attract someone's attention with **por favor**.

excuse me!
¡oiga por favor!
oy-ga por fa-**bor**

where is...?
¿dónde está...?
don-de es-**ta**...

where is the nearest...?
¿dónde está el/la ... más próximo(a)/cercano(a)?
don-de es-**ta** el/la ... mas **prok**-see-mo(a)/ther-**ka**-no(a)

how do I get to...?
¿cómo se va a...?
ko-mo se ba a...

is this the right way to...?
¿se va por aquí a...?
se ba por a-**kee** a...

to the station
a la estación
a la es-tath-**yon**

to the...museum
al museo...
al moo-**se**-o...

to the...hotel
al hotel...
alo-**tel**...

is it far?
¿está lejos?
es-**ta** le-khos

can I walk there?
¿puedo ir andando?
pwe-do eer an-**dan**-do

is there a bus that goes there?
¿hay algún autobús hasta allí?
aee al-**goon** ow-to-**boos** as-ta a-**yee**

we're looking for...
estamos buscando...
es-**ta**-mos boos-**kan**-do...

we're lost
nos hemos perdido
nos **e**-mos per-**dee**-do

can you show me where ... is on the map?
¿puede indicarme dónde está ... en el mapa?
pwe-de een-dee-**kar**-me **don**-de es-**ta** ... en el **ma**-pa

answers – Asking the Way

- Key words are 'right' **a la derecha** (a la de-re-cha), 'left' **a la izquierda** (a la eeth-**kyer**-da), and 'straight on' **recto** (**rek**-to).
- 'Street' is **calle** (**kal**-ye), or **paseo** (pa-se-o), 'square' is **plaza** (**pla**-tha), and 'roundabout' is **glorieta** (glor-**ye**-ta).
- In shopping centres, hotels, etc, 'floor' is **planta** (**plan**-ta); 'basement' is **sótano** (**so**-ta-no).

no, this is not the way to...
no, por aquí no se va a...
*no, por a-**kee** no se va a...*

turn left/right
gire a la izquierda/derecha
*khee-re a la eeth-**kyer**-da/de-**re**-cha*

keep straight on until you get to...
siga todo recto hasta llegar a...
*see-ga to-do **rek**-to **as**-ta lyeg-**ar** a...*

as far as...
hasta...
***as**-ta...*

you have to turn round
tiene que dar la vuelta
***tyen**-e ke dar la **bwel**-ta*

take...
coja/tome...
*ko-kha/**to**-me...*

the first on the right
la primera calle a la derecha
*la pree-**me**-ra **kal**-ye a la de-**re**-cha*

the second on the left
la segunda calle a la izquierda
*la se-**goon**-da **kal**-ye a la eeth-**kyer**-da*

the road to...
la carretera de...
*la ka-rre-**te**-ra de...*

follow the signs for...
siga las señales de...
***see**-ga las sen-**ya**-les de...*

Bus

● For long distance travel, coaches are often cheaper than the train. You can buy your ticket up to 2 months ahead – this is recommended at weekends and in the high season.
● You buy single tickets on the bus. You can get multi-journey tickets (**bonobús** or **metrobús**). All tickets have to be validated in the machine on the bus.

where is the bus station?
¿dónde está la estación de autobuses?
don-de es-ta la es-tath-yon de ow-to-boo-ses

I want to go...	**to the station**	**to the museum**
quiero ir...	**a la estación**	**al museo**
kyer-o eer...	*a la es-tath-yon*	*al moo-se-o*
	to the Prado	**to Toledo**
	al Prado	**a Toledo**
	al pra-do	*a to-le-do*

is there a bus that goes there?
¿hay un autobús que vaya allí?
aee oon ow-to-boos ke ba-ya a-yee

which bus do I take to go to...?
¿qué autobús se coge para ir a...?
ke ow-to-boos se ko-khe pa-ra eer a...

where do I get the bus to...?
¿dónde se coge el autobús para...?
don-de se ko-khe el ow-to-boos pa-ra...

how often are the buses?
¿cada cuánto hay autobuses?
ka-da kwan-to aee ow-to-boos-es

when is the last bus?
¿cuándo sale el último autobús?
kwan-do sa-le el ool-tee-mo ow-to-boos

can you tell me when to get off?
¿me dice cuándo tengo que bajarme?
me dee-the kwan-do ten-go ke ba-khar-me

Underground

● Madrid, Barcelona and Bilbao have Metro systems. Maps are available from station booths. A 10-trip ticket (**metrobús**) can be used on buses as well as the underground.
● Busy times are 8.30-10am and 3.30-8pm.
● For information, check out **www.metromadrid.es**, **www.metrobilbao.net** and **www.tmb./net/cast/home.htm**.

where is the metro station?
¿dónde está la estación de metro?
don-de es-ta la es-tath-yon de me-tro

are there any special discount tickets?
¿hay algún billete con descuento especial?
aee al-goon beel-ye-te kon des-kwen-to es-peth-yal

do you have an underground map?
¿tiene un plano del metro?
tyen-e oon pla-no del me-tro

I want to go to...
quiero ir a...
kyer-o eer a...

can I go by underground?
¿se puede ir en metro?
se pwe-de eer en me-tro

do I have to change?
¿tengo que cambiar de línea?
ten-go ke kam-byar de lee-ne-a

where?
¿dónde?
don-de

which line is it for...?
¿cuál es la línea para ir a...?
kwal es la lee-nea pa-ra eer a...

what is the next stop?
¿cuál es la próxima parada?
kwal es la prok-see-ma pa-ra-da

which is the station for the Prado?
¿cuál es la estación de metro para el Prado?
kwal es la es-ta-thyon de me-tro pa-ra el pra-do

please let me through
¿me deja pasar, por favor?
me de-kha pa-sar por fa-bor

Train

● A high-speed train service called AVE links Madrid with Seville. The TALGO 200 service is as good as AVE but cheaper (journeys take 15 minutes longer). AVE network's base is at the RENFE Atocha Station in Madrid.
● You can buy most tickets from railway stations and travel agents, who will charge a commission.

where is the station?
¿dónde está la estación?
don-de es-ta la es-tath-yon

to the station, please
a la estación, por favor
a la es-tath-yon por fa-bor

a single to…
uno a…
oo-no a…

2 singles to…
dos a…
dos a…

a return to…
uno de ida y vuelta a…
oo-no de ee-da ee bwel-ta a…

2 returns to…
dos de ida y vuelta a…
dos de ee-da ee bwel-ta a…

a child's return to…
un billete de niño, ida y vuelta a…
oon beel-ye-te de neen-yo ee-da ee bwel-ta a…

1st class/tourist
de clase preferente/turista
de kla-se pre-fe-ren-te/too-rees-ta

smoking
fumador
foo-ma-dor

non smoking
no fumador
no foo-ma-dor

I want to book a seat on the AVE to Madrid
quería reservar un asiento en el AVE a Madrid
ke-ree-a re-serbar un as-yen-to en el a-be a ma-dreed

when is the first/last train to…?
¿cuándo sale el primer/último tren para…?
kwan-do sa-le el pree-mer/col-tee-mo tren pa-ra…

when does it arrive in…?
¿cuándo llega a…?
kwan-do lyeg-a a…

is there a buffet service?
¿hay servicio de cafetería?
aee ser-beeth-yo de ka-fet-er-ee-a

- *Reduced fares are available for certain age groups (such as students and over-60s) on certain days of the year called **días azules** ('blue days').*
- *Check out **www.renfe.es**.*
- *Children under 4 travel free; those aged from 4 to 13 get a 40% discount.*

do I have to pay a supplement?
¿tengo que pagar suplemento?
ten-go ke pa-gar soo-ple-men-to

can I have a timetable?
¿me da un horario?
me da oon o-rar-yo

is this pass valid on this train?
¿es válido este pase en este tren?
es ba-lee-do es-te pa-se en es-te tren

I want to book...   **a seat**   **a couchette**
quiero reservar...   un asiento   una litera
kyer-o re-ser-bar...   *oon as-yen-to*   *oo-na lee-te-ra*

do I need to change?   **where?**
¿tengo que hacer transbordo?   ¿dónde?
ten-go ke a-ther trans-bor-do   *don-de*

which platform does it leave from?
¿de qué andén sale?
de ke an-den sa-le

does the train to ... leave from this platform?
¿el tren para ... sale de este andén?
el tren pa-ra ... sa-le de es-te an-den

is this the train for...?   **where is the left-luggage?**
¿es este el tren para...?   ¿dónde está la consigna?
es es-te el tren pa-ra...   *don-de es-ta la kon-seeg-na*

is this seat taken?
¿está ocupado (este asíento)?
es-ta o-koo-pa-do (es-te as-yen-to)

Taxi

● You can either hail a taxi or pick one up at a taxi stand. There may be surcharges for baggage and for travelling late at night and at weekends.
● Taxis are usually white and display a green light when free, and a red light when they're not.
● Tipping isn't common, but it's usual to round up the cost.

to the airport, please
al aeropuerto, por favor
*al aee-ro-**pwer**-to por fa-**bor***

to the station, please
a la estación, por favor
*a la es-tath-**yon** por fa-**bor***

take me to this address, please
lléveme a esta dirección, por favor
lyeb**-e-me a **es**-ta dee-rekth-**yon** por fa-**bor

how much will it cost?
¿cuánto puede costar?
kwan**-to **pwe**-de kos-**tar

how much is it to the centre?
¿cuánto cuesta hasta el centro?
***kwan**-to **kwes**-ta **as**-ta el **then**-tro*

it's too much
es demasiado
*es de-mas-**ya**-do*

where is the taxi stand?
¿dónde está la parada de taxis?
***don**-de es-**ta** la pa-**ra**-da de **tak**-sees*

please order me a taxi
por favor, ¿me pide un taxi?
*por fa-**bor** me **pee**-de oon **tak**-see*

can I have a receipt?
¿puede darme un recibo?
***pwe**-de **dar**-me oon re-**theeb**-o*

I've nothing smaller
no tengo cambio
*no **ten**-go **kam**-byo*

keep the change
quédese con la vuelta
***ke**-de-se kon la **bwel**-ta*

Boat

- There is a good ferry service from Valencia and Barcelona to the Balearic Islands on modern ships with excellent facilities.
- Fast ferry services link Andalucia to North Africa. The crossing from Tarifa to Tangiers takes 35 minutes.
- Boat and ferry timetables follow peak summer-season schedules.

1 ticket	2 tickets	single	round trip
un billete	**dos billetes**	**de ida**	**de ida y vuelta**
*oon beel-**ye**-te*	*dos beel-**ye**-tes*	*de **ee**-da*	*de **ee**-da ee **bwel**-ta*

is there a tourist ticket?
¿hay algún billete de clase turista?
*aee al-**goon** beel-**ye**-te de **kla**-se too-**rees**-ta*

are there any boat trips?
¿hay excursiones en barco?
*aee eks-koor-**syon**-es en **bar**-ko*

how long is the trip?
¿cuánto dura el viaje?
*kwan-to **doo**-ra el **bya**-khe*

when is the next boat?
¿cuándo sale el próximo barco?
*kwan-do **sa**-le el **prok**-see-mo **bar**-ko*

when is the next ferry?
¿cuándo sale el próximo ferry?
*kwan-do **sa**-le el **prok**-see-mo ferry*

when is the first/last boat?
¿cuándo sale el primer/último barco?
*kwan-do **sa**-le el **pree**-mer/**ool**-tee-mo **bar**-ko*

when do we arrive in?
¿a qué hora llegamos a...?
*a **ke o**-ra lyeg-**a**-mos a...*

when does the boat leave?
¿cuándo sale el barco?
*kwan-do **sa**-le el **bar**-ko*

is there a restaurant on board?
¿hay restaurante en el barco?
*aee rest-ow-**ran**-te en el **bar**-ko*

can we hire a boat?
¿podemos alquilar una barca?
*po-**de**-mos al-kee-**lar oo**-na **bar**-ka*

do you have a timetable?
¿tiene un horario?
***tyen**-e oon o-**ra**-ree-o*

Car – driving

- To drive in Spain you must have a valid pink EU driving licence and be at least 18 years old. Make sure you bring your licence and registration document with you.
- You pay a toll on some motorways. Look for the word **PEAJE**.
- Check out www.dgt.es and www.aseta.es for road and traffic information.

can I/we park here?
¿se puede aparcar aquí?
*se **pwe**-de a-par-**kar** a-**kee***

where can I park?
¿dónde puedo aparcar?
don**-de **pwe**-do a-par-**kar

is there a car park?
¿hay un parking?
aee oon parking

do I/we need a parking disc?
¿hace falta tique de aparcamiento?
***a**-the **fal**-ta **tee**-ke de a-par-ka-**myen**-to*

where can I get a parking disc?
¿dónde puedo comprar un tique de aparcamiento?
***don**-de **pwe**-do kom-**prar** oon **tee**-ke de a-par-ka-**myen**-to*

how long can I park here?
¿cuánto tiempo puedo aparcar aquí?
kwan**-to **tyem**-po **pwe**-do a-par-**kar** a-**kee

we're going to...
vamos a...
***ba**-mos a...*

what's the best route?
¿cuál es la mejor ruta?
*kwal es la me-**khor roo**-ta*

which exit is it for...
¿cuál es la salida de...?
***kwal** es la sa-**lee**-da de...*

how do I get onto the motorway?
¿por dónde se va a la autopista?
*por **don**-de se ba a la ow-to-**pees**-ta*

- *Petrol stations often still have attendants.*
- *Unleaded (**sin plomo**) pumps are always coloured green.*
- *Service stations are **áreas de servicio** – they often have cash dispensers, shops, eating places, play areas, etc. They are not common on toll motorways, but there are more of them on non-toll roads.*

is there a petrol station near here?
¿hay alguna gasolinera por aquí?
*aee al-**goo**-na ga-so-lee-**ne**-ra por a-**kee***

fill it up, please
lleno, por favor
lyen**-o por fa-**bor

15 euros worth of unleaded
15 euros de sin plomo
***keen**-the **eoo**-ros seen **plo**-mo*

pump number...
surtidor número...
*soor-tee-**dor noo**-me-ro...*

that is my car
ese es mi coche
*e-se es mee **ko**-che*

where is the air line?
¿dónde está el aire?
***don**-de es-**ta** el **aee**-re*

where is the water?
¿dónde está el agua?
***don**-de es-**ta** el **ag**-wa*

please check...
¿me revisa...?
*me re-**bee**-sa...*

the tyre pressure
la presión de los neumáticos
*la pres-**yon** de los neoo-**ma**-tee-kos*

the oil
el aceite
*el a-**they**-te*

the water
el agua
*el **ag**-wa*

can I pay with this credit card?
¿puedo pager con esta tarjeta de crédito?
***pwe**-do pa-**gar** kon **es**-ta tar-**khe**-ta de **kre**-dee-to*

which pump did you use?
¿qué surtidor ha usado?
*ke soor-tee-**dor** a co-**sa**-do*

Car – problems/breakdown

● Drivers should carry a first-aid kit, spare light bulbs and a warning triangle in case of an accident or breakdown.
● Motorways have SOS emergency buttons every 1.5km. You simply press the button and wait for assistance.
● If you break down, pull over, put your hazard lights on and place your warning triangle 50m behind your car.

I've broken down
tengo una avería
ten-go *oo*-na a-be-*ree*-a

what do I do?
¿qué hago?
ke a-go

I'm on my own *(female)*
estoy sola
es-*toy so*-la

there are children in the car
hay niños en el coche
aee neen-yos en el *ko*-che

where's the nearest garage?
¿dónde está el taller más cercano?
don-de es-*ta* el tal-*yer* mas ther-*ka*-no

is it serious?
¿es muy serio?
es mooy *ser*-yo

can you repair it?
¿puede arreglarlo?
pwe-de ar-re-*glar*-lo

when will it be ready?
¿para cuándo estará listo?
pa-ra *kwan*-do es-ta-*ra lees*-to

how much will it cost?
¿cuánto me costará?
kwan-to me kos-ta-*ra*

the car won't start
el coche no arranca
el *ko*-che no ar-*ran*-ka

I have a flat tyre
tengo una rueda pinchada
ten-go *oo*-na *rwe*-da peen-*cha*-da

the engine is overheating
el motor se calienta
el mo-*tor* se kal-*yen*-ta

the battery is flat
la batería está descargada
la ba-te-*ree*-a es-*ta* des-kar-*ga*-da

can you replace the windscreen?
¿me puede cambiar el parabrisas?
me *pwe*-de kam-*byar* el pa-ra-*bree*-sas

- Cars can be hired at airports and main railway stations, and drivers must be over 21 and hold a valid EU driver's licence.
- Check what's covered in the price, particularly insurance.
- Most hire companies give information, often in English, on what to do in case of accident or breakdown.
- Bigger companies will be able to provide baby seats, etc.

I want to hire a car
querría alquilar un coche
ke-ree-a al-kee-lar oon ko-che

for one day
para un día
pa-ra oon dee-a

for ... days
para ... días
pa-ra ... dee-as

I want...
quiero...
kyer-o...

a large car
un coche grande
oon ko-che gran-de

a small car
un coche pequeño
oon ko-che pe-ken-yo

an automatic
un coche automático
oon ko-che ow-to-mat-ee-ko

how much is it?
¿cúanto es?
kwan-to es

is fully comprehensive insurance included in the price?
¿el seguro a todo riesgo va incluido en el precio?
el se-goo-ro a to-do ryes-go ba een-kloo-ee-do en el preth-yo

what do we do if we break down?
¿qué hay que hacer si tenemos una avería?
ke aee ke a-ther see te-ne-mos oo-na a-be-ree-a

when must I return the car by?
¿para qué hora tengo que devolver el coche?
pa-ra ke o-ra ten-go ke de-bol-ber el ko-che

please show me the controls
¿me enseña cómo funcionan los mandos?
me en-sen-ya ko-mo foon-thyo-nan los man-dos

where are the documents?
¿dónde están los papeles del coche?
don-de es-tan los pa-pe-les del ko-che

Shopping – holiday

- Shop opening hours vary but are usually 10 till 1.30 and 5 till 8, although food shops open earlier and large department stores stay open at lunchtime.
- The **estanco** sells a wide range of useful things: stamps, cigarettes, bus tickets and postcards.
- Postboxes are yellow, priority mail boxes are red.

do you sell...?	**batteries for this camera**	**stamps**
¿vende...?	**pilas para esta cámara**	**sellos**
ben-de...	*pee*-las **pa**-ra **es**-ta **ka**-ma-ra	*sel*-yos

where can I buy...?
¿dónde puedo comprar...?
don-de **pwe**-do kom-**prar**...

films
carretes de fotos
ka-**rre**-tes de **fo**-tos

10 stamps
diez sellos
dyeth **sel**-yos

for postcards
para postales
pa-ra pos-**ta**-les

to Britain
para Gran Bretaña
pa-ra gran bre-**tan**-ya

a colour film
un carrete en color
oon ka-**rre**-te en ko-**lor**

a tape for this video camera
una cinta para esta videocámara
oo-na **theen**-ta **pa**-ra **es**-ta **bee**-deo-**ka**-ma-ra

I'm looking for a present...
estoy buscando un regalo...
es-**toy** boos-**kan**-do oon re-**ga**-lo...

for my mother/son
para mi madre/hijo
pa-ra mee **ma**-dre/**ee**-kho

have you anything cheaper?
¿tiene algo más barato?
tyen-e **al**-go mas ba-**ra**-to

it's a gift
es un regalo
es oon re-**ga**-lo

please wrap it up
envuélvamelo por favor
en-**bwel**-ba-me-lo por fa-**bor**

is there a market/street market?
¿hay mercado/mercadillo?
aee mer-**ka**-do mer-ka-**deel**-yo

which day?
¿qué día?
ke **dee**-a

clothes – Shopping

● Spain's largest department store is **El Corte Inglés**, which has branches in all major towns. It is generally open on the first Sunday of each month.
● If you want a refund you must produce your receipt, and you may be offered a replacement or a credit note instead of your money back.

can I try this on?
¿puedo probarme esto?
pwe-do pro-bar-me es-to

it's too big
es demasiado grande
es de-mas-ya-do gran-de

it's too small
es demasiado pequeño
es de-mas-ya-do pe-ken-yo

it's too expensive
es demasiado caro
es de-mas-ya-do ka-ro

I'm just looking
sólo estoy mirando
so-lo es-toy mee-ran-do

I'll take this one
me llevo esto
me lyeb-o es-to

I take a size ... shoe
uso el número ... (de zapatos)
oo-so el noo-me-ro ... (de tha-pa-tos)

what shoe size are you?
¿qué número usa?
ke noo-me-ro oo-sa

where are the changing rooms?
¿dónde están los probadores?
don-de es-tan los pro-ba-dor-es

have you a smaller size?
¿tiene una talla menor?
tyen-e oo-na tal-ya me-nor

have you a larger size?
¿tiene una talla mayor?
tyen-e oo-na tal-ya ma-yor

I take size ... clothes
uso la talla...
oo-so la tal-ya...

does it fit?
¿le queda bien?
le ke-da byen

Shopping – food

- The tendency in Spain is to shop more in small local shops than in supermarkets, which are located on the outskirts of towns.
- In supermarkets you may have to leave your bags in a locker at the entrance, or with an attendant who will give you a token to get them back.

where can I buy...?	fruit	bread	milk
¿dónde puedo comprar...?	fruta	pan	leche
*don-de **pwe**-do kom-**prar**...*	*froo-ta*	*pan*	*le-che*

where is...?	the supermarket	the baker's
¿dónde está...?	el supermercado	la panadería
*don-de es-**ta**...*	*el soo-per-mer-**ka**-do*	*la pa-na-de-**ree**-a*

where is the market?	which day is the market?
¿dónde está el mercado?	¿qué día hay mercado?
*don-de es-**ta** el mer-**ka**-do*	*ke **dee**-a aee mer-**ka**-do*

it's me next	that's enough
estoy yo ahora	basta
*es-**toy** yo a-**o**-ra*	***bas**-ta*

a litre of...	milk	water	beer
un litro de...	leche	agua	cerveza
*oon **lee**-tro de...*	*le-che*	***ag**-wa*	*ther-**be**-tha*

a bottle of...	water	wine	oil
una botella de...	agua	vino	aceite
*oo-na bo-**tel**-ya de...*	***ag**-wa*	***bee**-no*	*a-**they**-te*

a can of...	coke	beer	tonic water
una lata de...	coca-cola	cerveza	tónica
*oo-na **la**-ta de...*	*ko-ka-**ko**-la*	*ther-**be**-tha*	***to**-nee-ka*

a carton of...	orange juice	milk
un cartón de...	zumo de naranja	leche
*oon kar-**ton** de...*	***thoo**-mo de na-**ran**-kha*	*le-che*

food – Shopping

- Many shops (including supermarkets) will gift-wrap presents.
- Big supermarkets have petrol stations and cash dispensers.
- You generally have to get fruit and vegetables weighed before going to the checkout.
- Bakers sell fresh bread, milk, fruit juice and sometimes sweets and cakes. Milk is almost always long-life.

100 grams of...
cien gramos de...
*thyen **gra**-mos de...*

250 grams of...
un cuarto de kilo de...
*oon **kwar**-to **kee**-lo de...*

a kilo of...
un kilo de...
*oon **kee**-lo de...*

8 slices of...
ocho lonchas de...
*o-cho **lon**-chas de...*

a loaf of bread
una barra de pan
*oo-na **bar**-ra de pan*

a packet of...
un paquete de...
*oon pa-**ke**-te de...*

a tin of tomatoes
una lata de tomates
*oo-na **la**-ta de to-**ma**-tes*

what would you like?
¿qué desea?
*ke de-**se**-a*

cheese
queso
***ke**-so*

sausages
salchichas
*sal-**chee**-chas*

potatoes
patatas
*pa-**ta**-tas*

cooked ham
jamón de York
*kha-**mon** de york*

three yogurts
tres yogures
*tres yo-**goo**-res*

biscuits
galletas
*gal-**yet**-as*

a jar of jam
un tarro de mermelada
*oon **tar**-ro de mer-me-**la**-da*

anything else?
¿algo más?
***al**-go mas*

chorizo
chorizo
*cho-**ree**-tho*

mushrooms
champiñones
*cham-peen-**yo**-nes*

apples
manzanas
*man-**tha**-nas*

cured ham
jamón serrano
*kha-**mon** ser-**ra**-no*

half a dozen eggs
media docena de huevos
***med**-ya doth-**en**-a de **we**-bos*

sugar
azúcar
*a-**thoo**-kar*

Sightseeing

● Tourist offices provide town plans and info on accommodation, restaurants and attractions. Check out **www.spaintour.com**.
● Museum opening hours vary but are usually 10am-2pm and 5-8pm. They normally close on Mondays.
● In Madrid a 3-gallery ticket gives admission to the Reina Sofia Gallery, the Thyssen Gallery and the Prado.

where is the tourist office?
¿dónde está la oficina de turismo?
don-de es-**ta** la o-fee-**thee**-na de too-**rees**-mo

we'd like to visit...
queríamos visitar...
ke-**ree**-a-mos bee-see-**tar**...

have you any leaflets?
¿tiene algún folleto?
tyen-e al-**goon** fol-**ye**-to

when can we visit...?
¿cuándo se puede visitar...?
kwan-do se **pwe**-de bee-see-**tar**...

do you have a town guide?
¿tiene una guía de la cuidad?
tyen-e **oo**-na **gee**-a de la thyoo-**dad**

what day does it close?
¿qué día cierra?
ke **dee**-a **thyerr**-a

is it open to the public?
¿está abierto al público?
es-**ta** ab-**yer**-to al **poob**-lee-ko

we'd like to go to...
queríamos ir a...
ke-**ree**-a-mos eer a...

are there any excursions?
¿hay alguna excursión organizada?
aee al-**goo**-na eks-koor-**syon** or-ga-nee-**tha**-da

when does it leave?
¿a qué hora sale?
a ke **o**-ra **sa**-le

where does it leave from?
¿de dónde sale?
de **don**-de **sa**-le

how much is it to get in?
¿cúanto cuesta entrar?
kwan-to **kwes**-ta en-**trar**

is there a reduction for...?
¿hay descuento para...?
aee des-**kwen**-to **pa**-ra...

students
estudiantes
e-stoo-**dyan**-tes

seniors
jubilados
khoo-bee-**la**-dos

a Playas

- Beaches which meet European standards of cleanliness are allowed to fly a blue flag.
- A green flag flying on a beach means it's safe to swim, a yellow flag means swimming isn't recommended, and a red flag means it's dangerous.
- You can hire a sunshade (**hamaca**) per day.

is there a quiet beach?
¿hay alguna playa tranquila?
*aee al-**goo**-na **pla**-ya tran-**kee**-la*

how do I get there?
¿cómo se va hasta allí?
ko**-mo se ba **as**-ta a-**yee

is there a swimming pool?
¿hay piscina?
*aee pees-**thee**-na*

can we swim in the river?
¿podemos bañarnos en el río?
*po-**de**-mos ban-**yar**-nos en el **ree**-go*

is the water clean?
¿está limpia el agua?
*es-**ta leem**-pya el **ag**-wa*

is the water deep?
¿es muy profundo?
*es mooy pro-**foon**-do*

is the water cold?
¿está fría el agua?
*es-**ta free**-a el **ag**-wa*

is it dangerous?
¿es peligroso?
*es pe-lee-**gro**-so*

are there currents?
¿hay corrientes?
*aee korr-**yen**-tes*

where can we...?
¿dónde se puede hacer...?
***don**-de se **pwe**-de a-**ther**...*

windsurf
windsurfing
*ween-**soor**-feen*

waterski
esquí acuático
*e-**skee** a-**kwa**-tee-ko*

can I hire...?
¿puedo alquilar...?
***pwe**-do al-kee-**lar**...*

a beach umbrella
una sombrilla
***oo**-na som-**breel**-ya*

a jetski
una moto acuática
***oo**-na **mo**-to a-**kwa**-tee-ka*

a pedal boat/pedalo
un hidropedal
*oon ee-dro-pe-**dal***

Sport

- *Tourist offices will provide information on sports activities in their area.*
- *Swimming caps must be worn at all indoor pools.*
- *National parks generally have walking and cycling trails.*
- *If you want tickets to a local football match, go to the stadium ticket booth an hour before kick-off.*

where can we...?
¿dónde se puede...?
don-de se pwe-de...

how much is it...?
¿cuánto cuesta...?
kwan-to kwes-ta...

play tennis
jugar al tenis
khoo-gar al te-nees

go swimming
nadar
na-dar

go fishing
ir a pescar
eer a pes-kar

per hour
la hora
la o-ra

play golf
jugar al golf
khoo-gar al golf

hire bikes
alquilar bicis
al-kee-lar bee-thees

go riding
montar a caballo
mon-tar a ka-bal-yo

per day
por día
por dee-a

how do I book a court?
¿cómo se reserva una pista?
ko-mo se re-ser-ba oo-na pee-sta

can I hire rackets?
¿puedo alquilar raquetas?
pwe-do al-kee-lar ra-ke-tas

is there a football match?
¿hay algún partido de fútbol?
aee al-goon par-tee-do de foot-bol

do I need walking boots?
¿necesito botas de montaña?
ne-the-see-to bo-tas de mon-tan-ya

where is there a sports shop?
¿dónde hay una tienda de deportes?
don-de aee oo-na tyen-da de de-por-tes

Skiing

Sierra
Grazale

● There are good skiing facilities in the Sierra Nevada and Catalonia.
● Check out skiing conditions on **www.snow-forecast.com** or **www.bbc.co.uk/weather/sports/snowsports**.
● Take passport-sized photos with you for passes.
● Cross-country skiing is **esquí de fondo**.

can I hire skis?
¿puedo alquilar unos esquíes?
pwe-do al-kee-lar oo-nos es-kee-es

how much is a pass?
¿cuánto cuesta un forfait?
kwan-to kwes-ta oon for-faeet

I'm a beginner
soy principiante
soy preen-thee-yan-te

which is an easy run?
¿hay alguna pista fácil?
aee al-goo-na pee-sta fa-theel

what is the snow like today?
¿cómo está hoy la nieve?
ko-mo es-ta oy la nye-be

is there a map of the ski runs?
¿hay un mapa de pistas?
aee oon ma-pa de pee-stas

my skis are...
mis esquíes son...
mees es-kee-es son...

too long
demasiado largos
de-mas-ya-do lar-gos

too short
demasiado cortos
de-mas-ya-do kor-tos

my bindings are...
tengo las fijaciones...
ten-go las fee-khath-yon-es...

too loose
demasiado flojas
de-mas-ya-do flo-khas

very tight
muy prietas
mooy pryet-as

where can we go cross-country skiing?
¿dónde se puede hacer esquí de fondo?
don-de se pwe-de a-ther es-kee de fon-do

what length skis do you want?
¿de qué largo quiere los esquíes?
de ke lar-go kyer-e los es-kee-es

what is your shoe size?
¿qué número de zapato tiene?
ke noo-me-ro de tha-pa-to tyen-e

Nightlife – popular

● Spanish people tend to dine late and then go out afterwards. An evening out might not start until 10pm and typically involves visiting a series of bars, staying for only a short time in each one.
● The last film showing is usually at midnight when tickets are cheaper.

what is there to do at night?
¿qué se puede hacer por las noches?
*ke se **pwe**-de a-**ther** por las **no**-ches*

which is a good bar?
¿qué bares buenos hay?
*ke **ba**-res **bwe**-nos aee*

which is a good disco?
¿qué discotecas buenas hay?
*ke dees-ko-te-kas **bwe**-nas aee*

where can we hear live music?
¿dónde hay música en vivo?
***don**-de aee **moo**-see-ka en **bee**-bo*

is it expensive?
¿es caro?
*es **ka**-ro*

where can we hear flamenco/salsa?
¿dónde se puede escuchar flamenco/salsa?
***don**-de se **pwe**-de es-koo-**char** fla-**men**-ko/**sal**-sa*

where do local people go at night?
¿dónde va la gente de aquí por la noche?
***don**-de ba la **khen**-te de a-**kee** por la **no**-che*

is it a safe area?
¿es una zona segura?
*es **oo**-na **tho**-na se-**goo**-ra*

are there any concerts?
¿hay algún concierto?
*aee al-**goon** kon-**thyer**-to*

do you want to dance?
¿quieres bailar?
kyer**-es baee-**lar

my name is...
me llamo...
*me **lya**-mo...*

what's your name?
¿cómo te llamas?
***ko**-mo te **lya**-mas*

cultural – Nightlife

- *Museums sometimes reopen between 5 and 8 pm.*
- *There are many summer festivals featuring dance, music and drama, which generally begin around 10.30 or 11 pm.*
- *In large cities you can often find **La Guia del Ocio**, a magazine listing events. Newspapers usually carry a page called **Agenda Cultural** with local events.*

is there a list of cultural events?
¿hay alguna guía del ocio?
*aee al-**goo**-na **gee**-a del **oth**-yo*

when is the local festival?
¿cuándo son las fiestas de aquí?
*kwan-do son las **fyes**-tas de a-**kee***

we'd like to go...
queríamos ir...
*ke-**ree**-a-mos eer...*

to the theatre
al teatro
*al te-**a**-tro*

to the opera
a la ópera
*a la **o**-pe-ra*

to the ballet
al ballet
*al ba-**le***

to a concert
a un concierto
*a oon kon-**thyer**-to*

what's on?
¿qué ponen?
*ke **po**-nen*

do I need to get tickets in advance?
¿tengo que sacar antes las entradas?
***ten**-go ke sa-**kar an**-tes las en-**tra**-das*

how much are the tickets?
¿cuánto cuestan las entradas?
***kwan**-to **kwes**-tan las en-**tra**-das*

when does the performance end?
¿cuándo termina la representación?
kwan**-do ter-**mee**-na la re-pre-sen-tath-**yon

2 tickets...
dos entradas...
*dos en-**tra**-das...*

for tonight
para esta noche
***pa**-ra **es**-ta **no**-che*

for tomorrow
para mañana
***pa**-ra man-**ya**-na*

for 5th August
para el cinco de agosto
***pa**-ra el **theen**-ko de a-**gos**-to*

51

Hotel

- *Tourist offices have lists of hotels and other accommodation in their area. Hotels use a star grading system (from 1 to 5).*
- *Hostales and pensiones are generally family-owned guesthouses. The price doesn't usually include breakfast.*
- *Paradores are good-quality hotels, usually in monuments, castles, listed buildings etc. Check out www.parador.es.*

have you a room for tonight?
¿tiene una habitación para esta noche?
tyen-e oo-na a-bee-tath-yon pa-ra es-ta no-che

a room	**single**	**double**	**family**
una habitación	individual	doble	familiar
oo-na a-bee-tath-yon	*een-dee-bee-dwal*	*dob-le*	*fa-meel-yar*

with a shower	**with a bath**
con ducha	con baño
kon doo-cha	*kon ba-nyo*

how much is it per night?
¿cuánto cuesta por noche?
kwan-to kwes-ta por no-che

is breakfast included?
¿está incluido desayuno?
es-ta een-kloo-ee-do de-sa-yoo-no

I booked a room
tengo reservada una habitación
ten-go re-ser-ba-da oo-na a-bee-tath-yon

in the name of...
a nombre de...
a nom-bre de...

I'd like to see the room
quería ver la habitación
ke-ree-a ber la a-bee-tath-yon

have you anything cheaper?
¿tiene algo más barato?
tyen-e al-go mas ba-ra-to

I want a room with three beds
quiero una habitación con tres camas
kyer-o oo-na a-bee-tath-yon kon tres ka-mas

can I leave this in the safe?
¿puedo dejar esto en la caja fuerte?
pwe-do de-khar es-to en la ka-kha fwer-te

can I have my key, please?
¿puede darme la llave, por favor?
pwe-de dar-me la lya-be por fa-bor

are there any messages for me?
¿hay algún mensaje para mí?
aee al-goon men-sa-khe pa-ra mee

come in!
¡pase!
pa-se

please come back later
por favor, vuelva más tarde
por fa-bor bwel-ba mas tar-de

I'd like breakfast in my room
quería desayunar en la habitación
ker-ee-a de-sa-yoo-nar en la a-bee-tath-yon

please bring...
por favor, ¿me trae...?
por fa-bor me trae...

toilet paper
papel higiénico
pa-pel eekh-yen-ee-ko

soap
jabón
kha-bon

clean towels
toallas limpias
to-al-yas leemp-yas

a glass
un vaso
oon ba-so

could you clean...?
¿puede limpiar...?
pwe-de leem-pyar

my room
la habitación
la a-bee-tath-yon

the bath
el baño
el ban-yo

please call me...
por favor, despiérteme...
por fa-bor des-pyer-te-me...

at 8 o'clock
a las ocho
a las o-cho

do you have a laundry service?
¿tienen servicio de lavandería?
tyen-en ser-beeth-yo de la-ban-de-ree-a

we're leaving tomorrow
nos vamos mañana
nos ba-mos man-ya-na

please prepare the bill
¿me prepara la cuenta, por favor?
me pre-pa-ra la kwen-ta por fa-bor

Self-catering

- Gas in self-catering accommodation is usually bottled.
- Electricity is mostly 220 volts with 2-pin plugs. You'll need an adaptor for British appliances.
- Rubbish is collected from bins in the streets daily. Spanish people try to recycle as much as possible.
- Youth hostels (**albergues**) can be booked in advance.

which is the key for this door?
¿cuál es la llave de esta puerta?
kwal es la lya-be de es-ta pwer-ta

please show us how this works
enséñenos cómo funciona esto, por favor
es-sen-ye-nos ko-mo foonth-yon-a es-to por fa-bor

how does ... work?	**the waterheater**
¿cómo funciona...?	**el calentador del agua**
ko-mo foonth-yon-a...	*el ka-len-ta-dor del a-gwa*

the washing machine	**the cooker**
la lavadora	**la cocina**
la la-ba-do-ra	*la ko-thee-na*

who do I contact if there are any problems?
¿a quién aviso si hay algún problema?
a kyen a-bee-so see aee al-goon prob-le-ma

we need extra...	**cutlery**	**sheets**
nos hacen falta más...	**cubiertos**	**sábanas**
nos a-then fal-ta mas...	*koo-byer-tos*	*sab-a-nas*

the gas has run out	**what do I do?**
se ha acabado el gas	**¿qué hago?**
se a a-ka-ba-do el gas	*ke a-go*

where are the fuses?	**where do I put the rubbish?**
¿dónde están los fusibles?	**¿dónde se deja la basura?**
don-de es-tan los foo-seeb-les	*don-de se de-kha la ba-soo-ra*

Camping & Caravanning

- When camping in Spain you must use approved sites. Campsites are graded 1st, 2nd and 3rd. A useful website is **www.campinguia.com**.
- You usually pay per tent, per person and per car/caravan.
- If towing a caravan or trailer you must not exceed 50kph in built-up areas and 70 or 80 kph on other roads.

we're looking for a campsite
estamos buscando un camping
es-**ta**-mos boos-**kan**-do oon **kam**-peen

have you a list of campsites?
¿tiene una guía de campings?
tyen-e **oo**-na **gee**-a de **kam**-peens

where is the campsite?
¿dónde está el camping?
don-de es-**ta** el **kam**-peen

have you any vacancies?
¿tienen sitio?
tyen-en **seet**-yo

how much is it per night?
¿cuánto cuesta por noche?
kwan-to **kwes**-ta por **no**-che

we'd like to stay for ... nights
queríamos quedarnos ... noches
ke-**ree**-a-mos ke-**dar**-nos ... **no**-ches

is the campsite near the beach?
¿está el camping cerca de la playa?
es-**ta** el **kam**-peen **ther**-ka de la **pla**-ya

do you have a more sheltered site?
¿tienen algún sitio más resguardado?
tyen-en al-**goon** **see**-tyo mas res-gwar-**da**-do

it is very muddy here
aquí hay mucho barro
a-**kee** aee **moo**-cho **bar**-ro

is there another site?
¿hay otro sitio?
aee **o**-tro **see**-tyo

is there a shop on the site?
¿hay alguna tienda en el camping?
aee al-**goo**-na **tyen**-da en el **kam**-peen

can we camp here?
¿podemos acampar aquí?
po-**de**-mos a-kam-**par** a-**kee**

can we park our caravan here?
¿podemos aparcar la caravana aquí?
po-**de**-mos a-par-**kar** la ka-ra-**ba**-na a-**kee**

for the night
por esta noche
por **es**-ta **no**-che

Children

- Children are accepted almost everywhere in Spain and will often be out with the family until late at night.
- Children under 4 go free on trains and buses; those between 4 and 13 pay 60% of the full fare on trains.
- When travelling by car children must be restrained in appropriate seats at all times.

a child's ticket *(for transport)*
un billete de niño
oon beel-ye-te de neen-yo

(for entertainment)
una entrada de niño
oo-na en-tra-da de neen-yo

is there a reduction for children?
¿hay descuento para niños?
aee des-kwen-to pa-ra neen-yos

do you have a children's menu?
¿tienen menú para niños?
tyen-en me-noo pa-ra neen-yos

do you have...?
¿tiene...?
tyen-e...

a high chair
una trona
oo-na tro-na

a cot
una cuna
oo-na koo-na

what's there for children to do?
¿qué cosas hay para los niños?
ke ko-sas aee pa-ra los neen-yos

is there a playpark?
¿hay algún parque infantil?
aee al-goon par-ke een-fan-teel

is it safe for children?
¿es seguro para los niños?
es se-goo-ro pa-ra los neen-yos

is it dangerous?
¿es peligroso?
es pe-lee-gro-so

I have two children
tengo dos hijos
ten-go dos ee-khos

(s)he is 10 years old
tiene diez años
tyen-e dyeth an-yos

do you have children?
¿tiene hijos?
tyen-e ee-khos

Special Needs

- Tourist offices provide information on provision in their areas.
- Some youth hostels and a few hotels have facilities for disabled travellers.
- Check out disabled access carefully before your trip.
- Each town normally has a fleet of taxis designed to take wheelchairs. These have to be ordered specially.

is it possible to visit ... with a wheelchair?
¿se puede entrar en ... con silla de ruedas?
se **pwe**-de en-**trar** en ... kon **seel**-ya de **rwed**-as

do you have toilets for the disabled?
¿hay aseos para minusválidos?
aee a-**se**-os **pa**-ra mee-noos-**ba**-lee-dos

I need a bedroom on the ground floor
necesito una habitación en la planta baja
ne-the-**see**-to **oo**-na a-bee-tath-**yon** en la **plan**-ta **ba**-kha

is there a lift?
¿hay ascensor?
aee as-then-**sor**

where is the lift?
¿dónde está el ascensor?
don-de es-**ta** el as-then-**sor**

I can't walk far
no puedo andar mucho
no **pwe**-do an-**dar moo**-cho

are there many steps?
¿hay muchos escalones?
aee **moo**-chos es-ka-**lo**-nes

is there an entrance for wheelchairs?
¿hay acceso para sillas de ruedas?
aee ak-**the**-so **pa**-ra **seel**-yas de **rwed**-as

can I travel on this train with a wheelchair?
¿puedo viajar en este tren con silla de ruedas?
pwe-do bya-**khar** en **es**-te tren kon **seel**-ya de **rwed**-as

is there a reduction for the disabled?
¿hay descuento para minusválidos?
aee des-**kwen**-to **pa**-ra mee-noos-**ba**-lee-dos

Exchange Visitors

ESPAÑA CORREOS 0,26€

● These phrases are intended for families hosting Spanish-speaking visitors. We have used the more familiar **tú** form.
● Spanish people tend to eat dinner much later than in the UK, any time between 8.30 and 11 pm. They may not be used to eating their main meal of the day as early as 6pm!
● Spanish guests may never have eaten Indian or Chinese food.

what would you like for breakfast?
¿qué quieres de desayuno?
*ke **kyer**-es de de-sa-**yoo**-no*

do you eat...?
¿comes...?
ko-mes...

what would you like to eat?
¿qué quieres comer
*ke **kyer**-es ko-**mer***

what would you like to drink?
¿qué quieres beber?
*ke **kyer**-es be-**ber***

did you sleep well?
¿has dormido bien?
*as dor-**mee**-do byen*

would you like to take a shower?
¿quieres darte una ducha?
***kyer**-es **dar**-te **oo**-na **doo**-cha*

what would you like to do today?
¿qué quieres hacer hoy?
*ke **kyer**-es a-**ther** oy*

would you like to go shopping?
¿quieres ir de compras?
***kyer**-es eer de **kom**-pras*

I will pick you up at...
te iré a recoger a...
*te ee-**re** a re-ko-**kher** a...*

take care
ten cuidado
*ten kwee-**da**-do*

did you enjoy yourself?
¿te lo has pasado bien?
*te lo as pa-**sa**-do byen*

please be back by...
vuelve antes de...
***bwel**-be **an**-tes de...*

we'll be in bed when you get back
cuando vuelvas estaremos en la cama
*kwan-do **bwel**-bas es-ta-**re**-mos en la **ka**-ma*

Exchange Visitors

- *These phrases are intended for those people staying with Spanish-speaking families.*
- *Take care to use the more formal **usted** form until you are invited to use **tú**, especially with older people.*
- *Spanish families tend to dine together more formally than in the UK.*

I like...
me gusta...
*me **goos**-ta...*

I don't like...
no me gusta...
*no me **goos**-ta...*

that was delicious
estaba buenísimo
*es-**ta**-ba bwe-**nee**-see-mo*

thank you very much
muchas gracias
*moo-chas **grath**-yas*

may I phone home?
¿puedo llamar a casa?
***pwe**-do lya-**mar** a **ka**-sa*

may I make a local call?
¿puedo hacer una llamada local?
pwe**-do a-**ther** oo-na lya-**ma**-da lo-**kal

can I have a key?
¿me deja una llave?
*me **de**-kha oo-na **lya**-be*

can you take me by car?
¿puede llevarme en coche?
***pwe**-de lye-**bar**-me en **ko**-che*

can I borrow...?
¿me deja...?
*me **de**-kha...*

an iron
una plancha
*oo-na **plan**-cha*

a hairdryer
un secador
*oon se-ka-**dor***

what time do you get up?
¿a qué hora se levanta?
*a ke **o**-ra se le-**ban**-ta*

please could you call me at...?
¿me puede llamar a las...?
*me **pwe**-de lya-**mar** a las...*

I'm leaving in a week
me voy dentro de una semana
*me **boy den**-tro de **oo**-na se-**ma**-na*

thanks for everything
gracias por todo
***grath**-yas por **to**-do*

I've had a great time
lo he pasado muy bien
*lo e pa-**sa**-do mooy byen*

Problems

● Always try to speak in Spanish – however bad! And then ask if there is someone who does speak some English.
● Try to stay calm. Not understanding each other can often aggravate the situation.
● Try to be as polite as possible, using **señor** or **señora** and the polite **usted** form.

can you help me, please?
¿puede ayudarme, por favor?
pwe-de a-yoo-*dar*-me por fa-*bor*

I don't speak Spanish
no hablo español
no ab-lo es-pan-yol

do you speak English?
¿habla inglés?
ab-la een-*gles*

does anyone speak English?
¿hay alguien que hable inglés?
aee al-gyen ke *ab*-le een-*gles*

I'm lost
me he perdido
me e per-dee-do

how do I get to...?
¿cómo se va a...?
ko-mo se ba a...

I'm late
llego tarde
lyeg-o *tar*-de

I need to get to...
tengo que ir a...
ten-go se ba eer a...

I've missed...
he perdido...
e per-dee-do...

my plane
el vuelo
el bwe-lo

my connection
el enlace
el en-lath-e

I've lost...
he perdido...
e per-dee-do...

my wallet
la cartera
la kar-te-ra

my passport
el pasaporte
el pa-sa-por-te

my luggage has not arrived
no ha llegado mi equipaje
no a lyeg-a-do mee e-kee-pa-khe

I've left my bag in...
me he dejado la bolsa en...
me e de-kha-do la bol-sa en...

leave me alone!
¡déjeme en paz!
de-khe-me en path

go away!
¡váyase!
ba-ya-se

I have no money
no tengo dinero
no ten-go dee-ne-ro

Complaints

- The British might have a reputation for not complaining, but the Spanish complain even less.
- Complaining does sometimes work, but don't expect miracles as it is not a major part of Spanish culture.
- There is sometimes a lack of flexibility to standard rules and regulations.

the light
la luz
la looth

the air conditioning
el aire acondicionado
el aee-re a-kon-deeth-yon-a-do

...doesn't work
...no funciona
...no foonth-yon-a

the room is dirty
la habitación está sucia
la a-bee-tath-yon es-ta sooth-ya

the bath is dirty
el baño está sucio
el ban-yo es-ta sooth-yo

there is no...
no hay...
no aee...

hot water
agua caliente
a-wa kal-yen-te

toilet paper
papel higiénico
pa-pel eekh-yen-ee-ko

it is too noisy
hay demasiado ruido
aee de-mas-ya-do rwee-do

it is too small
es demasiado pequeño
es de-mas-ya-do pe-ken-yo

this isn't what I ordered
esto no es lo que he pedido
es-to no es lo ke e pe-dee-do

I want to complain
quiero hacer una reclamación
kyer-o a-ther oo-na re-kla-math-yon

I want my money back
quiero que me devuelvan el dinero
kyer-o ke me de-bwel-ban el dee-ne-ro

we've been waiting for a very long time
llevamos mucho tiempo esperando
lyeb-a-mos moo-cho tyem-po es-pe-ran-do

there is a mistake
hay un error
aee oon er-ror

this is broken
esto está roto
es-to es-ta ro-to

can you repair it?
¿puede arreglarlo?
pwe-de ar-reg-lar-lo

Emergencies

● Emergency numbers in Spain: Police (nationwide) – 091,
(local) – 092, Fire Brigade (Madrid, Barcelona & Seville) – 080,
(elsewhere) – check with the operator.
● For an ambulance, call the police and they will make
arrangements, or call 061 for emergencies. The ambulance
service is private.

help!
¡socorro!
*so-**kor**-ro*

can you help me?
¿me puede ayudar?
*me **pwe**-de a-yoo-**dar***

there's been an accident
ha habido un accidente
*a a-**bee**-do oon ak-thee-**den**-te*

someone is injured
hay un herido
*aee oon er-**ee**-do*

call...
llame a...
***lya**-me a...*

the police
la policía
*la po-lee-**thee**-a*

an ambulance
una ambulancia
***oo**-na am-boo-**lanth**-ya*

he was driving too fast
él iba demasiado rápido
*el **ee**-ba de-mas-**ya**-do **rap**-ee-do*

where's the police station?
¿dónde está la comisaría?
***don**-de es-**ta** la kom-ee-sa-**ree**-ya*

the insurance company requires me to report it
la compañía de seguros me exige que lo notifique
*la kom-pan-**yee**-ya de se-**goo**-ros me ek-**see**-khe ke lo no-tee-**fee**-ke*

I've been robbed
me han robado
*me an ro-**ba**-do*

I have no money
no tengo dinero
*no **ten**-go dee-**ne**-ro*

Emergencies

I've been attacked
me han agredido
*me an ag-re-**dee**-do*

I've been raped
me han violado
*me an byo-**la**-do*

my car has been broken into
me han entrado en el coche
*me an en-**tra**-do en el **ko**-che*

my car has been stolen
me han robado el coche
*me an ro-**ba**-do el **ko**-che*

that man keeps following me
ese hombre me está siguiendo
*e-se **om**-bre me es-**ta** seeg-**yen**-do*

how much is the fine?
¿cuánto es la multa?
***kwan**-to es la **mool**-ta*

I don't have enough
no tengo suficiente
*no **ten**-go soo-fee-**thyen**-te*

can I pay at the police station?
¿puedo pagar en la comisaría?
***pwe**-do pa-**gar** en la ko-mee-sa-**ree**-a*

I would like to phone my embassy
quisiera llamar a mi embajada
*kees-**yer**-a lya-**mar** a mee em-ba-**kha**-da*

where is the British Consulate?
¿dónde está el consulado británico?
***don**-de es-**ta** el kon-soo-**la**-do bree-**ta**-nee-ko*

I'm very sorry
lo siento mucho
*lo **syen**-to **moo**-cho*

we're on our way
ahora vamos para allá
*a-**o**-ra **ba**-mos **pa**-ra a-**ya***

Health

● Take a stamped E111 form (from post offices). You can keep it for future trips (unless you change address). This will entitle you to free emergency treatment during your stay.
● If you need to see a doctor, go to the nearest clinic by 9am and you may get an appointment that day. Make sure you're being treated as a National Health patient and not privately.

URGENCIA

have you something for...?
¿tiene algo para...
tyen-e al-go pa-ra...

car sickness
el mareo
el ma-re-o

diarrhoea
la diarrea
la dee-ar-re-a

is it safe for children to take?
¿lo pueden tomar los niños?
lo pwe-den to-mar los neen-yos

I don't feel well
no me encuentro bien
no me en-kwen-tro byen

I need a doctor
necesito un médico
ne-the-see-to oon med-ee-ko

my son/daughter is ill
mi hijo/hija está enfermo(a)
mee ee-kho/ee-kha es-ta en-fer-mo(a)

he/she has a temperature
tiene fiebre
tyen-e fyeb-re

I'm taking these drugs
estoy tomando estos medicamentos
es-toy to-man-do es-tos me-dee-ka-men-tos

I have high blood pressure
tengo la tensión alta
ten-go la ten-syon al-ta

I'm diabetic
soy diabético(a)
soy dya-be-tee-ko(a)

I'm pregnant
estoy embarazada
es-toy em-ba-ra-tha-da

I'm on the pill
estoy tomando la píldora
es-toy tom-an-do la peel-do-ra

I'm allergic to penicillin
soy alérgico(a) a la penicilina
soy a-ler-khee-ko(a) a la pen-ee-thee-lee-na

my blood group is...
mi grupo sanguíneo es...
*mee **groo**-po san-**gee**-ne-o es...*

I'm breastfeeding
estoy dando de mamar
*es-**toy** **dan**-do de ma-**mar***

is it safe to take?
¿tiene contraindicaciones?
***tyen**-e con-tra-een-dee-kath-**yon**-es*

will he/she have to go to hospital?
¿tendrá que ir al hospital?
*ten-**dra** ke eer al os-pee-**tal***

I need to go to casualty
tengo que ir a urgencias
***ten**-go ke eer a oor-**khenth**-yas*

where is the hospital?
¿dónde está el hospital?
don**-de es-**ta** el os-pee-**tal

when are visiting hours?
¿cuáles son las horas de visita?
***kwal**-es son las **o**-ras de bee-**see**-ta*

which ward?
¿qué planta?
*ke **plan**-ta*

I need to see the dentist
necesito ver al dentista
*ne-the-**see**-to ber al den-**tees**-ta*

I have toothache
me duele una muela
*me **dwe**-le **oo**-na **mwe**-la*

the filling has come out
se me ha caído el empaste
*se me a ka-**ee**-do el em-**pas**-te*

it hurts
me duele
*me **dwe**-le*

my dentures are broken
se me ha roto la dentadura postiza
*se me a **ro**-to la den-ta-**doo**-ra pos-**tee**-tha*

can you repair them?
¿puede arreglarla?
***pwe**-de ar-reg-**lar**-la*

I have an abscess
tengo un absceso
***ten**-go oon ab-**thes**-o*

I need a receipt for my insurance
necesito un recibo para el seguro
*ne-the-**see**-to oon re-**thee**-bo pa-ra el se-**goo**-ro*

Business

- *Office hours are generally 9am till 1pm, and 4 till 7pm.*
- *Government offices are open to the public from 9am till 2pm.*
- *Spanish company websites end .es.*
- *If a Spanish bank holiday falls on a Thursday people take Friday off to have a long weekend.*

I'm...
soy...
soy...

here's my card
aquí tiene mi tarjeta
a-kee tyen-e mee tar-khe-ta

I'm from Jones Ltd
soy de la empresa Jones
soy de la em-pre-sa Jones

I'd like to arrange a meeting with Mr/Ms...
quería tener una reunión con el señor/la señora...
ke-ree-a te-ner oo-na re-oon-yon kon el sen-yor/la sen-yor-a...

can we meet at a restaurant?
¿podemos vernos en un restaurante?
po-de-mos ber-nos en oon res-tow-ran-te

I will send a fax to confirm
se lo confirmaré por fax
se lo kon-feer-ma-re por faks

I'm staying at Hotel...
estoy en el Hotel...
es-toy en el o-tel...

how do I get to your office?
¿cómo se va a su oficina?
ko-mo se ba a soo o-fee-thee-na

here is some information about my company
aquí tiene información sobre mi empresa
a-kee tyen-e een-for-math-yon sob-re mee em-pre-sa

I have an appointment with...
tengo una cita con...
ten-go oo-na thee-ta kon...

at ... o'clock
a las...
a las...

I'm delighted to meet you
encantado(a) de conocerle
en-kan-ta-do(a) de ko-no-ther-le

my Spanish isn't very good
no hablo muy bien español
no ab-lo mooy byen es-pan-yol

what is the name of the managing director?
¿cómo se llama el director gerente?
ko-mo se lya-ma el dee-rek-tor khe-ren-te

I would like some information about the company
quería información sobre la empresa
ke-ree-a een-for-math-yon sob-re la em-pre-sa

do you have a press office?
¿tiene oficina de prensa?
tyen-e o-fee-thee-na de pren-sa

I need an interpreter
necesito un intérprete
ne-the-see-to oon een-ter-pre-te

can you photocopy this for me?
¿me puede fotocopiar esto?
me pwe-de fo-to-kop-yar es-to

is there a business centre?
¿hay algún centro de negocios?
aee al-goon then-tro de ne-go-thyos

do you have an appointment?
¿está usted citado(a)?
es-ta oo-sted thee-ta-do(a)

Phoning

● The international dialling code for the UK is 00 44. To phone Spain it is 00 34.

● You can buy phonecards (for 6 and 12 euros) from newspaper kiosks and tobacconists'.

● For calls within Spain you must dial the area code and number (even for local calls).

a phonecard
una tarjeta telefónica
oo-na tar-**khe**-ta te-le-**fo**-nee-ka

for ... euros
de ... euros
*de ... **eoo**-ros*

I want to make a phone call
quiero hacer una llamada
kyer-o a-**ther** oo-na lya-**ma**-da

I want to make a reverse charge call
quiero hacer una llamada a cobro revertido
kyer-o a-**ther** oo-na lya-**ma**-da a **ko**-bro re-ber-**tee**-do

can I speak to...?
¿puedo hablar con...?
pwe-do a-**blar** kon...

this is...
soy...
soy...

is Valle there?
¿está Valle?
*es-**ta** bal*-ye

with Señor Rugama, please
con el señor Rugama, por favor
*kon el sen-**yor** roo-**ga**-ma por fa-**bor***

I'll call back later/tomorrow
le volveré a llamar más tarde/mañana
*le bol-be-**re** a lya-**mar** mas **tar**-de ma-**nya**-na*

can you give me an outside line, please
¿me da línea, por favor?
*me da **lee**-ne-a por fa-**bor***

hello
¿diga?
dee-ga

who is calling?
¿de parte de quién?
*de **par**-te de kyen*

it's engaged
está comunicando
*es-**ta** ko-moo-nee-**kan**-do*

- There are a lot of internet cafés in Spain. Some deals look better than they actually are.
- www. is **tres uve dobles punto**. @ is either 'at' or **arroba**. Many English terms are used and understood.
- The ending for Spanish websites is **.es**.
- The Spanish word for 'password' is **contraseña**.

I want to send an e-mail
quiero mandar un email
kyer-o man-**dar** oon **ee**-meyl

what's your e-mail address?
cuál es su email?
kwal es soo **ee**-meyl

my e-mail address is...
mi dirección email es...
mee dee-rekth-**yon ee**-meyl es...

lydia.martin@villen.es
Lydia punto Martin arroba villen punto e s
lee-dya **poon**-to mar-**teen** ar-**ro**-ba **uil**-yen **poon**-to e **e**-se

did you get my e-mail?
¿le llegó mi email?
le lyeg-**o** mee **ee**-meyl

I want to send a fax
quiero mandar un fax
kyer-o man-**dar** oon faks

do you have a fax?
¿tiene fax?
tyen-e faks

what's your fax number?
¿cuál es su número de fax?
kwal es soo **noo**-me-ro de faks

did you get my fax?
¿le llegó mi fax?
le lyeg-**o** mee faks

can I send a fax from here?
¿puedo mandar un fax desde aquí?
pwe-do man-**dar** oon faks **des**-de a-**kee**

the fax is engaged
el fax está ocupado
el faks es-**ta** o-koo-**pa**-do

Numbers

0	cero *ther*-o	1st	primero/ primer 1º/1ᵉʳ *pree-**me**-ro*
1	uno **oo**-no		
2	dos *dos*		
3	tres *tres*	2nd	segundo 2º *se-**goon**-do*
4	cuatro **kwat**-ro		
5	cinco **theen**-ko		
6	seis *seyss*	3rd	tercero/tercer 3º/3ᵉʳ *ter-**the**-ro*
7	siete **syet**-e		
8	ocho **o**-cho		
9	nueve **nwe**-be	4th	cuarto 4º **kwar**-to
10	diez *dyeth*		
11	once **on**-the		
12	doce **doth**-e	5th	quinto 5º **keen**-to
13	trece **treth**-e		
14	catorce ka-**torth**-e		
15	quince **keenth**-e	6th	sexto 6º **seks**-to
16	dieciséis dyeth-ee-**seyss**		
17	diecisiete dyeth-ee-**syet**-e	7th	séptimo 7º **sept**-ee-mo
18	dieciocho dyeth-ee-**o**-cho		
19	diencinueve dyeth-ee-**nwe**-be	8th	octavo 8º ok-**ta**-bo
20	veinte **beyn**-te		
21	veintiuno beyn-tee-**oo**-no		
22	veintidós beyn-tee-**dos**	9th	noveno 9º no-**be**-no
30	treinta **treyn**-ta		
40	cuarenta kwa-**ren**-ta	10th	décimo 10º **deth**-ee-mo
50	cincuenta theen-**kwen**-ta		
60	sesenta se-**sen**-ta		
70	setenta se-**ten**-ta		
80	ochenta o-**chen**-ta		
90	noventa no-**ben**-ta		
100	cien *thyen*		
110	ciento diez **thyen**-to dyeth		
200	doscientos dos-**thyen**-tos		
500	quinientos keen-**yen**-tos		
1000	mil *meel*		
million	un millón oon meel-**yon**		

Days & Months

Monday	lunes *loo*-nes
Tuesday	martes *mar*-tes
Wednesday	míercoles *myer*-ko-les
Thursday	jeuves *khwe*-bes
Friday	viernes *byer*-nes
Saturday	sábado *sa*-ba-do
Sunday	domingo do-*meen*-go
January	enero e-*ne*-ro
February	febrero feb-*re*-ro
March	marzo *mar*-tho
April	abril av-*reel*
May	mayo *ma*-yo
June	junio *khoon*-yo
July	julio *khool*-yo
August	agosto a-*gos*-to
September	septiembre sep-*tyem*-bre
October	octubre ok-*toob*-re
November	noviembre nov-*yem*-bre
December	diciembre deeth-*yem*-bre

what's the date?
¿qué fecha es hoy?
ke fe-cha es oy

which day?
¿qué día?
ke dee-a

which month?
¿qué mes?
ke mes

March 5th
el cinco de marzo
el theen-ko de mar-tho

July 6th
el seis de julio
el se-ees de khool-yo

2004
dos mil cuatro
dos meel kwat-ro

on Saturday
el sábado
el sa-ba-do

on Saturdays
los sábados
los sa-ba-dos

every Saturday
todos los sábados
to-dos los sa-ba-dos

this Saturday
este sábado
es-te sa-ba-do

next Saturday
el próximo sábado
el prok-see-mo sa-ba-do

last Saturday
el sábado pasado
el sa-ba-do pa-sa-do

please can you confirm the date?
¿me puede confirmar la fecha?
me pwe-de kon-feer-mar la fe-cha

Time

- am = **de la mañana** (de la man-ya-na)
- pm = **de la tarde** (de la **tar**-de)
- *The 24-hour clock is used a lot more in Europe than in Britain.*
- *With the 24-hour clock the words **cuarto** (quarter) and **media** (half) aren't used.*

what time is it, please?
¿qué hora es por favor?
ke **o**-ra es por fa-**bor**

am
de la mañana
de la man-**ya**-na

pm
de la tarde
de la **tar**-de

it's 1 o'clock
es la una
es la **oo**-na

it's 2/3 o'clock
son las dos/tres
son las dos/tres

it's half past 8
son las ocho y media
son las **o**-cho ee **med**-ya

it is half past 10
son las diez y media
son las dyeth ee **med**-ya

in an hour
dentro de una hora
den-tro de **oo**-na **o**-ra

in half an hour
dentro de media hora
den-tro de **med**-ya **o**-ra

until 8 o'clock
hasta las ocho
as-ta las **o**-cho

until 4 o'clock
hasta las cuatro
as-ta las **kwat**-ro

at 10 am
a las diez de la mañana
a las dyeth de la man-**ya**-na

at 2200
a las veintidós horas
a las beyn-tee-**dos** **o**-ras

at midday
a las doce de la mañana
a las **doth**-e de la man-**ya**-na

at midnight
a medianoche
a med-ya-**no**-che

soon
pronto
pron-to

later
más tarde
mas **tar**-de

La cocina española

One of the greatest pleasures of travelling in Spain is the discovery of regional cooking. Spain is a large country and its many provinces, so different in character and history, have developed their own distinctive dishes using the best of local produce.

Sampling the many tastes and textures of Spanish food couldn't be easier: just stop at a bar (**bar**) and order **tapas**. **Tapas** seem to have originated in Andalucia, but they are a way of life in the whole of Spain and have become fashionable even outside the country. They have the advantage of allowing you to taste lots of dishes at once **Tapas** are ideal as a quick snack or light meal – often very welcome when you consider how late the meals are served in Spain. Some people have become addicted to visiting various bars, one after the other, to eat a few of their mini dishes instead of having a main meal. This can be great fun, especially in big cities, where there is an incredible variety of **tapas**.

The rich diversity of regional cooking, based on fresh local ingredients, reflects the diversity of Spain's landscape and climate. However, some elements are common to all areas, such as the use of **chorizo** (spicy pork sausage with paprika), peppers, olive oil and garlic. A number of regional dishes have become associated with Spain as a whole, such as **paella** (a rice dish), **tortilla** (potato omelette) and **fabada** (bean stew), but, fortunately, regional traditions continue to thrive.

As far as eating out in Spain is concerned, the general rule is that you must expect meals to be served late. It may be possible to start lunch at 1 pm but late lunches, starting at 2 pm at the earliest and going on until nearly 4 pm are more common. This also makes for a very late dinner, lighter than lunch (see below).

Breakfast (**el desayuno**) is normally light, consisting of coffee/milk with bread and olive oil or butter. The main meal is still eaten at lunchtime (2–3 pm) and this is very much a family event. Lunch (**el almuerzo**) is usually a 3-course meal, with the second course often being a piece of meat with no accompaniment. When people eat in the evening (**la cena**), either at home or out, their meal may not start until 10 pm or later.

Ordering drinks

● Tea in Spain tends to be served weak and with lemon.
If you want milk, ask for it to be served separately (*aparte*
a-par-te), otherwise you may get a cup of hot milk with a
teabag in it.
● If you want a strong black coffee, ask for **un café solo**.
● A white coffee is often served in a glass mug, **en caña**.

a black coffee un café solo *oon ka-fe so-lo*	**a white coffee** un café con leche *oon ka-fe kon le-che*	**a tea** un té *oon te*

with milk con leche *kon le-che*	**with lemon** con limón *kon lee-mon*	**a lager** una cerveza *oo-na ther-be-tha*	**a dry sherry** un fino *oon fee-no*

a hot chocolate with churros, please
un chocolate con churros por favor
oon cho-ko-la-te kon choor-ros por fa-bor

a bottle of mineral water
una botella de agua mineral
oo-na bo-tel-ya de ag-wa mee-ne-ral

sparkling
con gas
kon gas

still
sin gas
sin gas

a glass of red wine
un vaso de tinto
oon ba-so de teen-to

a glass of white wine
un vaso de vino blanco
oon ba-so de vee-no blan-ko

a bottle of wine
una botella de vino
oo-na bo-tel-ya de bee-no

red
tinto
teen-to

white
blanco
blan-ko

the wine list, please
la carta de vinos, por favor
la kar-ta de bee-nos por fa-bor

another bottle, please
otra botella, por favor
o-tra bo-tel-ya por fa-bor

would you like a drink?
¿quiere tomar algo?
kyer-e to-mar al-go

what will you have?
¿qué quiere tomar?
ke kyer-e to-mar

- In Spain, lunch is usually between 1 and 3pm and dinner between 8.30 and 11pm.
- Eating **tapas** in various bars is a good way of trying out various foods and lets you eat earlier.
- The equivalent to 'Bon appétit!' is **¡Qué aproveche!** The reply is **¡Gracias, igualmente!** (thanks, you too!)

can you recommend a good restaurant?
¿puede recomendarme un buen restaurante?
pwe-de re-ko-men-dar-me oon bwen res-tow-ran-te

I'd like to book a table
quería reservar una mesa
ke-ree-a re-ser-bar oo-na me-sa

for ... people
para ... personas
pa-ra ... per-so-nas

for tonight
para esta noche
pa-ra es-ta no-che

at 8 pm
a las ocho
a las o-cho

the menu, please
la carta por favor
la kar-ta por fa-bor

is there a dish of the day?
¿hay plato del día?
aee pla-to del dee-a

have you a set-price menu?
¿tiene un menú del día?
tyen-e oon me-noo del dee-a

I'll have this
yo voy a tomar esto
yo boy a to-mar es-to

what do you recommend?
¿qué recomienda?
ke re-kom-yen-da

I don't eat meat
no como carne
no ko-mo kar-ne

do you have any vegetarian dishes?
¿tiene algún plato vegetariano?
tyen-e al-goon pla-to be-khe-tar-ya-no

excuse me!
¡oiga, por favor!
oy-ga por fa-bor

more bread
más pan
mas pan

more water
más agua
mas ag-wa

the bill, please
la cuenta, por favor
la kwen-ta por fa-bor

is service included?
¿está incluido el servicio?
es-ta een-klwee-do el ser-beeth-yo

Special requirements

- The words for gluten free are **sin gluten**.
- **Biológico** or **bio** means organic.
- On labels, **hidratos de carbono** are carbohydrates. **Grasos** are fats.
- Health foods (**productos dietéticos**) are available in large supermarkets and specialist shops (**herbolarios**).

I'm vegetarian
soy vegetariano/a
*soy ve-khe-tar-**ya**-no/a*

what is in this?
¿qué lleva esto?
*ke **lyeb**-a **es**-to*

I don't eat meat/pork
no como carne/cerdo
*no **ko**-mo **kar**-ne/**ther**-do*

I don't eat fish/shellfish
no como pescado/mariscos
*no **ko**-mo pes-**ka**-do/ma-**rees**-kos*

I'm allergic to shellfish
soy alérgico(a) al marisco
*soy a-**ler**-khee-ko(a) al ma-**rees**-ko*

I can't eat raw eggs
no puedo comer huevos crudos
*no **pwe**-do ko-**mer** hwe-bos **kroo**-dos*

I can't eat liver
no puedo comer higado
*no **pwe**-do ko-**mer** ee-ga-do*

I am on a diet
estoy a dieta
*es-**toy** a **dyet**-a*

I am allergic to peanuts
soy alérgico(a) a los cacahuetes
*soy a-**ler**-khee-ko(a) a los ka-ka-**we**-tes*

is it raw?
¿está crudo?
*es-**ta kroo**-do*

I don't drink alcohol
no bebo alcohol
*no **be**-bo al-**kol**

is it made with unpasteurised milk?
¿está hecho con leche sin pasteurizar?
*es-**ta e**-cho kon **le**-che seen past-e-oo-ree-**thar**

76

BAKERS sell fresh bread, milk, juice and other basic items. You can get both breakfast and lunch there.

It is normal to pay for drinks as you leave the bar. However, in some outdoor cafés, the waiter will present you with the bill as he gives you the drink and you are expected to pay there and then.

RESTAURANT/TAVERN Eating places must display menus and prices.

MARKET Daily or weekly, you will find cheese and local specialities as well as tomatoes and fruit for the perfect picnic.

At restaurants, be prepared to spend time at the table. You can order à la carte or opt for the set menu, in which case you will be served more quickly. But take into consideration the large portions generally served. In Spain salads and vegetable dishes are considered as separate items and normally brought to the table before the main dish. Bread is always provided but not butter. Flexibility is often the key here. For example, if you want boiled potatoes instead of chips, ask and they will probably be able to do it.

| fried fish | fish | shellfish | meat |

Pizza and other Italian food are widely available in Spain.

PIZZERIA

CAFE - BAR - HELADERIA
MEZQUITA

HELADERIA = ICE-CREAM PARLOUR

Comedor

DINING ROOM

pequeña = small
mediana = medium
grande = large

PEQUEÑA MEDIANA GRANDE

PLATOS COMBINADOS

batidos = milkshakes

BATIDOS

granizados = iced drinks such as iced lemon

GRANIZADOS

Platos combinados consist normally of meat or fish with rice, potatoes or chips and vegetables, i.e. a full dish.

If what you order isn't a *plato combinado* and you order, for example, a piece of fish, you will only get fish. The waiter will usually ask you if you want it with chips or vegetables.

CAKE SHOPS AND CAFÉS

Pastelería

CONFITERIA CAFETERIA

A *cafetería* normally serves some dishes (toasted sandwiches, *sándwiches*) as well as some cakes, *pasteles*.

Look out for local specialities. Here, *ensaimadas*, spiral-shaped cakes from Majorca. These can be either sweet or savoury.

Beach bars/restaurants are called *Chiringuitos*.

desayuno = breakfast
comidas = meals

Kiosks are good for soft drinks, crisps, sweets and ice creams.

Snacks are often sold on the street, especially in shopping areas and during fiestas.

ALMENDRAS	100G	1€	almonds
AVELLANAS	100G	1€	hazelnuts
PISTACHOS	250G	1€	pistacchios
CONGUITOS	100G	0.5€	chocolate peanuts
PIPAS	1 BOLSA	1€	sunflower seeds
PATATAS F BTAS	1 BOLSA	1€	crisps (*bolsa*=bag)

TODOS LOS DIAS

ENTREPANS / BOCADILLOS

PAN CON TOMATE Y ACEITE

PAN TOMATE Y ACEITE	1,00 €
MORTADELA	1,50 €
SALCHICHÓN	1,50 €
CHORIZO	1,50 €
JAMÓN YORK	1,50 €
ATÚN	1,50 €
SARDINAS	1,65 €
ANCHOAS	1,85 €
JAMÓN SERRANO	2,10 €
FIAMBRE DE PAVO	1,50 €

SUPLEMENTOS

1/2 BARRA	0,25 €
CALIENTE	0,25 €
ACEITUNAS RELLENAS ANCHOA	0,25 €
QUESO BARRA	0,50 €
QUESO MANCHEGO Ó MAHONES	1,00 €

Bocadillos are sandwiches
pan = bread
aceite = olive oil
mortadela = liver sausage
salchichón = salami
chorizo = spicy salami
jamón york = cooked ham
atún = tuna
sardinas = sardines
anchoas = anchovies
jamón serrano = cured ham
fiambre de pavo = turkey
barra = baguette
caliente = hot
aceitunas rellenas anchoa
= olives stuffed with anchovy
queso barra = slice of cheese
queso manchego = hard cheese

The menu will indicate the various types of dishes served, dividing them into categories, i.e. soups, starters, fish dishes, and so on, in more or less detail, according to the type of restaurant.

La Carta

Entremeses
*Starters (also **entrantes fríos** or **calientes** – starters, cold or hot)*

Sopas *Soups*

Plato del día *Dish of the day*

Primer plato *First course*

Ensalada *Salad*

Verduras *Vegetables*

Huevos *Egg dishes*

Revueltos *Scrambled eggs (generally cooked with something like mushrooms, asparagus or spinach)*

Pastas *Pasta dishes*

Arroces *Rice dishes. (Many rice dishes, such as paella, are normally only prepared for a minimum of two people)*

Parrilladas *Grilled food*

Pescados *Fish dishes*

Carnes *Meats*

Postres *Desserts*

Quesos *Cheeses*

Many set-price menus (*menú del día*) will include wine (*vino*). See the bottom section of board which says *pan, postre, vino* (bread, dessert, wine) included. *1º* (= *primero* = first), *2º* (= *segundo* = second). *Sólo arriba en el comedor* means 'only upstairs in the dining room'. *El menú* is a set-price menu, *la carta* is the actual printed menu.

MENU CASERO=7€

Casero means homemade

SNACK
"SOLO MEDIO DIA"
"ONLY LUNCH TIME"

Some dishes (usually snacky ones) will only be available at lunchtime, *sólo a medio día*. Here the house speciality (*especialidad de la casa*) is *caldereta de langosta* (lobster stew).

ESPECIALIDAD DE LA CALDERETA DE LANG

In *tapas* bars, there are usually two sets of prices, the lower one for sitting at the bar and the other for sitting at a table. If you are at the bar, ordering *tapas* is simply a matter of pointing at what you want. Spaniards don't often drink without picking at some small *tapas* or snack. *Tapas* allow you to taste lots of dishes at once, because, although they can just be appetizers such as cured ham (*jamón serrano*) or cheese (*queso*), they are often small portions of main dishes. Almost any dish can be served as *tapas*. Often each person orders two or three different tapas, so if you are eating with a group of friends you will have a dozen or so to share. *Tapas* are ideal as a quick snack or light meal – often very welcome when you consider how late meals are served in Spain.

croquetas
(fish or meat croquettes)

chorizo
(spicy salami-type sausage)

calamares fritos
(squid in batter)

chanquetes
(whitebait)

patatas bravas
(fried potato cubes with spicy tomato sauce)

jamón serrano
(cured ham)

gambas
(prawns)

queso
(cheese)

A **ración** is a larger serving of **tapas**.

Tapas y Raciones		
	TAPA	RACIÓN
ESTOFADO	2,85	4,30

almejas
(clams)

aceitunas
(olives)

COFFEE comes in many varieties, the most common is *café con leche*; *café solo*, black coffee is like an espresso. If you want decaff, be careful to ask for *descafeinado de máquina* (from the espresso machine), or you are likely to get a cup of warm milk and a sachet of Nescafé. *Café con leche* is usually served in a glass (*en caña*). If you want it in a cup ask for it *en taza*.

Ordering a tea with milk will often get you a teabag put into hot milk, so you have to be quite specific and ask for a tea with cold milk separately, *un té con leche fría aparte.*

té

REFRESCOS

SOFT DRINKS

GOFRES
HELADOS · GRANIZADOS
REFRESCOS ·

helados = ice cream
granizados = iced drinks
refrescos = soft drinks

CHOCOLATE CON CHURROS
A popular breakfast and late afternoon snack (*merienda*) is thick hot chocolate with *churros*, fried batter sticks for dipping.

San Miguel
ELABORADA EN ESPAÑA
TRADICIÓN

Beer in Spain means lager. Local brews are very good. You can order a bottle *un botellín* or a draught beer *una caña*, usually about half a pint.

servicio no incluido

SERVICE NOT INCLUDED
If you wish to tip, between 5 and 10% of the bill is fairly standard.

CALIENTE HOT

FRÍO COLD

READING THE WINE LABEL

Cosecha means vintage

The *DO* (*denominación de origen*) system is based on regions. In this case, Penedès. *DOC* (adding the word *calificada* indicates tighter growing and production controls) only applies to Rioja at present. If you like good wine, stick to *DO* and *DOC* and avoid lowlier *vino de la tierra* and *vino de mesa*. Other terms to look out for are *sin crianza* (new wine, so not aged), *crianza* (1 year aging and often the best bet), *reserva* (3 year aging) and *gran reserva* (5 year aging). Rioja wine is aged in oak barrels, so if you don't like too much oak, go for *sin crianza* or *crianza*.

At 13% the alcohol content is quite high. 11.5% is about average, 14% is pretty hefty.

Mesón is a traditional-style tavern/restaurant. *Cervecería* means beerhouse.

Carta de vinos

WINE LIST

Jerez **SHERRY** is named after one of the main sherry towns, Jerez. The other two towns are El Puerto de Santa María and Sanlúcar. Avoid the cheapies.

Fino — Dry, lean, subtle and lemony from Jerez. Drink chilled.

Amontillado — An aged *fino*, it is rich and nutty.

Manzanilla — Briny, dry and yeasty.

Palo Cortado — Halfway between *Amontillado* and *Oloroso*.

Oloroso — Rich, spicy and Christmassy.

Bodega is the word for wine cellar and is the term for a wine bar which usually also serves food. Menus are displayed outside.

Tapas

There are many different varieties of **tapas** depending on the region. This is a list of some of the most common **tapas** that can be found in any part of Spain. A larger portion of **tapas** is called a **ración**. A **pincho** is another word for a **tapa**.

Asadillo/Asadura de pimientos roasted red peppers marinated in olive oil and garlic

Berenjenas fritas fried aubergines

Boquerones en vinagre fresh anchovies marinated in garlic, parsley and olive oil

Croquetas de carne/pescado meat/fish croquettes with bechamel

Ensaladilla rusa potato salad with vegetables, tuna, hard-boiled eggs and mayonnaise

Frituría de pescado assorted deep-fried fish

Gambas al ajillo grilled shrimps sautéed in olive oil, garlic, parsley and dry white wine

Gambas plancha grilled shrimps

Japuta/Cazón en adobo marinated pomfret/dogfish

Montadito de lomo grilled pork fillet marinated in paprika and garlic, served on toasted bread

Patatas alioli potato in garlic and olive oil vinaigrette

Patatas bravas fried potato cubes with a spicy tomato sauce

Pinchitos morunos grilled skewers of pork tenderloin marinated in spices, garlic and olive oil

Pincho de tortilla small portion of Spanish omelette

Pulpo a la vinagreta octopus marinated in garlic, onions, peppers, olive oil and lemon juice

Rabo de toro en salsa oxtail stew

Salmorejo thick cold tomato soup made with tomatoes, bread, garlic and olive oil

A

...a la/al in the style of

...a la Navarra stuffed with ham

...a la parilla/plancha grilled

...a la romana fried in batter

...al horno baked/roast

aceite oil
  aceite de oliva olive oil

aceitunas olives
  aceitunas rellenas stuffed olives

acelgas Swiss chard

adobo, ...en marinated

agua water
  agua mineral mineral water
  agua con gas sparkling water
  agua sin gas still water

aguardiente a kind of clear grape brandy distilled from fermented fruit juice

ahumado smoked

ajetes garlic shoots

ajillo, ...al with garlic

ajo garlic
  ajo blanco kind of garlic, bread and almond soup served cold. Sometimes served with diced apple and raisins

ajo de las manos *sliced, boiled potatoes mixed with a garlic, oil and vinegar dressing, and flavoured with red chillies*

albahaca *basil*

albaricoque *apricot*

albóndigas *meatballs in sauce*

alcachofas *artichokes*
  alcachofas a la vinagreta *artichokes served with a strong vinaigrette*
  alcachofas con jamón *sautéed artichoke hearts with cured ham*
  alcachofas rellenas *stuffed artichokes*

alcaparras *capers*

aliño *dressing*

alioli/allioli *olive oil and garlic mashed together into a creamy paste similar to mayonnaise. Served with meat, potatoes or fish*

almejas *clams*
  almejas a la marinera *steamed clams cooked with parsley, wine and garlic*

almendras *almonds*

alubias *large white beans found in many stews*

amontillado *medium-dry to dry sherry, very prized*

ancas de rana *frogs' legs*

anchoa *anchovy*

anguila *eel*

angulas *baby eels, highly prized*
  angulas al ajillo *baby eels cooked with garlic*
  angulas en cazuelita *garlic-flavoured, fried baby eels seasoned with hot pepper*

anís (seco or **dulce)** *aniseed liqueur, dry or sweet, normally drunk as a long drink with water and ice*

apio *celery*

arenque *herring*

arroz *rice*
  arroz a banda *a dish of rice and fish. The dish is served in two courses: first the rice cooked with saffron is served and then the fish that has been cooked in it*
  arroz a la cubana *rice with fried egg and tomato sauce*
  arroz a la levantina *rice with shellfish, onions, artichokes, peas, tomatoes and saffron*
  arroz a la marinera *rice with seafood*
  arroz a la valenciana *Valencian version of paella, sometimes cooked with eel*
  arroz a la zamorana *rice with pork, peppers and garlic*
  arroz blanco *boiled rice*
  arroz con costra *rice with chicken, rabbit, sausages, chickpeas and pork meatballs baked in oven with egg topping*
  arroz con leche *rice pudding flavoured with cinnamon*
  arroz con pollo *rice with chicken, garnished with peas and peppers*
  arroz negro *black rice (with squid in its own ink)*
  arroz santanderino *rice cooked with salmon and milk*

asado *roasted*

asadillo *roasted sliced red peppers in olive oil and garlic*

atún *tuna (usually fresh)*
  atún con salsa de tomate *tuna fish in tomato sauce*

avellana *hazelnut*

azafrán *saffron*

azúcar *sugar*

B

bacalao *salt cod, cod*
  bacalao a la vizcaína *salt cod cooked with dried peppers, onions and parsley*
  bacalao al ajo arriero *salt cod fried with garlic to which is added vinegar, paprika and parsley*
  bacalao al pil-pil *a Basque speciality – salt cod cooked in a creamy garlic and olive oil sauce*
  bacalao con patatas *salt cod slowly baked with potatoes, peppers, tomatoes, onions, olives and bay leaves*
  bacalao de convento *salt cod cooked with spinach and potato*

bajoques farcides *peppers stuffed with rice, pork and tomatoes spices*

bandeja de quesos *cheese platter*

barbacoa, ...a la *barbecued*

berenjena *aubergine (eggplant)*
  berenjenas a la catalana *aubergines with tomato sauce, Catalan style*
  berenjenas rellenas *stuffed aubergines (usually with mince)*
  berenjenas salteadas *aubergines sautéed with tomatoes and onions*

besugo *red bream*

bistec *steak*

bizcocho *sponge*

bizcocho borracho *sponge soaked in wine and syrup*

blanco y negro *a milky coffee with ice*

bocadillo *sandwich (French bread)*

bogavante *lobster*

bonito *tunny fish, lighter than tuna, good grilled*

boquerones *fresh anchovies*
  boquerones fritos *fried anchovies*

brasa, ...a la *barbecued*

buñuelos *type of fritter. Savoury ones are filled with cheese, ham, mussels or prawns. Sweet ones can be filled with fruit*
  buñuelos de bacalao *salt cod fritters*

butifarra *special sausage from Catalonia*
  butifarra blanca *white sausage containing pork and tripe*
  butifarra negra *black sausage containing pork blood, belly and spices*

C

caballa *mackerel*

cabello de ángel *sweet pumpkin filling*

cabrito *kid (goat)*
  cabrito al horno *roast kid*

cacahuete *peanut*

cachelada *chopped boiled potatoes and cabbage with garlic, red pepper and fried bacon. Often served with* ***chorizo***

café *coffee*
  café con leche *white coffee*
  café cortado *coffee with only*

a little milk
café descafeinado decaffeinated coffee
café helado iced coffee
café solo black coffee

calabacines courgettes
calabacines rellenos stuffed courgettes

calabaza guisada stewed pumpkin

calamares squid
calamares a la romana fried squid rings in batter
calamares en su tinta squid cooked in its own ink
calamares fritos fried squid
calamares rellenos stuffed squid

calçotada roasted spring onion laced with olive oil and almonds. Typical of Tarragona

caldeirada fish soup from Galicia

caldereta stew/casserole
caldereta de cordero lamb casserole
caldereta de langosta lobster stew
caldereta de pescado fish stew

caldo clear soup
caldo de pescado fish soup
caldo gallego clear soup with green vegetables, beans, pork and **chorizo**

caliente hot

callos tripe

callos a la madrileña fried tripe casseroled in a spicy paprika sauce with tomatoes and **chorizo**

camarones shrimps

canela cinnamon

cangrejo crab

caracoles snails

caracoles de mar winkles

caracolillos winkles

carajillo black coffee with brandy which may be set alight depending on regional customs

cardo cardoon, plant related to the artichoke

carne meat
carne de buey beef
carne picada minced meat

carnero mutton

cassolada pork and vegetable stew from Catalonia

castaña chestnut

cava champagne-style sparkling wine

cazuela de fideos legumes, meat and noodle stew

cebolla onion
cebollas rellenas stuffed onions

centollo spider crab

cerdo pork
cerdo asado roast pork

cerezas cherries

cerveza beer

champán champagne

champiñones mushrooms

chanfaina a stew made from pig's liver and other parts

chanquetes whitebait

chilindrón, ...al sauce made with pepper, tomato, fried onions and meat (pork or lamb)

chistorra spicy sausage from Navarra

chocolate drinking chocolate (thickened)

chorizo spicy red sausage. The larger type is eaten like salami, the thinner type is cooked in various dishes

choto *kid/calf*
  choto albaicinero *kid fried with garlic from Granada*

chuleta *chop*
  chuleta de cerdo *pork chop*
  chuleta de ternera *veal/beef chop*
  chuletas de cordero *grilled lamb chops*

chuletón *large steak*

churrasco *barbecued steak*

churros *fried batter sticks sprinkled with sugar, usually eaten with thick hot chocolate*

ciervo *deer (venison)*

cigalas *king prawns*

ciruelas *plums*

coca (coques) *type of pizza with meat, fish or vegetables served in the Balearic Islands. They can also be sweet*

cochinillo *roast suckling pig*

cocido *stew made with various meats, vegetables and chickpeas. There are regional variations of this dish and it is worth trying the local version*
  cocido de lentejas *thick stew of lentils and* **chorizo**
  cocido de pelotas *a rich spicy stew with mince wrapped in cabbage leaves containing pork and chickpeas*

coco *coconut*

cóctel de gambas *prawn cocktail*

codillo de cerdo *pig's trotter*

codornices asadas *roast quail*

codorniz *quail*

col *cabbage*

coles de Bruselas *Brussels sprouts*

coliflor *cauliflower*

comino *cumin*

coñac *brandy; it can be on the dry side or sweet and fragrant, as the Spaniards prefer*

conchas finas *large scallops*

conejo *rabbit*

consomé *consommé*
  consomé al jerez *consommé with sherry*
  consomé de gallina *chicken consommé*

copa *goblet*
  copa de helado *ice-cream sundae*

coques *see* **coca**
  coques de torró *wafers filled with almonds, sold at Christmas in Majorca*

cordero *lamb*
  cordero al chilindrón *lamb in a spicy pepper sauce*
  cordero asado *roast lamb*
  cordero asado a la manchega *spit-roasted young lamb*
  cordero relleno trufado *lamb stuffed with truffles*

costillas *ribs*
  costillas de cerdo *pork ribs*

crema *cream soup/cream*
  crema catalana *similar to crème brûlée*
  crema de espárragos *cream of asparagus*
  crema de tomate *cream of tomato soup*

crema *generic name given to smooth liqueurs, e.g.* **crema de naranja** *(orange cream)*

cremat *coffee with brandy and rum, served in Catalonia*

croquetas *croquettes (made with thick bechamel sauce)*

croquetas de camarones shrimp croquettes

crudo raw

cuajada cream-based dessert served with honey or sugar

cubalibre coca-cola mixed with rum or gin

culantro coriander

D

dátiles dates

descafeinado decaffeinated

dorada sea bream
  dorada a la sal sea bream cooked in the oven, covered only with salt, forming a crust
  dorada al horno baked sea bream

dulce sweet

E

embutido sausage, cold meat

empanada pastry/pie filled with meat or fish and vegetables

empanadilla pasty/small pie filled with meat or fish

empanado breadcrumbed and fried

ensaimada sweet spiral-shaped yeast bun from Majorca

ensalada (mixta/verde) (mixed/green) salad
  ensalada de la casa lettuce, tomato and onion salad (may include tuna)
  ensalada de huevos salad with hard boiled eggs

ensaladilla rusa diced cooked vegetables and potatoes in mayonnaise

entrecot entrecôte steak

entremeses starters
  entremeses de fiambre cold meat hors d'œuvres
  entremeses de pescado fish hors d'œuvres

escabeche, ...en pickled
  escabeche de pescado fish marinated in oil and served cold

escalfado poached

escalivada salad of chargrilled vegetables such as peppers and aubergines soaked in olive oil

escalope de ternera veal/beef escalope

escarola endive

escudella meat, vegetable and chickpea stew. Traditionally served as two courses: a soup and then the cooked meat and vegetables
  escudilla de pages white bean, sausage, ham and pork soup

espárragos asparagus
  espárragos con mahonesa asparagus with mayonnaise

espinacas gratinadas spinach au gratin

esqueixada salad made with salt cod

estofado braised/stewed
  estofado de cordero lamb stew
  estofado de ternera veal/beef stew

estragón tarragon

F

fabada asturiana pork, cured ham, black pudding, large butter beans or sausage stew with **chorizo** and **morcilla**

fabes large white haricot beans

faisán pheasant

farinatos fried sausages served
with eggs

fiambre cold meat
fiambre de tenera veal pâté
fiambres surtidos assorted cold
meats

fideos noodles/thin ribbons of
pasta (vermicelli)
fideos a la cazuela noodles
cooked with pork, sausages,
ham and **sofrito** (fried onions,
garlic and tomato)

fideuà amb marisc seafood dish
with fine pasta (vermicelli)

filete fillet steak
filete de ternera veal/beef steak
filete a la plancha grilled fillet
steak

filetes de lenguado sole fillets

fino the finest sherry, light and
dry, equally good when young
or after being aged

flan crème caramel

frambuesas raspberries

fresas strawberries
fresas con nata strawberries
and cream

frijoles beans (name used
in the Canary Islands)

frío cold

frite pieces of lamb fried
in olive oil and paprika

frito fried

fritura de pescado fried
assortment of fish

fruta fruit
fruta del tiempo fruit in season

frutos secos nuts

G

galleta biscuit

gallina hen

gambas prawns
gambas a la plancha grilled
prawns
gambas al ajillo grilled prawns
with garlic
gambas pil-pil sizzling prawns
cooked with chillies

ganso goose

garbanzos chickpeas
garbanzos con espinacas
chickpeas with spinach

garrotxa goat's cheese

gazpacho traditional cold creamy
tomato soup of southern Spain.
There are many different
recipes. Basic ingredients are
water, tomatoes, garlic, fresh
breadcrumbs, salt, vinegar and
olive oil. Should be served
chilled with diced cucumbers,
hard-boiled eggs and cured
ham (in some Southern parts
they add other vegetables)
gazpacho extremeño a version
of gazpacho made with finely
chopped green peppers and
onions

ginebra gin

gofio toasted corn meal often
rolled into balls and eaten as a
bread substitute in the Canary
Islands

gran reserva classification given
to aged wines of exceptional
quality

granada pomegranate

granizado fruit drink with
crushed ice

gratinado au gratin

grelos young turnip tops
guindilla chilli
guisado stew or casserole
guisantes peas
  guisantes a la española boiled peas with cured ham, lettuce, carrots and onions

H

habas broad beans
  habas a la catalana broad beans cooked in pork fat often served with **chorizo**
  habas con jamón broad beans with cured ham
hamburguesa hamburger
helado ice cream
hervido boiled
hígado liver
  hígado con cebolla fried calf's liver with onions
higos figs
  higos secos dried figs
horchata de chufas cool drink made with tiger nuts
horno, ...al baked (in oven)
huevos eggs
  huevos a la española stuffed eggs with a cheese sauce
  huevos a la flamenca baked eggs with tomatoes, peas, peppers, asparagus and **chorizo**
  huevos al plato eggs baked in butter
  huevos con jamón fried eggs and cured ham

I

infusión herbal tea
intxaursalsa whipped cream and walnut pudding

J

jamón ham
  jamón de Jabugo Andalusian prime-quality cured ham
  jamón de York cooked ham
  jamón serrano dark red cured ham
jengibre ginger
jerez sherry
jibia cuttlefish
judías beans
  judías blancas haricot beans
  judías verdes green beans
  judías verdes a la castellana/española boiled green beans mixed with fried parsley, garlic and peppers
jurel horse mackerel

K

kokotxas hake's cheek usually fried

L

lacón con grelos salted pork with young turnip tops and white cabbage
langosta lobster
  langosta a la catalana potatoes with a lobster filling served with mayonnaise
langostinos king prawns
  langostinos a la plancha grilled king prawns
  langostinos a la vinagreta casseroled crayfish with hardboiled eggs served in a vinaigrette sauce
laurel bay leaf
lechazo young lamb (roasted)
leche milk

leche caliente *hot milk*
leche fría *cold milk*
leche frita *very thick custard dipped into an egg and breadcrumb mixture, fried and served hot in squares*
leche merengada *type of ice cream made with egg whites, sugar and cinnamon (can be drunk as a milkshake)*
lechuga *lettuce*
legumbres *fresh or dried pulses*
lengua *tongue*
lenguado *sole*
  lenguado a la romana *sole fried in batter*
  lenguados fritos *fried fillets of sole often served on a bed of mixed sautéed vegetables*
  lenguados rellenos *fillets of sole stuffed with shrimps or prawns*
lentejas *lentils (very popular in Spain)*
licor *liqueur*
liebre *hare*
  liebre estofada *stewed hare*
limón *lemon*
limonada *lemonade (normally canned and fizzy)*
lomo *loin of pork*
longaniza *spicy pork sausage*
  longaniza con judías blancas *spicy pork sausage with white beans*
lubina *sea bass*
  lubina a la asturiana *Asturian-style sea bass, with cider*
  lubina al horno *baked sea bass with potatoes, onion, tomato and garlic*

M

macarrones *macaroni*

macedonia de fruta *fruit salad*
magras con tomate *slices of fried ham dipped into tomato sauce*
mahonesa *mayonnaise*
maíz *sweetcorn*
majorero *goat's cheese from Canary Islands*
manitas de cerdo *pig's trotters*
mantequilla *butter*
manzana *apple*
  manzanas rellenas *stuffed baked apples*
manzanilla *camomile tea (not to be confused with manzanilla as a sherry)*
manzanilla *very dry special sherry*
marinado *marinated*
mariscada *mixed shellfish*
marisco *shellfish ; seafood*
marmitako *tuna fish and potato stew*
mayonesa *mayonnaise*
mazapán *marzipan*
medallón *thick steak (medallion)*
mejillones *mussels*
  mejillones a la marinera *mussels steamed in wine*
  mejillones al vapor *mussels (steamed)*
melocotón *peach*
  melocotón en almíbar *peaches in syrup*
melón *melon*
  melón con jamón *melon and cured ham*
membrillo *quince jelly*
menestra de verduras *fresh vegetable stew often cooked with cured ham*
merluza *hake, one of the most*

popular fish in Spain
merluza a la asturiana *boiled hake served with mayonnaise and garnished with hard boiled eggs*
merluza a la sidra *hake baked with clams, onions and cider*
merluza en salsa verde *hake with green sauce (with parsley)*
mermelada *jam*
mero *grouper*
miel *honey*
migas *cubes of bread (like croûtons) usually fried in garlic, olive oil with streaky bacon and sometimes* **chorizo**
migas con jamón *ham with breadcrumbs*
migas extremeñas *breadcrumbs fried with egg and spicy sausage*
mollejas *sweetbreads*
mojama *cured tuna fish, a delicacy*
mojo *a sauce made from olive oil, vinegar, garlic and different spices. Paprika is added for the red mojo. Predominantly found in the Canaries*
mojo picón *spicy* **mojo** *made with chilli peppers*
mojo verde *made with fresh coriander*
mollejas *sweetbreads*
mollejas de ternera *calves' sweetbreads*
morcilla *black pudding*
moros y cristianos *boiled rice, black beans and onions served with garlic sausage*
moscatel *muscat grape wine, sweet and fragrant*
mostaza *mustard*

N

nabo *turnip*
naranja *orange*
naranjada *orangeade*
nata *cream*
natillas *custard*
navajas *razor clams*
nécora *sea crab*
nectarinas *nectarines*
naranja *orange*
níspero *loquat*
nuez moscada *nutmeg*

O

olla *stew made traditionally with white beans, beef and bacon*
olla gitana *thick stew/soup made with chickpeas, pork and vegetables and flavoured with almonds and saffron*
olla podrida *thick cured ham, vegetable and chickpea stew/soup*
oloroso *sweet, darker sherry*
orejas de cerdo a la plancha *grilled pigs' ears*
ostras *oysters*

P

paella *one of the most famous of Spanish dishes. Paella varies from region to region but usually consists of rice, chicken, shellfish, vegetables, garlic and saffron. The dish's name derives from the large shallow pan in which it is cooked. The traditional paella Valenciana contains rabbit, chicken and sometimes eel*
paella de mariscos *rice and shellfish paella*

pan bread
  pan de higos dried figs pressed together in the shape of a small cake
panades lamb pasties eaten at Easter in Balearics
panchineta almond and custard tart
panecillo bread roll
panelleta small cakes with pine nuts and almonds
papas arrugadas potatoes cooked in skins in salty water
parrilla, ...a la grilled
parrillada mixed grill (can be meat or fish)
  parrillada de mariscos mixed grilled shellfish
pasas raisins
pasta pasta
pastel cake/pastry
  pastel de carne meat pie
  pastel de ternera veal/beef pie
patatas potatoes
  patatas arrugadas potatoes cooked in their skins
  patatas bravas sliced boiled potatoes mixed with a garlic, oil and vinegar dressing and flavoured with tomatoes and red chilli peppers
  patatas con chorizo potatoes cooked with **chorizo**
  patatas fritas chips/crisps
  patatas nuevas new potatoes
pato duck
  pato a la sevillana joints of wild duck cooked with sherry, onion, tomatoes, herbs and garlic, served in an orange and olive sauce
pavo turkey
  pavo relleno stuffed turkey
pechuga de pollo chicken breast

pechugas en bechamel chicken breasts in bechamel sauce
Pedro Ximénez sweet, rich sherry-type dessert wine
pepino cucumber
pepitoria de pavo/pollo turkey/chicken fricassée
pera pear
percebes goose-neck barnacle, a Galician shellfish
perdices con chocolate partridges with a chocolate sauce
perdiz partridge
perejil parsley
pescado fish
pescaíto frito mixed fried fish
pez espada swordfish
picada sauce made of chopped parsley, almonds, pine nuts and garlic
pichones young pigeon
pimentón (sweet) paprika; (spicy) cayenne pepper
pimienta pepper (spice)
pimientos red and green peppers, one of the typical Spanish flavours
  pimientos de piquillo pickled red peppers
  pimientos morrones sweet red peppers
  pimientos rellenos peppers stuffed with meat or fish
piña pineapple
pinchos small tapas
  pinchos morunos pork grilled on a skewer
piperrada type of scrambled eggs with red and green peppers, tomato, onion, garlic and paprika. A typical dish from the Basque country.

pipirrana *a salad of fish, roast red peppers, tomatoes, hard-boiled eggs and onions, from Andalusia*

pisto manchego *a mixture of sautéed peppers, onions, aubergines, tomatoes, garlic and parsley. Similiar to French ratatouille. Served hot or cold*

plancha, …a la *grilled*

plátano *banana*

platija *plaice (flounder)*

plato *dish*

plato del día *dish of the day*

platos combinados *quick meal usually eaten in a bar; consists of assorted food served together on one plate*

pollo *chicken*
   pollo al chilindrón *chicken cooked with onion, ham, garlic, red pepper and tomatoes*
   pollo asado *roast chicken*
   pollo con patatas *chicken and chips*
   pollo en pepitoria *breaded chicken pieces fried, then casseroled with herbs, almonds, garlic and sherry*
   pollo estofado *chicken stewed with potatoes, mushrooms, shallots, bay leaves and mushrooms*
   pollo relleno *stuffed chicken*

polvorones *very crumbly cakes made with almonds and often eaten with a glass of anís*

pomelo *grapefruit*

porras *fried sticks of batter*

postres *desserts*

potaje *thick soup/stew often with pork and pulses*

potaje murciano *red bean, french bean and rice soup*

pote *thick soup with beans and sausage which has many regional variations*
   pote gallego *thick soup made with cabbage, white kidney beans, potatoes, pork and sausage*

primer plato *first course*

puchero *hotpot made from meat or fish*
   puchero canario *salted fish and potatoes served with mojo sauce*

puerros *leeks*

pulpo *octopus*

puré de garbanzos *thick chickpea soup*

puré de patatas *mashed potatoes*

Q

queimada *warm drink made with aguardiente (clear brandy) sweetened with sugar and flamed, a speciality from Galicia*

quesada *dessert similar to cheesecake*

queso *cheese*
   queso de Burgos *curd cheese from Burgos*
   queso de cabrales *strong blue cheese from Asturias*
   queso de Idiazábal *smoked sheep's milk cheese from the Basque country*
   queso de Mahón *strong hard cheese from Menorca*
   queso de oveja *mild sheep's cheese from León*
   queso de Roncal *hard, smoked sheep's cheese*

queso de tetilla *soft, white cheese made in the form of a woman's breast*

queso fresco *green cheese*

queso manchego *hard sheep's curd cheese from La Mancha*

R

rábanos *radishes*

rabo de toro *bull's tail, usually cooked in a stew*

rancio *dessert wine*

ración *portion of tapas*

rape *monkfish*
  rape a la marinera *monkfish cooked with wine*

raya *skate*

rebozado *in batter*

refresco de fruta *fruit drink with ice*

rehogado *lightly fried*

relleno *stuffed*

remolacha *beetroot*

repollo *cabbage*

requesón *cottage cheese*

reserva *wines of good quality that have been aged, but not as long as* **gran reserva**

revuelto *scrambled eggs often cooked with another ingredient*
  revuelto de champiñones *scrambled eggs with mushrooms*
  revuelto de espárragos *scrambled eggs with asparagus*
  revuelto de espinacas *scrambled eggs with spinach*
  revuelto de gambas *scrambled eggs with prawns*
  revuelto de morcilla *scrambled eggs with black pudding*

riñones al jerez *kidneys in sherry sauce*

rodaballo *turbot*

romana, ...a la *fried in batter (generally squid –* **calamares***)*

romero *rosemary*

romesco *sauce made traditionally with olive oil, red pepper and bread. Other ingredients are often added, such as almonds and garlic*
  romesco de pescado *fish in a sauce of peppers, olive oil and bread with almonds*

ron *rum*

rosco *type of doughnut*
  roscón de reyes *a large bun-like cake in the shape of a ring, similar to Italian panettone and eaten at Epiphany*

S

sal *salt*

salchicha *sausage*

salchichón *salami-type sausage*

salmón *salmon*
  salmón a la parilla *grilled salmon*
  salmón a la ribereña *salmon fried with ham cooked with cider*
  salmón ahumado *smoked salmon*

salmonete *red mullet*
  salmonete frito *fried red mullet*

salpicón *chopped seafood or meat with tomato, onion, garlic and peppers*

salsa *sauce*
  salsa de tomate *tomato sauce*
  salsa romesco *sauce made of almonds and hazelnuts with mild chilli. Often served with fish and chicken*

salsa verde *garlic, olive oil and parsley sauce often served with fish*

salteado *sautéed*

samfaina *a dish of peppers, aubergines and tomatoes to which meat is often added*

sandía *watermelon*

sándwich *sandwich (usually toasted)*

sangría *red wine mixed with fruit, lemonade, sugar and ice often with cinnamon added*

sardinas *sardines*
  sardinas a la santanderina *sardines cooked with tomato, Santander style*
  sardinas asadas *barbecued sardines*
  sardinas frescas/fritas *fresh/fried sardines*
  sardinas rebozadas *sardines cooked in batter*

sargo *type of bream*

seco *dry*

sepia *cuttlefish*

sesos *brains*
  sesos a la romana *brains fried in batter*
  sesos fritos *fried brains*

setas *wild mushrooms*

sidra *cider*

sifón *soda water*

sobrasada *a paprika-flavoured pork sausage from Mallorca*

sofrito *basic sauce made with slowly fried onions, garlic and tomato*

solomillo *sirloin*
  solomillo de ternera *veal/beef sirloin*

sopa *soup*
  sopa castellana *see* **sopa de ajo**

sopa de ajo *garlic soup with bread. May contain poached egg or cured ham*

sopa de arroz *rice soup*

sopa de cebolla *onion soup*

sopa de cocido *meat soup*

sopa de fideos *noodle soup*

sopa de gallina *chicken soup*

sopa de rabo *oxtail/bulltail soup*

sopa mallorquina *tomato, onion and pepper soup thickened with breadcrumbs*

sopa de mariscos *shellfish soup*

sopa de pescado *fish soup*

sopa de pollo *chicken soup*

sopa de verduras *vegetable soup*

sorbete *sorbet*
  sorbetes de frutas *fruit sorbets*

suquet *fish, potato and tomato stew*

suspiros *meringues*
  suspiros de monja *meringues served with thick custard*

T

tapas *appetizers ; snacks*

tarta *cake/tart/gâteau*
  tarta de manzana *apple tart*
  tarta de Santiago *flat almond cake*
  tarta helada *ice-cream cake*

té *tea*
  té con leche *tea with milk*
  té con limón *tea with lemon*
  té helado *iced tea*

ternasco *young lamb*

ternera *veal/beef*
  ternera con naranja *veal/beef cooked with orange*
  ternera rellena *stuffed veal/beef*

tisana *herbal tea*

tocinillo (de cielo) *sweet made with egg yolk and sugar*

tocino *bacon*

tomates *tomatoes*
  tomates rellenos *stuffed tomatos*

tomillo *thyme*

toronja *grapefruit*

torrija *bread dipped in milk and then fried and sprinkled with sugar and cinnamon*

tortilla (española) *omelette cooked with potatoes. Often sliced and served as a tapa*
  tortilla de champiñones *mushroom omelette*
  tortilla de chorizo *omelette with chorizo*
  tortilla de espárragos *asparagus omelette*
  tortilla de jamón *cured ham omelette*
  tortilla murciana *tomato and pepper omelette*

trucha *trout*
  trucha a la navarra *trout stuffed with cured ham slices*
  trucha con almendras *fried trout with almonds*

tumbet *layers of peppers, aubergine and tomato cooked with potato in an earthenware dish. Originally from Majorca*

turrón *nougat*
  turrón de Alicante *hard nougat*
  turrón de Jijona *soft nougat*

txangurro *spider crab*

U

uvas *grapes*

V

vapor, ...al *steamed*

verduras *vegetables*

verduras con patatas *boiled potatoes with greens*

vermú *vermouth*

vieiras *scallops*
  vieiras de Santiago *scallops served in their shell, cooked in brandy, topped with breadcrumbs and grilled*

vinagre *vinegar*

vinagreta *vinaigrette*

vino *wine*
  vino blanco *white wine*
  vino clarete *rosé wine*
  vino de jerez *sherry*
  vino de mesa *table wine*
  vino rosado *rosé wine*
  vino tinto *red wine*

Y

yemas *small cakes that look like egg yolks*

yogur *yoghurt*

Z

zanahorias *carrots*

zarzuela de mariscos *mixed seafood with wine and saffron*

zarzuela de pescado *fish stew*

zumo *juice*
  zumo de fruta *fruit juice*
  zumo de albaricoque *apricot juice*
  zumo de lima *lime juice*
  zumo de melocotón *peach juice*
  zumo de naranja *orange juice*
  zumo de piña *pineapple juice*
  zumo de tomate *tomato juice*

zurrukutuna *salt cod cooked with green peppers*

DICTIONARY
English-Spanish
Spanish-English

A

a(n) un(a)
abbey la abadía
able: *to be able* poder
abortion el aborto
about *(concerning)* sobre
  about 2 o'clock alrededor de
  las dos
above arriba ; por encima
abroad en el extranjero
abscess el absceso
accelerator el acelerador
accent *(pronunciation)* el acento
to accept aceptar
  do you accept this card? ¿acepta
  esta tarjeta?
access el acceso
  wheelchair access el acceso para
  sillas de ruedas
accident el accidente
accident & emergency department
  Urgencias
accommodation el alojamiento
to accompany acompañar
account *(bank, etc)* la cuenta
account number el número de
  cuenta
to ache doler
  my head aches me duele la cabeza
  it aches duele
acid el ácido
actor/actress el actor/la actriz
adaptor el adaptador
address la dirección
  what is the address?
  ¿cuál es la dirección?
address book la agenda
admission charge/fee el precio
  de entrada
to admit *(to hospital)* ingresar
adult el/la adulto(a)
  for adults para adultos
advance: *in advance* por adelantado
advertisement el anuncio
to advise aconsejar

A&E Urgencias
aeroplane el avión
aerosol el aerosol
afraid: *to be afraid of...* tener miedo
  de...
after después
afternoon la tarde
  this afternoon esta tarde
  in the afternoon por la tarde
  tomorrow afternoon mañana por
  la tarde
aftershave el aftershave
again otra vez
against contra
age la edad
agency la agencia
ago: *a week ago* hace una semana
to agree estar de acuerdo
agreement el acuerdo
AIDS el sida
airbag *(in car)* el airbag
air bed el colchón inflable
air conditioning el aire
  acondicionado
air freshener el ambientador
airline la linea aérea
air mail: *by airmail* por avión
airplane el avión
airport el aeropuerto
airport bus el autobús del
  aeropuerto
air ticket el billete de avión
aisle el pasillo
alarm la alarma
alarm clock el despertador
alcohol el alcohol
alcohol-free sin alcohol
alcoholic alcohólico(a)
  is it alcoholic? ¿tiene alcohol?
all todo(a)/todos(as)
allergic to alérgico(a) a
  I'm allergic to... soy alérgico(a) a...
allergy la alergia
to allow permitir
  it's not allowed no está permitido

all right (agreed) de acuerdo
  (OK) vale
  are you all right? ¿está bien?
almost casi
alone solo(a)
alphabet el alfabeto
already ya
also también
altar el altar
always siempre
a.m. de la mañana
amber (traffic light) amarillo ; ámbar
ambulance la ambulancia
America Norteamérica
American norteamericano(a)
amount el total
anaesthetic la anestesia
  local anaesthetic la anestesia local
  general anaesthetic la anestesia
  general
anchor el ancla
ancient antiguo(a)
and y
angina la angina (de pecho)
angry enfadado(a)
animal el animal
aniseed el anís
ankle el tobillo
anniversary el aniversario
to announce anunciar
announcement el anuncio
annual anual
another otro(a)
  another beer, please otra cerveza,
  por favor
answer la respuesta
to answer responder
answerphone el contestador
  (automático)
antacid el antiácido
antibiotic el antibiótico
antifreeze el anticongelante
antihistamine el antihistamínico
anti-inflammatory
  antiinflamatorio(a)

antiques las antigüedades
antique shop el anticuario
antiseptic el antiséptico
any alguno(a)
  have you any pears? ¿tiene peras?
anyone alguien
anything algo
anywhere en cualquier parte
apartment el apartamento
appendicitis la apendicitis
apple la manzana
application form el impreso de
  solicitud
appointment (meeting) la cita
  (dentist, hairdresser) la hora
approximately aproximadamente
April abril
apricot el albaricoque
apron el delantal
architect el/la arquitecto(a)
architecture la arquitectura
arm el brazo
armbands (to swim) los manguitos
  de nadar
armchair el sillón
to arrange organizar
to arrest detener
arrival la llegada
to arrive llegar
art el arte
art gallery la galería de arte
arthritis la artritis
artificial artificial
artist el/la artista
ashtray el cenicero
to ask (question) preguntar
  (to ask for something) pedir
asparagus el espárrago
aspirin la aspirina
asthma el asma
  I have asthma tengo asma
at a ; en
  at home en casa
  at 8 o'clock a las ocho
  at once ahora mismo
  at night por la noche

Atlantic Ocean el Océano Atlántico
attack *(terrorist)* el atentado
 (medical) el ataque
to attack atacar
attractive atractivo(a)
aubergine la berenjena
auction la subasta
audience el público
August agosto
aunt la tía
au pair el/la au pair
Australia Australia
Australian australiano(a)
author el/la autor(a)
automatic automático(a)
automatic car el coche automático
auto-teller el cajero automático
autumn el otoño
available disponible
avalanche la avalancha
avenue la avenida
average medio(a)
to avoid *(issue)* evitar
 (obstacle) esquivar
awake: *to be awake* estar
 despierto(a)
away: *far away* lejos
awful espantoso(a)
axle *(in car)* el eje

B

baby el bebé
baby food los potitos
baby milk la leche infantil
baby's bottle el biberón
babyseat *(in car)* el asiento del bebé
babysitter el/la canguro
baby wipes las toallitas infantiles
back *(of body)* la espalda
backpack la mochila
bacon el beicon/bacon
bad *(weather, news)* mal/malo(a)
 (fruit and vegetables) podrido(a)
badminton el bádminton

bag la bolsa
baggage el equipaje
baggage allowance el equipaje
 permitido
baggage reclaim la recogida de
 equipajes
bail bond la fianza
bait *(for fishing)* el cebo
baked al horno
baker's la panadería
balcony el balcón
bald *(person)* calvo(a)
 (tyre) gastado(a)
ball *(large: football, etc)* el balón
 (small: golf, tennis, etc) la pelota
ballet el ballet
balloon el globo
banana el plátano
band *(rock)* el grupo
bandage la venda
bank el banco
 (river) la ribera
bank account la cuenta bancaria
banknote el billete
bar el bar
bar of chocolate la tableta de
 chocolate
barbecue la barbacoa
 to have a barbecue hacer una
 barbacoa
barber's la barbería
to bark ladrar
barn el granero
barrel *(wine/beer)* el barril
basement el sótano
basil la albahaca
basket la cesta
basketball el baloncesto
bat *(baseball, cricket)* el bate
 (creature) el murciélago
bath el baño
 to have a bath bañarse
bathing cap el gorro de baño
bathroom el cuarto de baño
 with bathroom con baño

battery (radio, camera, etc) la pila
(in car) la batería
bay (along coast) la bahía
Bay of Biscay el golfo de Vizcaya
to be estar ; ser
beach la playa
  private beach la playa privada
  sandy beach la playa de arena
  nudist beach la playa nudista
beach hut la caseta de playa
bean la alubia
beard la barba
beautiful hermoso(a)
beauty salon el salón de belleza
because porque
to become hacerse ; convertirse
en ; llegar a ser
bed la cama
  double bed la cama de matrimonio
  single bed la cama individual
  sofa bed el sofá-cama
  twin beds las camas individuales
bed and breakfast alojamienta y
desayuno
bed clothes la ropa de cama
bedroom el dormitorio
bee la abeja
beef la ternera
beer la cerveza
before antes de
  before breakfast antes de
desayunar/del desayuno
to begin empezar
behind detrás de
  behind the house detrás de la casa
beige beige ; beis
to believe creer
bell (church) la campana
(door bell) el timbre
to belong to pertenecer a
(club) ser miembro de
below debajo, por debajo
belt el cinturón
bend (in road) la curva
berth la litera

beside (next to) al lado de
  beside the bank al lado del banco
best el/la mejor
bet la apuesta
to bet on apostar por
better mejor
  better than mejor que
between entre
bib el babero
bicycle la bicicleta
  by bicycle en bicicleta
bicycle repair kit la caja
de herramientas
bidet el bidé
big grande
  bigger than mayor que
bike (pushbike) la bicicleta
(motorbike) la moto
bike lock el candado de la bicicleta
bikini el bikini
bill la factura
(in restaurant) la cuenta
bin el cubo ; la papelera
bin liner la bolsa de la basura
binoculars los prismáticos
bird el pájaro
biro el boli
birth el nacimiento
birth certificate la partida de
nacimiento
birthday el cumpleaños
  happy birthday! ¡feliz cumpleaños!
  my birthday is on... mi cumpleaños
es el...
birthday card la tarjeta de
cumpleaños
birthday present el regalo de
cumpleaños
biscuits las galletas
bit: a bit of un poco de
bite (insect) la picadura
(animal) la mordedura
to bite morder
(insect) picar
bitten (by animal) mordido(a)
(by insect) picado(a)

bitter *(taste)* amargo(a)
black negro(a)
black ice la capa invisible de hielo en la carretera
blanket la manta
bleach *(household)* la lejía
to bleed sangrar
blender *(for food)* la licuadora
blind *(person)* ciego(a)
blind *(for window)* la persiana
   (roman) el estor
blister la ampolla
blocked *(road)* cortado(a)
   (pipe) obstruido(a)
blond *(person)* rubio(a)
blood la sangre
blood group el grupo sanguíneo
blood pressure la presión sanguínea
blood test el análisis de sangre
blouse la blusa
blow-dry el secado a mano
blue azul
   dark blue azul marino
   light blue azul claro
blunt *(knife, blade)* desafilado(a)
boar el jabalí
to board *(train, etc)* subir
boarding card/pass la tarjeta de embarque
boarding house la pensión
boat *(large)* el barco
   (small) la barca
boat trip la excursión en barco
body el cuerpo
to boil hervir
boiled hervido(a)
boiler la caldera
bomb la bomba
bone el hueso
   (fish bone) la espina
bonfire la hoguera
bonnet *(car)* el capó
book el libro
to book reservar
booking la reserva

booking office *(train)* la ventanilla de billetes
bookshop la librería
boot *(car)* el maletero
boots las botas
border *(of country)* la frontera
boring aburrido(a)
born: I was born in... nací en...
to borrow pedir prestado
boss el/la jefe(a)
both ambos(as)
bottle la botella
   a bottle of wine una botella de vino
   a half-bottle media botella
bottle opener el abrebotellas
bottom *(of pool, garden)* el fondo
bowl *(for soup, etc)* el bol
bow tie la pajarita
box la caja
box office la taquilla
boxer shorts los calzoncillos
boy el chico
boyfriend el novio
bra el sujetador
bracelet la pulsera
brain el cerebro
brake el freno
to brake frenar
brake fluid el líquido de frenos
brake light la luz de freno
brake pads las pastillas de freno
branch *(of tree)* la rama
   (of bank, etc) la sucursal
brand *(make)* la marca
brass el latón
brave valiente
bread el pan
   wholemeal bread el pan integral
   French bread la barra de pan
   sliced bread el pan de molde
bread roll el panecillo
to break romper
breakable frágil
breakdown *(car)* la avería
   (nervous) la crisis nerviosa

breakdown van la grúa
breakfast el desayuno
breast el pecho
to breast-feed amamantar
to breathe respirar
brick el ladrillo
bride la novia
bridegroom el novio
bridge el puente
briefcase la cartera
bright (colour) vivo(a)
Brillo pads® el nanas®
to bring traer
Britain Gran Bretaña
British británico(a)
broccoli el brócoli
brochure el folleto
broken roto(a)
   my leg is broken me he roto la
   pierna
broken down (car, etc) averiado(a)
bronchitis la bronquitis
bronze el bronce
brooch el broche
broom (brush) la escoba
brother el hermano
brother-in-law el cuñado
brown marrón
bruise el moratón ; el cardenal
brush el cepillo
to brush cepillar
bubble bath el baño de espuma
bucket el cubo
buckle la hebilla
buffet car el coche comedor
to build construir
building el edificio
bulb (electric) la bombilla
bull el toro
bullfight la corrida de toros
bullfighter el torero
bullring la plaza de toros
bumbag la riñonera
bumper (car) el parachoques

bunch (of flowers) el ramo
   (grapes) el racimo
bungee jumping el banyi
buoy la boya
bureau de change la oficina de
   cambio
burger la hamburguesa
burglar el/la ladrón/ladrona
burglar alarm la alarma antirrobo
to burn quemar
burnt (food) quemado(a)
to burst reventar
bus el autobús
bus pass el bonobús
bus station la estación de autobuses
bus stop la parada de autobús
bus ticket el billete de autobús
business el negocio
   on business de negocios
business card la tarjeta de visita
business class la clase preferente
businessman/woman
   el hombre/la mujer de negocios
business trip el viaje de negocios
busy ocupado(a)
but pero
butcher's la carnicería
butter la mantequilla
butterfly la mariposa
button el botón
to buy comprar
by (via) por
   (beside) al lado de
   by bus en autobús
   by car en coche
   by train en tren
   by ship en barco
bypass (road) la carretera
   de circunvalación

C

cab (taxi) el taxi
cabaret el cabaré
cabin (on boat) el camarote
cabin crew la tripulación de cabina

cablecar el teleférico
café el café
  internet café el cibercafé
cafetiere la cafetera
cake *(big)* la tarta
  (little) el pastel
cake shop la pastelería
calculator la calculadora
calendar el calendario
call *(telephone)* la llamada
  a long distance call una
  conferencia
to call *(phone)* llamar por teléfono
calm tranquilo(a)
camcorder la videocámara
  (digital) la cámara digital
camera la cámara
camera case la funda de la cámara
camera shop la tienda de fotografía
to camp acampar
camping gas el camping gas
camping stove el hornillo de gas
campsite el camping
to can *(to be able)* poder
  I can puedo
  we can podemos
  I cannot no puedo
  we cannot no podemos
can la lata
can opener el abrelatas
Canada (el) Canadá
Canadian canadiense
canal el canal
to cancel anular ; cancelar
cancellation la cancelación
cancer el cáncer
candle la vela
canoe la canoa
canoeing: *to go canoeing* hacer
  piragüismo
cap *(hat)* la gorra
  (diaphragm) el diafragma
capital *(city)* la capital
car el coche
car alarm la alarma de coche

car ferry el transbordador ; el ferry
car hire el alquiler de coches
car insurance el seguro del coche
car keys las llaves del coche
car park el aparcamiento
car parts los accesorios para
  el coche
car radio la radio del coche
car seat *(child)* el asiento para niños
car wash el lavado (automático)
  de coches
carafe la jarra
caravan la caravana
carburettor el carburador
card *(greetings, business)* la tarjeta
  playing cards las cartas
cardboard el cartón
cardigan la chaqueta de punto
careful cuidadoso(a)
  be careful! ¡ten cuidado!
carpet *(rug)* la alfombra
  (fitted) la moqueta
carriage *(railway)* el vagón
carrot la zanahoria
to carry llevar
carton la caja
  (of cigarettes) el cartón
case *(suitcase)* la maleta
cash el dinero en efectivo
to cash *(cheque)* cobrar
cash desk la caja
cash dispenser el cajero automático
cashier el/la cajero(a)
cashpoint el cajero automático
casino el casino
casserole la cazuela
cassette el casete
cassette player el radiocasete
castanets las castañuelas
castle el castillo
casualty department urgencias
cat el gato
cat food la comida para gatos
catalogue el catálogo

to catch *(bus, train, etc)* coger
cathedral la catedral
Catholic católico(a)
cauliflower la coliflor
cave la cueva
cavity *(in tooth)* la caries
CD el CD
CD player el lector de CD
ceiling el techo
cellar la bodega
cemetery el cementerio
centimetre el centímetro
central central
central heating la calefacción central
central locking *(car)* el cierre centralizado
centre el centro
century el siglo
ceramic la cerámica
cereal los cereales
certain *(sure)* seguro(a)
certificate el certificado
chain la cadena
chair la silla
chairlift el telesilla
chalet el chalet
chambermaid la camarera
Champagne el champán
change el cambio
  (small coins) el suelto
  (money returned) la vuelta
to change cambiar
  (clothes) cambiarse
  (train) hacer transbordo
  to change money cambiar dinero
changing room el probador
chapel la capilla
charcoal el carbón vegetal
charge *(fee)* el precio
to charge cobrar
  please charge it to my account cárguelo a mi cuenta, por favor
charger *(for battery)* el cargador
charter flight el vuelo chárter

cheap barato(a)
cheaper más barato(a)
cheap rate la tarifa baja
to check revisar ; comprobar
to check in *(at airport)* facturar el equipaje
  (at hotel) registrarse
check-in la facturación
cheek la mejilla
cheers! ¡salud!
cheese el queso
chef el chef
chemist's la farmacia
cheque el cheque
cheque book el talonario
cheque card la tarjeta bancaria
cherry la cereza
chest *(of body)* el pecho
chewing gum el chicle
chicken el pollo
chickenpox la varicela
child *(boy)* el niño
  (girl) la niña
children *(infants)* los niños
  for children para niños
child safety seat *(car)* el asiento de niños
chilli la guindilla ; el chile
chimney la chimenea
chin la barbillla
china la porcelana
chips las patatas fritas
chocolate el chocolate
chocolates los bombones
choir el coro
to choose escoger
chop *(meat)* la chuleta
chopping board la tabla de cortar
christening el bautizo
Christian name el nombre de pila
Christmas la Navidad
  Merry Christmas! ¡Feliz Navidad!
Christmas card la tarjeta de Navidad
Christmas Eve la Nochebuena
church la iglesia

cigar el puro
cigarette el cigarrillo
cigarette lighter el mechero
cigarette paper el papel de fumar
cinema el cine
circle *(theatre)* el anfiteatro
circuit breaker el cortacircuitos
circus el circo
cistern la cisterna
city la ciudad
city centre el centro de la ciudad
class: *first class* primera clase
  second class segunda clase
clean limpio(a)
to clean limpiar
cleaner *(person)* el/la encargado/a
  de la limpieza
cleanser *(for face)* la crema
  limpiadora
clear claro(a)
client el/la cliente
cliff *(along coast)* el acantilado
  (in mountains) el precipicio
to climb *(mountains)* escalar
climbing boots las botas
  de escalar
Clingfilm® el rollo de plástico
  transparente
clinic la clínica
cloakroom el guardarropa
clock el reloj
close by muy cerca
to close cerrar
closed *(shop, etc)* cerrado(a)
cloth *(rag)* el trapo
  (fabric) la tela
clothes la ropa
clothes line el tendedero
clothes peg la pinza
clothes shop la tienda de ropa
cloudy nublado(a)
club el club
clutch *(in car)* el embrague
coach *(bus)* el autocar
coach station la estación
  de autobuses

coach trip la excursión en autocar
coal el carbón
coast la costa
coastguard el/la guardacostas
coat el abrigo
coat hanger la percha
cockroach la cucaracha
cocktail el cóctel
cocoa el cacao
code el código
coffee el café
  black coffee el café solo
  white coffee el café con leche
  cappuccino el capuchino
  decaffeinated coffee
  el (café) descafeinado
coil *(IUD)* el DIU
coin la moneda
Coke® la Coca Cola®
colander el colador
cold frío(a)
  I'm cold tengo frío
  it's cold hace frío
  cold water el agua fría
cold *(illness)* el resfriado
  I have a cold estoy resfriado(a)
cold sore la calentura
collar el cuello
collar bone la clavícula
colleague el/la compañero(a)
  de trabajo
to collect recoger
collection la recogida
colour el color
colour-blind daltónico(a)
colour film *(for camera)* el carrete
  en color
comb el peine
to come venir
  (to arrive) llegar
to come back volver
to come in entrar
  come in! ¡pase!
comedy la comedia
comfortable cómodo(a)
company *(firm)* la empresa

compartment el compartimento

compass la brújula

to complain reclamar

complaint la reclamación ; la queja

complete completo(a)

to complete terminar

compulsory obligatorio(a)

computer el ordenador

computer disk (floppy) el disquete

computer game el juego de ordenador

computer program el programa de ordenador

concert el concierto

concert hall la sala de conciertos ; el auditorio

concession el descuento

concussion la conmoción cerebral

conditioner el suavizante

condom el condón

conductor (on bus) el/la cobrador(a) (on train) el/la revisor(a)

conference el congreso

to confirm confirmar *please confirm* por favor, confirme

confirmation (flight, booking) la confirmación

congratulations! ¡enhorabuena!

connection (train, etc) el enlace

constipated estreñido(a)

consulate el consulado

to consult consultar

to contact ponerse en contacto con

contact lens la lentilla

contact lens cleaner la solución limpiadora para lentillas

to continue continuar

contraceptive el anticonceptivo

contract el contrato

convenient: *is it convenient?* ¿le viene bien?

convulsions las convulsiones

to cook cocinar

cooked preparado(a)

cooker la cocina

cookies las galletas

cool fresco(a)

cool-box la nevera portátil

copper el cobre

copy (duplicate) la copia (of book) el ejemplar

to copy copiar

coral el coral

cork el corcho

corkscrew el sacacorchos

corner la esquina

cornflakes los copos de maíz

corridor el pasillo

cortisone la cortisona

cosmetics los cosméticos

cost (price) el precio

to cost costar *how much does it cost?* ¿cuánto cuesta?

costume (swimming) el bañador

cot la cuna

cottage la casita de campo

cotton el algodón (hidrófilo)

cotton buds los bastoncillos

cotton wool el algodón

couchette la litera

to cough toser

cough la tos

cough mixture el jarabe para la tos

cough sweets los caramelos para la tos

counter (in shop) el mostrador (in bar) la barra

country (not town) el campo (nation) el país

countryside el campo

couple (2 people) la pareja *a couple of...* un par de ...

courgette el calabacín

courier service el servicio de mensajero

course (of study) el curso (of meal) el plato

cousin el/la primo(a)

cover charge (in restaurant) el cubierto

cow la vaca
crafts la artesanía
craftsperson el/la artesano(a)
cramps los calambres
crash (car) el accidente
to crash (car) chocar
crash helmet el casco protector
cream (lotion) la crema
  (on milk) la nata
  soured cream la nata cortada
  whipped cream la nata montada
credit card la tarjeta de crédito
crime el delito
crisps las patatas fritas
cross (crucifix) la cruz
to cross (road) cruzar
cross-channel ferry el ferry (que
  cruza el Canal de la Mancha)
cross country skiing el esquí de
  fondo
crossing (sea) la travesía
crossroads el cruce
crossword puzzle el crucigrama
crowd la multitud
crowded concurrido(a)
crown la corona
cruise el crucero
crutches las muletas
to cry (weep) llorar
crystal el cristal
cucumber el pepino
cufflinks los gemelos
cul-de-sac el callejón sin salida
cup la taza
cupboard el armario
currant la pasa (de Corinto)
currency la moneda
current la corriente
curtain la cortina
cushion el cojín
custom (tradition) la costumbre
customer el/la cliente
customs (control) la aduana
customs declaration la declaración
  aduanera

cut el corte
to cut cortar
cutlery los cubiertos
to cycle ir en bicicleta
cycle track el carril bici
cycling el ciclismo
cyst el quiste
cystitis la cistitis

D

daily (each day) cada día ; diario
dairy produce los productos lácteos
dam la presa
damage el/los daño(s)
damp húmedo(a)
dance el baile
to dance bailar
danger el peligro
dangerous peligroso(a)
dark oscuro(a)
  after dark por la noche
date la fecha
date of birth la fecha de nacimiento
daughter la hija
daughter-in-law la cuñada
dawn el amanecer
day el día
  every day todos los días
  per day al día
dead muerto(a)
deaf sordo(a)
dear (on letter) querido(a)
  (expensive) caro(a)
debt la deuda
decaffeinated coffee
  el descafeinado
  have you decaff?
  ¿tiene descafeinado?
December diciembre
deck chair la tumbona
to declare declarar
  nothing to declare nada que
  declarar
deep profundo(a)
deep freeze el ultracongelador

deer el ciervo
to defrost descongelar
to de-ice descongelar
delay el retraso
 how long is the delay?
 ¿cuánto lleva de retraso?
delayed retrasado(a)
delicatessen la charcutería
delicious delicioso(a)
demonstration la manifestación
dental floss el hilo dental
dentist el/la dentista
dentures la dentadura postiza
deodorant el desodorante
department *(gen)* el departamento
 (in shop) la sección
department store los grandes almacenes
departure lounge la sala de embarque
departures las salidas
deposit la fianza
to describe describir
description la descripción
desk *(in hotel, airport)* el mostrador
dessert el postre
details los detalles
 (personal) los datos personales
detergent el detergente
detour el desvío
to develop *(photos)* revelar
diabetes la diabetes
diabetic diabético(a)
 I'm diabetic soy diabético(a)
to dial marcar
dialling code el prefijo
dialling tone el tono de marcar
diamond el diamante
diapers los pañales
diaphragm *(in body, contraception)* el diafragma
diarrhoea la diarrea
diary la agenda
dice los dados
dictionary el diccionario

to die morir
diesel el diesel ; el gasóleo
diet la dieta
 I'm on a diet estoy a dieta
 special diet la dieta especial
different distinto(a)
difficult difícil
digital camera la cámara digital
digital radio la radio digital
to dilute diluir
dinghy el bote
dining room el comedor
dinner *(evening meal)* la cena
 to have dinner cenar
diplomat el/la diplomático(a)
direct *(train, etc)* directo(a)
directions *(instructions)*
 las instrucciones
 to ask for directions
 preguntar el camino
directory *(phone)* la guía telefónica
directory enquiries la información telefónica
dirty sucio(a)
disability la discapacidad
disabled discapacitado(a) ; minusválido(a)
to disagree no estar de acuerdo
to disappear desaparecer
disaster el desastre
disco la discoteca
discount el descuento
to discover descubrir
disease la enfermedad
dish el plato
dishtowel el paño de cocina
dishwasher el lavavajillas
dishwasher powder el detergente para lavavajillas
disinfectant el desinfectante
disk *(floppy)* el disquete
to dislocate *(joint)* dislocarse
disposable desechable
distance la distancia
distant distante ; lejano(a)

distilled water el agua destilada
district el barrio
to disturb molestar
ditch la cuneta
to dive tirarse al agua
diversion el desvío
divorced divorciado(a)
DIY shop la tienda de bricolaje
dizzy mareado(a)
to do hacer
doctor el/la médico(a)
documents los documentos
dog el perro
dog food la comida para perros
dog lead la correa del perro
doll la muñeca
dollar el dólar
domestic (flight) nacional
donor card la tarjeta de donante
door la puerta
doorbell el timbre
double doble
double bed la cama de matrimonio
double room la habitación doble
doughnut el donut
down: to go down bajar
to download descargar
downstairs abajo
dozen la dozena
drain el desagüe
draught (of air) la corriente
  there's a draught hay corriente
draught lager la cerveza de barril
to draw dibujar
drawer el cajón
drawing el dibujo
dress el vestido
to dress (to get dressed) vestirse
dressing (for food) el aliño
  (for wound) el vendaje
dressing gown la bata
drill (tool) la taladradora
drink la bebida
to drink beber

drinking water el agua potable
to drive conducir
driver el/la conductor(a)
driving licence el carné de conducir
drought la sequía
to drown ahogarse
drug la droga
  (medicine) la medicina
drunk borracho(a)
dry seco(a)
to dry secar
dry-cleaner's la tintorería ;
  la limpieza en seco
due: when is it due? ¿para cuándo
  está previsto?
dummy (for baby) el chupete
during durante
dust el polvo
duster el trapo del polvo
dustpan and brush el cepillo y
  recogedor
duty-free libre de impuestos
duvet el edredón (nórdico)
duvet cover la funda de edredón
  (nórdico)
dye el tinte
dynamo la dinamo

E

each cada
ear (outside) la oreja
  (inside) el oído
earache el dolor de oído(s)
  I have earache me duele el oído
earlier antes
early temprano
to earn ganar
earphones los auriculares
earplugs los tapones para los oídos
earrings los pendientes
earth la tierra
earthquake el terremoto
east el este
Easter la Pascua ; la Semana Santa

easy fácil
to eat comer
egg el huevo
 fried egg el huevo frito
 hard-boiled egg el huevo duro
 scrambled eggs los huevos revueltos
 soft-boiled egg el huevo pasado por agua
eggplant la berenjena
either... or... o... o...
elastic band la goma
elastoplast la tirita
elbow el codo
electric eléctrico(a)
electric blanket la manta eléctrica
electric razor la maquinilla de afeitar
electrician el/la electricista
electricity la electricidad
electricity meter el contador de electricidad
electric point el enchufe
electric shock la descarga eléctrica
elevator el ascensor
e-mail el email ; el correo electrónico
 to e-mail s.o. mandar un email a alguien
e-mail address el email
embassy la embajada
emergency la emergencia
emergency exit la salida de emergencia
empty vacío(a)
end el fin
engaged *(to marry)* prometido(a)
 (toilet, phone) ocupado(a)
engine el motor
England Inglaterra
English inglés/inglesa
 (language) el inglés
Englishman/-woman el inglés/la inglesa
to enjoy *(to like)* gustar
 I enjoy swimming me gusta nadar

I enjoy dancing me gusta bailar
 enjoy your meal! ¡qué aproveche!
to enjoy oneself divertirse
enough bastante
 that's enough ya basta
enquiry desk la información
to enter entrar en
entertainment el entretenimiento
entrance la entrada
entrance fee el precio de entrada
envelope el sobre
epileptic epiléptico(a)
epileptic fit el ataque epiléptico
equal igual
equipment el equipo
eraser la goma (de borrar)
error el error
escalator la escalera mecánica
to escape escapar
espadrilles las alpargatas
essential imprescindible
estate agent's la agencia inmobiliaria
euro el euro
eurocheque el eurocheque
Europe Europa
European el/la europeo(a)
European Union la Unión Europea
even *(not odd)* par
evening la tarde
 this evening esta tarde
 tomorrow evening mañana por la tarde
 in the evening por la tarde
evening dress *(man's)* el traje de etiqueta
 (woman's) el traje de noche
evening meal la cena
every cada
everyone todo el mundo ; todos
everything todo
everywhere en todas partes
examination el examen
example: *for example* por ejemplo
excellent excelente

except excepto
excess baggage el exceso de equipaje
exchange el cambio
to exchange cambiar
exchange rate el tipo de cambio
exciting emocionante
excursion la excursión
excuse: *excuse me!* perdón
exercise el ejercicio
exhaust pipe el tubo de escape
exhibition la exposición
exit la salida
expenses los gastos
expensive caro(a)
expert el/la experto(a)
to expire *(ticket, etc)* caducar
to explain explicar
explosion la explosión
to export exportar
express *(train)* el expreso
express: *to send a letter express* enviar una carta por correo urgente
extension *(electrical)* el alargador
extra *(in addition)* de más
 (more) extra ; adicional
eye el ojo
eyebrows las cejas
eye drops el colirio
eyelashes las pestañas
eyeliner el lápiz de ojos
eye shadow la sombra de ojos

F

fabric la tela
face la cara
face cloth la toallita
facial la limpieza de cutis
facilities las instalaciones
fact el hecho
factory la fábrica
to fade desteñir
to faint desmayarse

fainted desmayado(a)
fair *(hair)* rubio(a)
 (just) justo(a)
fair *(funfair)* la feria
fake falso(a)
fall *(autumn)* el otoño
to fall caer ; caerse
 he/she has fallen se ha caído
false teeth la dentadura postiza
family la familia
famous famoso(a)
fan *(electric)* el ventilador
 (hand-held) el abanico
 (football, etc) el/la hincha
 (jazz, etc) el/la aficionado(a)
fan belt la correa del ventilador
fancy dress el disfraz
far lejos
 is it far? ¿está lejos?
 how far is it? ¿a cuánto está?
farm la granja
farmer el/la granjero(a)
farmhouse la granja
fashionable de moda
fast rápido(a)
 too fast demasiado rápido
to fasten *(seatbelt, etc)* abrocharse
fat *(plump)* gordo(a)
 (in food, on person) la grasa
 saturated fats las grasas saturadas
 unsaturated fats las grasas insaturadas
father el padre
father-in-law el suegro
fault *(defect)* el defecto
 it's not my fault no tengo la culpa
favour el favor
favourite favorito(a) ; preferido(a)
to fax mandar por fax
fax el fax
 by fax por fax
fax number el número de fax
February febrero
to feed dar de comer
to feel sentir
 I don't feel well no me siento bien
 I feel sick estoy mareado(a)

feet los pies
felt-tip pen el rotulador
female mujer
ferry el ferry ; el transbordador
festival el festival
to fetch (to bring) traer
  (to go and get) ir a buscar
fever la fiebre
few pocos(as)
  a few algunos(as)
fiancé(e) el/la novio(a)
field el campo
to fight luchar
file (computer) el fichero
  (nail) la lima
to fill llenar
  (form) rellenar
  fill it up, please! (car) lleno,
  por favor
fillet el filete
filling (in tooth) el empaste
film (at cinema) la película
  (for camera) el carrete
filter el filtro
to find encontrar
fine (to be paid) la multa
finger el dedo
to finish acabar
finished terminado(a)
fire (flames) el fuego
  (blaze) el incendio
  fire! ¡fuego!
fire alarm la alarma de incendios
fire brigade los bomberos
fire engine el coche de bomberos
fire escape la salida de incendios
fire exit la salida de incendios
fire extinguisher el extintor
fireplace la chimenea
fireworks los fuegos artificiales
firm (company) la empresa
first primero(a)
first aid los primeros auxilios
first aid kit el botiquín de
  primeros auxilios

first class de primera clase
first name el nombre de pila
fish (food) el pescado
  (alive) el pez
to fish pescar
fisherman el pescador
fishing permit la licencia de pesca
fishing rod la caña de pescar
fishmonger's la pescadería
fit (seizure) el ataque
to fit (clothes) quedar bien
  it doesn't fit no queda bien
to fix arreglar
  can you fix it? ¿puede arreglarlo?
fizzy con gas
flag la bandera
flames las llamas
flash (for camera) el flash
flashlight la linterna
flask (thermos) el termo
flat (apartment) el piso
flat llano(a)
  (battery) descargado(a)
  (beer) sin gas
  it's flat ya no tiene gas
flat tyre la rueda pinchada
flavour el sabor
  which flavour? ¿qué sabor?
flaw el defecto
fleas las pulgas
flesh la carne
flex el cable eléctrico
flight el vuelo
flip flops las chancletas
flippers las aletas
flood la inundación
  flash flood la riada
floor (of building) el piso
  (of room) el suelo
  which floor? ¿qué piso?
  on the ground floor en la planta
  baja
  on the first floor en el primer piso
  on the second floor en el segundo
  piso
floorcloth la bayeta

florist's shop la floristería
flour la harina
flower la flor
flu la gripe
fly la mosca
to fly volar
fly sheet el toldo impermeable
fog la niebla
foggy: *it's foggy* hay niebla
foil *(tinfoil)* el papel de estaño
to fold doblar
to follow seguir
food la comida
food poisoning la intoxicación
  por alimentos
foot el pie
  on foot a pie
football el fútbol
football match el partido de fútbol
football pitch el campo de fútbol
football player el/la futbolista
footpath *(in country)* el sendero
for para ; por
  for me para mí
  for you para usted/ti
  for him/her/us para él/ella/
  nosotros
forbidden prohibido(a)
forehead la frente
foreign extranjero(a)
foreign currency la moneda
  extranjera
foreigner el/la extranjero(a)
forest el bosque
forever para siempre
to forget olvidar
fork *(for eating)* el tenedor
  (in road) la bifurcación
form *(document)* el impreso
formal dress el traje de etiqueta
fortnight quince días
forward adelante
foul *(football)* la falta
fountain la fuente
four-wheel drive la tracción a
  cuatro ruedas

fox el zorro
fracture la fractura
fragile frágil
fragrance el perfume
frame *(picture)* el marco
France Francia
free *(not occupied)* libre
  (costing nothing) gratis
freezer el congelador
French francés/francesa
  (language) el francés
French bean la judía verde
French fries las patatas fritas
frequent frecuente
fresh fresco(a)
fresh water el agua dulce
Friday el viernes
fridge el frigorífico
fried frito(a)
friend el/la amigo(a)
frisbee® el frisbee®
frog la rana
from de ; desde
  from Scotland de Escocia
  from England de Inglaterra
front la parte delantera
  in front of delante de
front door la puerta de la calle
frost la helada
frozen congelado(a)
fruit la fruta
  dried fruit la fruta seca
fruit juice el zumo (de fruta)
fruit salad la macedonia
to fry freír
frying pan la sartén
fuel *(petrol)* la gasolina
fuel gauge el indicador
  de la gasolina
fuel tank el depósito de gasolina
fuel pump *(in car)* el surtidor de
  gasolina
full lleno(a)
  (occupied) ocupado(a)
full board pensión completa

fumes *(of car)* los gases
fun la diversión
funeral el funeral
funfair la feria
funny *(amusing)* divertido(a)
fur la piel
furnished amueblado(a)
furniture los muebles
fuse el fusible
fuse box la caja de fusibles
future el futuro

G

gallery la galería
gallon = approx. 4.5 litres
game el juego
  (animal) la caza
garage el garaje
  (for repairs) el taller
  (for petrol) la gasolinera
garden el jardín
garlic el ajo
gas el gas
gas cooker la cocina de gas
gas cylinder la bombona de gas
gastritis la gastritis
gate *(airport)* la puerta
gay *(person)* gay
gear la marcha
  first gear la primera
  second gear la segunda
  third gear la tercera
  fourth gear la cuarta
  neutral el punto muerto
  reverse la marcha atrás
gearbox la caja de cambios
generous generoso(a)
gents *(toilet)* los servicios
  de caballeros
genuine auténtico(a)
German alemán/alemana
  (language) el alemán
German measles la rubeola
Germany Alemania

to get *(to obtain)* conseguir
  (to receive) recibir
  (to bring) traer
to get in *(vehicle)* subir (al)
to get out *(of vehicle)* bajarse de
gift el regalo
gift shop la tienda de regalos
girl la chica
girlfriend la novia
to give dar
to give back devolver
glacier el glaciar
glass *(for drinking)* el vaso
  (substance) el cristal
  a glass of water un vaso de agua
  a glass of wine un vaso de vino
glasses *(spectacles)* las gafas
glasses case la funda de gafas
gloves los guantes
glue el pegamento
to go ir
  I'm going to ... voy a...
  we're going to ... vamos a...
  to go home irse a casa
to go back volver
to go in entrar (en)
to go out salir
goat la cabra
God Dios
goggles *(for swimming)* las gafas
  de natación
  (for skiing) las gafas de esquí
gold el oro
golf el golf
golf ball la pelota de golf
golf clubs los palos de golf
golf course el campo de golf
good bueno(a)
  very good muy bueno
good afternoon buenas tardes
goodbye adiós
good day buenos días
good evening buenas tardes
  (when dark) buenas noches
good morning buenos días
good night buenas noches

goose el ganso
gram(me) el gramo
grandchild el/la nieto(a)
granddaughter la nieta
grandfather el abuelo
grandmother la abuela
grandparents los abuelos
grandson el nieto
grapefruit el pomelo
grapes las uvas
grass la hierba
grated *(cheese, etc)* rallado(a)
grater *(for cheese, etc)* el rallador
greasy grasiento(a)
great *(big)* grande
   (wonderful) estupendo(a)
Great Britain Gran Bretaña
green verde
green card la carta verde
greengrocer's la frutería
greetings card la tarjeta de
   felicitación
grey gris
grill el grill
   (barbecue) la parrilla
to grill gratinar
   (on barbecue) asar a la parrilla
grilled gratinado(a)
   (on barbecue) a la parrilla
grocer's la tienda de alimentación
ground el suelo
ground floor la planta baja
   on the ground floor en la planta
   baja
groundsheet el suelo (de tela)
   impermeable
group el grupo
guarantee la garantía
guard *(on train)* el/la jefe(a) de tren
guest el/la invitado(a)
   (in hotel) el/la huésped
guesthouse la pensión
guide *(tour guide)* el/la guía
to guide guiar
guidebook la guía turística

guided tour la visita con guía
guitar la guitarra
gun la pistola
gym el gimnasio
gym shoes las zapatillas de deporte

H

haemorrhoids las hemorroides
hail el granizo
hair el pelo
hairbrush el cepillo del pelo
haircut el corte de pelo
hairdresser el/la peluquero(a)
hairdryer el secador de pelo
hair dye el tinte de pelo
hair gel el gel (para el pelo)
hairgrip la horquilla
hair mousse la espuma del pelo
hair spray la laca
half medio(a)
   half an hour media hora
half board media pensión
half fare el billete reducido
   para niños
half-price a mitad de precio
ham el jamón
   (cooked) el jamón de York
   (cured) el jamón serrano
hamburger la hamburguesa
hammer el martillo
hand la mano
handbag el bolso
hand luggage el equipaje de mano
hand-made hecho(a) a mano
handicapped discapacitado(a) ;
   minusválido(a)
handkerchief el pañuelo
handle *(of cup)* el asa
   (of door) el pomo
handlebars el manillar
hands-free phone el teléfono de
   manos libres
handsome guapo(a)
hang gliding el vuelo con ala delta

hangover la resaca
to hang up *(phone)* colgar
to happen pasar
  what happened? ¿qué ha pasado?
happy feliz
  happy birthday! ¡feliz cumpleaños!
harbour el puerto
hard duro(a)
  (difficult) difícil
hard disk el disco duro
hardware shop la ferretería
to harm *(person)* hacer daño a
  (crops, etc) dañar
harvest la cosecha
hat el sombrero
to have tener
  I have... tengo
  I don't have... no tengo...
  we have... tenemos...
  we don't have... no tenemos...
  do you have...? ¿tiene...?
to have to tener que
hay fever la alergia al polen
he él
head la cabeza
headache el dolor de cabeza
  I have a headache me duele
  la cabeza
headlights los faros
headphones los auriculares
head waiter el maître
health la salud
health food shop la tienda de
  dietética
healthy sano(a)
to hear oír
hearing aid el audífono
heart el corazón
heart attack el infarto
heartburn el ardor de estómago
heater el calentador
heating la calefacción
to heat up *(food)* calentar
heavy pesado(a)
heel *(of foot)* el talón
  (of shoe) el tacón

heel bar la tienda de reparación
  de calzado en el acto
height la altura
helicopter el helicóptero
hello hola
  (on phone) ¿diga?
helmet *(for bike, etc)* el casco
help! ¡socorro!
to help ayudar
  can you help me? ¿puede
  ayudarme?
hem el dobladillo
hepatitis la hepatitis
her su
herb la hierba
herbal tea la infusión
here aquí
  here is... aquí tiene...
  here is my passport aquí tiene
  mi pasaporte
hernia la hernia
hi! ¡hola!
to hide *(something)* esconder
  (oneself) esconderse
high alto(a)
high blood pressure la tensión alta
high chair la silla alta para niños
high tide la marea alta
hill la colina
hill-walking el montañismo
him él
hip la cadera
hip replacement la prótesis de
  cadera
hire *(bike, boat, etc)* el alquiler
  car hire el alquiler de coches
  bike hire el alquiler de bicicletas
  boat hire el alquiler de barcas
to hire alquilar
hired car el coche de alquiler
his su
historic histórico(a)
history la historia
to hit pegar
to hitchhike hacer autostop ;
  hacer dedo

HIV positive seropositivo(a)
hobby el hobby ; el pasatiempo
to hold tener
  (to contain) contener
hold-up (traffic jam) el atasco
hole el agujero
holiday las vacaciones
  (public) la fiesta
  on holiday de vacaciones
holiday rep el/la guía turístico(a)
home la casa
  at home en casa
homesick: to be homesick tener
  morriña
  I'm homesick tengo morriña
homosexual homosexual
honest sincero(a)
honey la miel
honeymoon la luna de miel
hood (jacket) la capucha
hook (fishing) el anzuelo
to hope esperar
  I hope so/not espero que sí/no
horn (car) el claxon
hors d'oeuvre los entremeses
horse el caballo
horse racing la hípica
horse riding la equitación
hosepipe la manguera
hospital el hospital
hostel el hostal
hot caliente
  I'm hot tengo calor
  it's hot (weather) hace calor
  hot water el agua caliente
hot-water bottle la bolsa de agua
  caliente
hotel el hotel
hour la hora
  half an hour media hora
house la casa
housewife/husband la/el ama(o)
  de casa
house wine el vino de la casa
housework las tareas domésticas
how (in what way) cómo

how much? ¿cuánto?
how many? ¿cuántos?
how are you? ¿cómo está?
hungry: to be hungry tener hambre
to hunt cazar
hunting permit el permiso de caza
hurry: I'm in a hurry tengo prisa
to hurt (injure) hacer daño
  my back hurts me duele la espalda
  that hurts eso duele
husband el marido
hut (bathing/beach) la caseta
  (mountain) el refugio
hydrofoil el hidrodeslizador
hypodermic needle la aguja
  hipodérmica

I

I yo
ice el hielo
  (cube) el cubito
  with/without ice con/sin hielo
ice box la nevera
icecream el helado
ice lolly el polo
ice rink la pista de patinaje
to ice skate patinar sobre hielo
ice skates los patines de hielo
iced tea el té helado
idea la idea
identity card el carné de identidad
if si
ignition el encendido
ignition key la llave de contacto
ill enfermo(a)
illness la enfermedad
immediately inmediatamente ; en
  seguida
immersion heater el calentador
  eléctrico
immigration la inmigración
immunisation la inmunización
to import importar
important importante
impossible imposible

to improve mejorar
in dentro de ; en
  in 10 minutes dentro de diez
  minutos
  in London en Londres
in front of delante de
inch la pulgada = approx. 2.5 cm
included incluido(a)
inconvenient inoportuno(a)
to increase aumentar
indicator *(in car)* el intermitente
indigestion la indigestión
indigestion tablets las pastillas para
  la indigestión
indoors dentro
infection la infección
infectious contagioso(a)
information la información
information desk la información
ingredients los ingredientes
inhaler *(for medication)* el inhalador
injection la inyección
to injure herir
injured herido(a)
injury la herida
ink la tinta
inn la pensión
inner tube la cámara
inquiries información
inquiry desk la información
insect el insecto
insect bite la picadura de insecto
insect repellent el repelente
  contra insectos
inside dentro de
instant coffee el café instantáneo
instead of en lugar de
instructor el/la instructor(a)
insulin la insulina
insurance el seguro
insurance certificate la póliza
  de seguros
to insure asegurar
insured asegurado(a)
to intend to pensar

interesting interesante
international internacional
internet el/la Internet
  internet café el cibercafé
interpreter el/la intérprete
interval *(theatre, etc)* el descanso ;
  el intermedio
interview la entrevista
into en
  into town al centro
to introduce to presentar a
invitation la invitación
to invite invitar
invoice la factura
Ireland Irlanda
Irish irlandés/irlandesa
iron *(for clothes)* la plancha
  (metal) el hierro
to iron planchar
ironing board la tabla de planchar
ironmonger's la ferretería
island la isla
it lo/la
Italian italiano(a)
  (language) el italiano
Italy Italia
itch el picor
to itch picar
  it itches pica
item el artículo
itemized bill la factura detallada

J

jack *(for car)* el gato
jacket la chaqueta
jam *(food)* la mermelada
jammed *(stuck)* atascado(a)
January enero
jar *(honey, jam, etc)* el tarro
jaundice la ictericia
jaw la mandíbula
jealous celoso(a)
jeans los vaqueros
jelly *(dessert)* la gelatina

jellyfish la medusa
jet ski la moto acuática
jetty el embarcadero
Jewish judío(a)
jeweller's la joyería
jewellery las joyas
job el empleo
to jog hacer footing
to join (club, etc) hacerse socio de
to join in participar en
joint (body) la articulación
to joke bromear
joke la broma
journalist el/la periodista
journey el viaje
judge el/la juez(a)
jug la jarra
juice el zumo
  a carton of juice un brik de zumo
July julio
to jump saltar
jumper el jersey
jump leads (for car) los cables
  de arranque
junction (road) la bifurcación
June junio
jungle la jungla
just: just two sólo dos
  I've just arrived acabo de llegar

K

to keep (to retain) guardar
kennel la caseta (del perro)
kettle el hervidor (de agua)
key la llave
  card key (used in hotel) la llave
  tarjeta
keyboard el teclado
keyring el llavero
to kick dar una patada a
kid (child) el/la crío(a)
kidneys los riñones
to kill matar
kilo(gram) el kilo(gramo)

kilometre el kilómetro
kind (person) amable
kind (sort) la clase
  what kind? ¿qué clase?
king el rey
kiosk el quiosco
kiss el beso
to kiss besar
kitchen la cocina
kitchen paper el papel de cocina
kite la cometa
knee la rodilla
knee highs las medias cortas
knickers las bragas
knife el cuchillo
to knit hacer punto
to knock (on door) llamar
to knock down (car) atropellar
to knock over (vase, glass) tirar
knot el nudo
to know (have knowledge of) saber
  (person, place) conocer
  I don't know no sé
to know how to saber
  to know how to swim saber nadar
kosher kosher

L

label la etiqueta
lace (fabric) el encaje
laces (for shoes) los cordones
ladder la escalera (de mano)
ladies (toilet) los servicios de señoras
lady la señora
lager la cerveza (rubia)
  bottled lager la cerveza (rubia)
  de botella
  draught lager la cerveza (rubia)
  de barril
lake el lago
lamb el cordero
lamp la lámpara
lamppost la farola
lampshade la pantalla (de lámpara)

land el terreno
to land aterrizar
landlady la dueña (de la casa)
landlord el dueño (de la casa)
landslide el desprendimiento
de tierras
lane el carril
language el idioma ; la lengua
language school la escuela/
academia de idiomas
laptop el ordenador portátil
large grande
last último(a)
the last bus el último autobús
the last train el último tren
last night anoche
last week la semana pasada
last year el año pasado
last time la última vez
late tarde
the train is late el tren viene con
retraso
sorry I'm late siento llegar tarde
later más tarde
to laugh reírse
launderette la lavandería
automática
laundry service el servicio de
lavandería
lavatory *(in house)* el wáter
(in public place) los servicios
law la ley
lawn el césped
lawyer el/la abogado(a)
laxative el laxante
layby la zona de descanso
lead *(electric)* el cable
lead *(metal)* el plomo
lead-free sin plomo
leaf la hoja
leak *(of gas, liquid)* la fuga
(in roof) la gotera
to leak: *it's leaking* *(radiator, etc)*
está goteando
to learn aprender
lease *(rental)* el alquiler

leather el cuero
to leave *(a place)* irse de
(leave behind) dejar
when does the train leave?
¿a qué hora sale el tren?
leek el puerro
left: *on/to the left* a la izquierda
left-handed *(person)* zurdo(a)
left-luggage *(office)* la consigna
left-luggage locker la consigna
automática
leg la pierna
legal legal
leisure centre el polideportivo
lemon el limón
lemonade la gaseosa
to lend prestar
length la longitud
lens *(phototgraphic)* el objetivo
(contact lens) la lentilla
lesbian lesbiana
less menos
less than menos de que
lesson la clase
to let *(to allow)* permitir
(to hire out) alquilar
letter la carta
(of alphabet) la letra
letterbox el buzón
lettuce la lechuga
level crossing el paso a nivel
library la biblioteca
licence el permiso
(driving) el carné de conducir
lid la tapa
lie *(untruth)* la mentira
to lie down acostarse
lifebelt el salvavidas
lifeboat el bote salvavidas
lifeguard el/la socorrista
life insurance el seguro de vida
life jacket el chaleco salvavidas
life raft la balsa salvavidas
lift *(elevator)* el ascensor
can you give me a lift? ¿me lleva?

lift pass *(on ski slopes)* el forfait
light *(not heavy)* ligero(a)
light la luz
  have you a light? ¿tiene fuego?
light bulb la bombilla
lighter el encendedor ; el mechero
lighthouse el faro
lightning el relámpago
like *(similar to)* como
to like gustar
  I like coffee me gusta el café
  I don't like... no me gusta...
  I'd like to... me gustaría...
  we'd like to... nos gustaría...
lilo® la colchoneta hinchable
lime *(fruit)* la lima
line *(row, queue)* la fila
  (telephone) la línea
linen el lino
lingerie la lencería
lips los labios
lip-reading la lectura de labios
lip salve el cacao para los labios
lipstick la barra de labios
liqueur el licor
list la lista
to listen to escuchar
litre el litro
litter *(rubbish)* la basura
little pequeño(a)
  a little... un poco...
to live vivir
  I live in Edinburgh vivo
  en Edimburgo
  he lives in a flat vive en un piso
liver el hígado
living room el salón
loaf el pan de molde
local de la región ; del país
lock *(on door, box)* la cerradura
  the lock is broken la cerradura
  está rota
to lock cerrar con llave
locker *(luggage)* la consigna
locksmith el/la cerrajero(a)
log *(for fire)* el leño

log book *(car)* los papeles del coche
lollipop la piruleta ; el chupón
London Londres
  in London en Londres
  to London a Londres
long largo(a)
  for a long time (por) mucho tiempo
long-sighted hipermétrope
to look after cuidar
to look at mirar
to look for buscar
loose suelto(a)
  it's come loose se ha soltado
lorry el camión
to lose perder
lost perdido(a)
  I've lost... he perdido...
  I'm lost me he perdido
lost property office
  la oficina de objetos perdidos
lot: *a lot of* mucho
lotion la loción
lottery la lotería
loud *(sound, voice)* fuerte
  (volume) alto(a)
lounge el salón
love el amor
to love *(person)* querer
  I love swimming me encanta nadar
  I love you te quiero
lovely precioso(a)
low bajo(a)
low-alcohol con baja graduación
low-fat bajo(a) en calorías
low tide la marea baja
luck la suerte
lucky: *to be lucky* tener suerte
luggage el equipaje
luggage allowance el equipaje
  permitido
luggage rack el portaequipajes
luggage tag la etiqueta
luggage trolley el carrito
lump *(swelling)* el bulto
  (on head) el chichón
lunch la comida

lunch break la hora de la comida
lung el pulmón
luxury de lujo

M

machine la máquina
mad loco(a)
magazine la revista
maggot el gusano
magnet el imán
magnifying glass la lupa
maid (in hotel) la camarera
maiden name el apellido de soltera
mail el correo
  by mail por correo
main principal
main course (of meal) el plato
  principal
main road la carretera principal
Majorca Mallorca
make (brand) la marca
to make hacer
make-up el maquillaje
male masculino(a)
mallet el mazo
man el hombre
to manage (be in charge of) dirigir
manager el/la gerente
manual (gear change) manual
many muchos(as)
map (of region, country) el mapa
  (of town) el plano
marble el mármol
March marzo
margarine la margarina
marina el puerto deportivo
mark (stain) la mancha
market el mercado
  where is the market? ¿dónde está
  el mercado?
  when is the market? ¿cuándo hay
  mercado?
market place la plaza (del mercado)
marmalade la mermelada de
  naranja

married casado(a)
  I'm married estoy casado(a)
  are you married? ¿está casado(a)?
to marry casarse con
marsh la marisma
mascara el rímel®
masher (potato) el pasapurés
mass (in church) la misa
mast el mástil
masterpiece la obra maestra
match (game) el partido
matches las cerillas
material (cloth) la tela
to matter importar
  it doesn't matter no importa
  what's the matter? ¿qué pasa?
mattress el colchón
May mayo
mayonnaise la mayonesa
maximum máximo(a)
meal la comida
to mean querer decir
  what does this mean? ¿qué quiere
  decir esto?
measles el sarampión
to measure medir
meat la carne
mechanic el/la mecánico(a)
medical insurance el seguro médico
medical treatment el tratamiento
  médico
medicine la medicina
medieval medieval
Mediterranean el Mediterráneo
medium rare (meat) medio(a)
  hecho(a)
to meet (by chance) encontrarse con
  (by arrangement) ver
  I'm meeting her tomorrow
  he quedado con ella mañana
meeting la reunión
meeting point el punto de reunión
melon el melón
to melt derretir
member (of club, etc) el/la socio(a)

membership fee la cuota de socio
memory el recuerdo
memory card la tarjeta de memoria
men los hombres
to mend arreglar
meningitis la meningitis
menu la carta
  set menu el menú del día
message el mensaje
metal el metal
meter el contador
metre el metro
metro *(underground)* el metro
metro station la estación de metro
microwave oven el microondas
midday las doce del mediodía
middle el medio
middle-aged de mediana edad
midge el mosquito enano
midnight la medianoche
  at midnight a medianoche
migraine la jaqueca ; la migraña
  I've a migraine tengo jaqueca
mile la milla
milk la leche
  fresh milk la leche fresca
  hot milk la leche caliente
  long-life milk la leche de larga
  duración (UHT)
  powdered milk la leche en polvo
  semi-skimmed milk la leche
  semidesnatada
  skimmed milk la leche desnatada
  soya milk la leche de soja
  with milk con leche
milkshake el batido
millimetre el milímetro
mince *(meat)* la carne picada
mind: *do you mind if...?* ¿le importa
  que...?
  I don't mind no me importa
mineral water el agua mineral
minibar el minibar
minimum el mínimo
minister *(political)* el/la ministro(a)
  (church) el/la pastor(a)

minor road la carretera secundaria
mint *(herb)* la menta
  (sweet) la pastilla de menta
minute el minuto
mirror el espejo
miscarriage el aborto no provocado
to miss *(train, etc)* perder
Miss la señorita
missing *(lost)* perdido(a)
  my son is missing se ha perdido
  mi hijo
mistake el error
misty: *it's misty* hay neblina
misunderstanding
  la equivocación
to mix mezclar
mixer *(food processor)* el robot
  (de cocina)
  (hand-held) la batidora
mobile (phone) el (teléfono) móvil
modem el módem
modern moderno(a)
moisturizer la leche/crema
  hidratante
mole *(on skin)* el lunar
moment el momento
  just a moment un momento
monastery el monasterio
Monday el lunes
money el dinero
  I've no money no tengo dinero
moneybelt la riñonera
money order el giro postal
month el mes
  this month este mes
  last month el mes pasado
  next month el mes que viene
monthly mensualmente ; mensual
monument el monumento
moon la luna
mooring el atracadero
mop la fregona
moped el ciclomotor
more más
  more than más que
  more wine más vino

morning la mañana
  in the morning por la mañana
  this morning esta mañana
  tomorrow morning mañana por la mañana
morning-after pill la píldora (anticonceptiva) del día después
mosque la mezquita
mosquito el mosquito
mosquito bite la picadura de mosquito
mosquito net la mosquitera
mosquito repellent el repelente contra mosquitos
most: *most of* la mayor parte de ; la mayoría de
moth *(clothes)* la polilla
mother la madre
mother-in-law la suegra
motor el motor
motorbike la moto
motorboat la lancha motora
motorway la autopista
mountain la montaña
mountain bike la bicicleta de montaña
mountain rescue el rescate de montaña
mountaineering el montañismo
mouse *(animal, computer)* el ratón
moustache el bigote
mouth la boca
mouthwash el enjuague bucal
to move mover
  it isn't moving no se mueve
movie la película
to mow cortar
Mr el señor (Sr.)
Mrs la señora (Sra.)
Ms la señora (Sra.)
much mucho(a)
  too much demasiado(a)
muddy embarrado(a)
mugging el atraco
mumps las paperas
muscle el músculo

museum el museo
mushrooms los champiñones
music la música
musical musical
must *(to have to)* deber
  I must debo
  we must debemos
  I musn't no debo
  we musn't no debemos
mustard la mostaza
my mi

N

nail *(fingernail)* la uña
  (metal) el clavo
nailbrush el cepillo de uñas
nail clippers el cortaúñas
nail file la lima (de uñas)
nail polish el esmalte de uñas
nail polish remover el quitaesmalte
nail scissors las tijeras de uñas
name el nombre
  my name is... me llamo...
  what's your name? ¿cómo se llama?
nanny la niñera
napkin la servilleta
nappies los pañales
narrow estrecho(a)
national nacional
national park el parque nacional
nationality la nacionalidad
natural natural
nature la naturaleza
nature reserve la reserva natural
navy blue azul marino
near to cerca de
  near to the bank cerca del banco
  is it near? ¿está cerca?
necessary necesario(a)
neck el cuello
necklace el collar
nectarine la nectarina
to need necesitar
  I need... necesito...
  we need... necesitamos...
  I need to go tengo que ir

needle la aguja
  a needle and thread una aguja
  e hilo
negative *(photo)* el negativo
neighbour el/la vecino(a)
nephew el sobrino
net la red
  the Net la Red ; el/la Internet
never nunca
  I never drink wine nunca bebo vino
new nuevo(a)
news *(TV, radio, etc)* las noticias
newsagent's la tienda de prensa
newspaper el periódico
newsstand el kiosko de prensa
New Year el Año Nuevo
  Happy New Year! ¡Feliz Año Nuevo!
New Year's Eve la Nochevieja
New Zealand Nueva Zelanda
next próximo(a)
  next to al lado de
  next week la próxima semana
  the next stop la próxima parada
  the next train el próximo tren
nice *(person)* simpático(a)
  (place, holiday) bonito(a)
niece la sobrina
night la noche
  at night por la noche
  last night anoche
  per night por noche
  tomorrow night mañana por
  la noche
  tonight esta noche
night club el club nocturno
nightdress el camisón
night porter el guarda nocturno
no no
  no entry prohibida la entrada
  no smoking prohibido fumar
  (without) sin
  no sugar sin azúcar
  no ice sin hielo
  no problem ¡por supuesto!
nobody nadie
noise el ruido
  it's very noisy hay mucho ruido

non-alcoholic sin alcohol
none ninguno(a)
non-smoker el/la no fumador(a)
non-smoking no fumador
normal normal
north el norte
Northern Ireland Irlanda del Norte
nose la nariz
nosebleed la hemorragia nasal
not no
  I am not... no estoy... ; no soy...
note *(banknote)* el billete
  (written) la nota
note pad el bloc
nothing nada
  nothing else nada más
notice *(sign)* el anuncio
  (warning) el aviso
notice board el tablón de anuncios
novel la novela
November noviembre
now ahora
nowhere en ninguna parte
nuclear nuclear
nudist beach la playa nudista
number el número
numberplate *(car)* la matrícula
nurse la/el enfermera(o)
nursery school la guardería (infantil)
nursery slope la pista para
  principiantes
nut *(for bolt)* la tuerca
nuts *(to eat)* los frutos secos

O

oar el remo
oats los copos de avena
to obtain obtener
occupation *(work)* la profesión
ocean el océano
October octubre
odd *(strange)* raro(a)
  (not even) impar
of de

a glass of wine un vaso de vino
made of... hecho(a) de...
off *(light, etc)* apagado(a)
  (rotten) pasado(a)
office la oficina
often a menudo
  how often? ¿cada cuánto?
oil el aceite
oil filter el filtro de aceite
oil gauge el indicador del aceite
ointment la pomada
OK ¡vale!
old viejo(a)
  how old are you? ¿cuántos años
  tiene?
  I'm ... years old tengo ... años
old age pensioner el/la pensionista
  (de la tercera edad)
olive la aceituna
olive oil el aceite de oliva
olive tree el olivo
on *(light, TV, engine)* encendido(a)
on sobre ; encima
  on the table sobre la mesa
  on time a la hora
once una vez
  at once en seguida
one-way dirección única
onion la cebolla
only sólo
open abierto(a)
to open abrir
opera la ópera
operation la operación
operator *(phone)* el/la telefonista
opposite (to) enfrente (de)
  opposite the bank enfrente del
  banco
  quite the opposite! ¡todo lo
  contrario!
optician's la óptica
or o
orange *(fruit)* la naranja
  (colour) naranja
orange juice el zumo de naranja
orchestra la orquesta

order: *out of order* averiado(a)
to order *(in restaurant)* pedir
  can I order? ¿puedo pedir?
organic biológico(a) ; ecológico(a)
to organize organizar
ornament el adorno
other: *the other one* el/la otro(a)
  have you any others? ¿tiene
  otros(as)?
ounce = approx. 30 g
our nuestro(a)
out *(light)* apagado(a)
  he's (gone) out ha salido
outdoor *(pool, etc)* al aire libre
outside: *it's outside* está fuera
oven el horno
ovenproof dish resistente al horno
over *(on top of)* (por) encima de
to be overbooked tener overbooking
to overcharge cobrar de más
overdone *(food)* demasiado hecho(a)
overdose la sobredosis
to overheat recalentar
to overload sobrecargar
to oversleep quedarse dormido(a)
to overtake *(in car)* adelantar
to owe deber
  I owe you... le debo...
  you owe me... me debe...
owner el/la propietario(a)
oxygen el oxígeno

P

pace el ritmo
pacemaker el marcapasos
to pack *(luggage)* hacer las maletas
package el paquete
package tour el viaje organizado
packet el paquete
padded envelope el sobre
  acolchado
paddling pool la piscina hinchable
padlock el candado

page la página
paid pagado(a)
  I've paid he pagado
pain el dolor
painful doloroso(a)
painkiller el analgésico ; el calmante
to paint pintar
paintbrush el pincel
painting *(picture)* el cuadro
pair el par
palace el palacio
pale pálido(a)
pan *(saucepan)* la cacerola
  (frying) la sartén
pancake el crep(e)
panniers *(for bike)* las alforjas
panties las bragas
pants *(men's underwear)*
  los calzoncillos
panty liner el salvaslip
paper el papel
paper hankies los pañuelos
  de papel
paper napkins las servilletas
  de papel
papoose *(for carrying baby)*
  la mochila portabebés
paragliding el parapente
paralysed paralizado(a)
parcel el paquete
pardon? ¿cómo?
  I beg your pardon! ¡perdón?
parents los padres
park el parque
to park aparcar
parking disk el tique de
  aparcamiento
parking meter el parquímetro
parking ticket *(fine)* la multa por
  aparcamiento indebido
partner *(business)* el/la socio(a)
  (boy/girlfriend) el/la compañero(a)
party *(group)* el grupo
  (celebration) la fiesta
  (political) el partido

pass *(mountain)* el puerto
  (train) el abono
  (bus) el bonobús
passenger el/la pasajero(a)
passport el pasaporte
passport control el control
  de pasaportes
password
pasta la pasta
pastry *(dough)* la masa
  (cake) el pastel
path el camino
patient *(in hospital)* el/la paciente
pavement la acera
to pay pagar
  I'd like to pay quisiera pagar
  where do I pay ¿dónde se paga?
payment el pago
payphone el teléfono público
peace la paz
peach el melocotón
peak rate la tarifa máxima
pear la pera
pearls las perlas
peas los guisantes
pedal el pedal
pedalo el hidropedal
pedestrian el peatón
pedestrian crossing el paso
  de peatones
to pee hacer pipí
to peel *(fruit)* pelar
peg *(for clothes)* la pinza
  (for tent) la estaca
pen el bolígrafo ; el boli
pencil el lápiz
penfriend el/la amigo(a) por
  correspondencia
penicillin la penicilina
penis el pene
penknife la navaja
pensioner el/la jubilado(a) ;
  el/la pensionista
people la gente

pepper *(spice)* la pimienta
  (vegetable) el pimiento
per por
  per day al día
  per hour por hora
  per week a la semana
  per person por persona
  50 km per hour 50 km por hora
perfect perfecto(a)
performance la función
perfume el perfume
perhaps quizá(s)
period *(menstruation)* la regla
perm la permanente
permit el permiso
person la persona
personal organizer la agenda
personal stereo el walkman®
pet el animal doméstico
pet food la comida para animales
pet shop la pajarería
petrol la gasolina
  4-star petrol la gasolina súper
  unleaded petrol la gasolina sin
  plomo
petrol cap el tapón del depósito
petrol pump el surtidor
petrol station la gasolinera
petrol tank el depósito
pharmacy la farmacia
phone el teléfono
  (mobile) el móvil
  (hands free) el teléfono 'manos
  libres'
  by phone por teléfono
to phone llamar por teléfono
phonebook la guía (telefónica)
phonebox la cabina (telefónica)
phone call la llamada (telefónica)
phonecard la tarjeta telefónica
photocopy la fotocopia
to photocopy fotocopiar
photograph la fotografía
  to take a photograph hacer una
  fotografía
phrase book la guía de conversación

piano el piano
to pick *(choose)* elegir
  (pluck) coger
pickled en vinagre
pickpocket el/la carterista
picnic el picnic
  to have a picnic ir de picnic
picnic area el merendero
picnic hamper la cesta de
  la merienda
picnic rug la mantita
picture *(painting)* el cuadro
  (photo) la foto
pie *(fruit)* la tarta
  (meat) el pastel de carne
  (and/or vegetable) la empanada
piece el trozo
pier el embarcadero ; el muelle
pig el cerdo
pill la píldora
  to be on the pill tomar la píldora
pillow la almohada
pillowcase la funda de almohada
pilot el/la piloto
pin el alfiler
pineapple la piña
pink rosa
pint = approx. 0.5 litre
pipe *(smoker's)* la pipa
  (drain, etc) la tubería
pity: *what a pity* ¡qué pena!
pizza la pizza
place el lugar
place of birth el lugar de
  nacimiento
plain *(yoghurt)* natural
plait la trenza
plan *(of town)* el plano
plane *(airplane)* el avión
plant la planta
plaster *(sticking)* la tirita®
  (for broken limb) la escayola
plastic *(made of)* de plástico
plastic bag la bolsa de plástico
plate el plato

platform el andén
  which platform? ¿qué andén?
play *(theatre)* la obra
to play *(games)* jugar
play area la zona recreativa
play park el parque infantil
playroom el cuarto de juegos
pleasant agradable
please por favor
pleased contento(a)
  pleased to meet you encantado(a)
  de conocerle(la)
pliers los alicates
plug *(electrical)* el enchufe
  (for sink) el tapón
to plug in enchufar
plum la ciruela
plumber el/la fontanero(a)
plumbing *(pipes)* las cañerías
  (craft) la fontanería
plunger *(for sink)* el desatascador
p.m. de la tarde
poached *(egg, fish)* escalfado(a)
pocket el bolsillo
point el punto
points *(in car)* los platinos
poison el veneno
poisonous venenoso(a)
police *(force)* la policía
policeman/woman el/la policía
police station la comisaría
polish *(for shoes)* el betún
  (for furniture) el limpiamuebles
pollen el polen
polluted contaminado(a)
pony el poni
pony-trekking la excursión a caballo
pool la piscina
pool attendant el/la encargado(a)
  de la piscina
poor pobre
pop socks los calcetines cortos
popular popular
pork el cerdo

port *(seaport)* el puerto
  (wine) el oporto
porter *(hotel)* el portero
  (at station) el mozo
portion la porción ; la ración
Portugal Portugal
Portuguese portugués/portuguesa
  (language) el portugués
possible posible
post: *by post* por correo
to post echar al correo
postbox el buzón
postcard la postal
postcode el código postal
poster el póster
postman/woman el/la cartero(a)
post office la oficina de correos
to postpone aplazar
pot *(for cooking)* la olla
potato la patata
  baked potato la patata asada
  boiled potatoes las patatas hervidas
  fried potatoes las patatas fritas
  mashed potatoes el puré de patatas
  roast potatoes las patatas asadas
  sautéed potatoes las patatas
  salteadas
potato masher el pasapurés
potato peeler el pelador
potato salad la ensalada de patatas
pothole el bache
pottery la cerámica
pound *(weight)* = approx. 0.5 kilo
  (money) la libra
to pour echar ; servir
powder el polvo
  in powder form en polvo
powdered milk la leche en polvo
power *(electicity)* la electricidad
power cut el apagón
pram el cochecito (de bebé)
to pray rezar
to prefer preferir
pregnant embarazada
  I'm pregnant estoy embarazada
to prepare preparar

to prescribe prescribir
prescription la receta médica
present *(gift)* el regalo
preservative el conservante
president el/la presidente(a)
pressure la presión
pretty bonito(a)
price el precio
price list la lista de precios
priest el sacerdote ; el cura
prime minister el/la primer(a) ministro(a)
print *(photo)* la copia
to print imprimir
printer la impresora
prison la cárcel
private privado(a)
prize el premio
probably probablemente
problem el problema
professor el/la catedrático(a)
programme *(TV, radio)* el programa
prohibited prohibido(a)
promise la promesa
to promise prometer
to pronounce pronunciar
  how's it pronounced? ¿cómo se pronuncia?
Protestant protestante
to provide proporcionar
public público(a)
public holiday la fiesta (oficial)
pudding el postre
to pull tirar
  I've pulled a muscle me ha dado un tirón en el músculo
to pull over *(car)* hacerse a un lado
pullover el jersey
pump *(bike, etc)* la bomba
  (petrol) el surtidor
puncture el pinchazo
puncture repair kit el kit para reparar pinchazos
puppet la marioneta

puppet show el espectáculo de marionetas
purple morado(a)
purpose el propósito
  on purpose a propósito
purse el monedero
to push empujar
pushchair la sillita de paseo
to put *(place)* poner
pyjamas el pijama
Pyrenees los Pirineos

Q

quality la calidad
quantity la cantidad
quarantine la cuarentena
to quarrel discutir ; pelearse
quarter el cuarto
quay el muelle
queen la reina
query la pregunta
question la pregunta
queue la cola
to queue hacer cola
quick rápido(a)
quickly de prisa
quiet *(place)* tranquilo(a)
quilt el edredón (nórdico)
quite bastante
  it's quite good es bastante bueno
  quite expensive bastante caro
quiz el concurso

R

rabbit el conejo
rabies la rabia
race *(sport)* la carrera
race course *(horses)* el hipódromo
racket *(tennis, etc)* la raqueta
radiator *(car, heater)* el radiador
radio la radio
  (digital) la radio digital
  (car) la radio del coche

railcard el carné de descuento para el tren
railway el ferrocarril
railway station la estación de tren
rain la lluvia
to rain: *it's raining* está lloviendo
raincoat el impermeable
rake el rastrillo
rape la violación
to rape violar
rare *(unique)* excepcional
   (steak) poco hecho(a)
rash *(skin)* el sarpullido
raspberry la frambuesa
rat la rata
rate *(price)* la tarifa
rate of exchange el tipo de cambio
raw crudo(a)
razor la maquinilla de afeitar
razor blades las hojas de afeitar
to read leer
ready listo(a)
   to get ready prepararse
real verdadero(a)
to realize darse cuenta de
rearview mirror el (espejo) retrovisor
receipt el recibo
receiver *(phone)* el auricular
reception desk la recepción
receptionist el/la recepcionista
to recharge *(battery, etc)* recargar
recharger el cargador
recipe la receta
to recognize reconocer
to recommend recomendar
to record *(on tape, etc)* grabar
   (facts) registrar
to recover *(from illness)* recuperarse
to recycle reciclar
red rojo(a)
to reduce reducir
reduction el descuento
to refer to referirse a
refill el recambio

refund el reembolso
to refuse negarse
regarding con respecto a
region la región
register el registro
to register *(at hotel)* registrarse
registered *(letter)* certificado(a)
registration form la hoja de inscripción
to reimburse reembolsar
relation *(family)* el/la pariente
relationship la relación
to remain *(stay)* quedarse
to remember acordarse (de)
   I don't remember no me acuerdo
remote control el mando a distancia
removal firm la empresa de mudanzas
to remove quitar
rent el alquiler
to rent alquilar
rental el alquiler
repair la reparación
to repair reparar
to repeat repetir
to reply contestar
report el informe
to report informar
request la solicitud
to request solicitar
to require necesitar
to rescue rescatar
reservation la reserva
to reserve reservar
reserved reservado(a)
resident el/la residente
resort el centro turístico
rest *(repose)* el descanso
   (remainder) el resto
to rest descansar
restaurant el restaurante
restaurant car el coche restaurante
retired jubilado(a)
to return *(to go back)* volver
   (to give back something) devolver

return *(ticket)* de ida y vuelta
to reverse dar marcha atrás
to reverse the charges llamar a cobro revertido
reverse charge call la llamada a cobro revertido
reverse gear la marcha atrás
rheumatism el reumatismo
rib la costilla
rice el arroz
rich *(person)* rico(a)
  (food) pesado(a)
to ride a horse montar a caballo
right *(correct)* correcto(a)
  to be right tener razón
right: *on/to the right* a la derecha
right of way el derecho de paso
to ring *(bell, to phone)* llamar
  it's ringing está sonando
ring el anillo
ring road la carretera de circunvalación
ripe maduro(a)
river el río
road la carretera
road sign la señal de tráfico
roadworks las obras
roast asado(a)
roll *(bread)* el panecillo
rollerblades los patines en línea
romantic romántico(a)
roof el tejado
roof-rack la baca
room *(in house, hotel)* la habitación
  (space) sitio
  double room la habitación doble
  single room la habitación individual
  family room la habitación familiar
room number el número de habitación
room service el servicio de habitaciones
root la raíz
rope la cuerda
rose la rosa
rosé wine el (vino) rosado

rotten *(fruit, etc)* podrido(a)
rough *(sea)* picado(a)
round *(shape)* redondo(a)
roundabout *(traffic)* la rotonda
row *(line, theatre)* la fila
to row *(boat)* remar
rowing *(sport)* el remo
rowing boat el bote de remos
royal real
rubber *(material)* la goma
  (eraser) la goma de borrar
rubber band la goma
rubber gloves los guantes de goma
rubbish la basura
rubella la rubeola
rucksack la mochila
rug la alfombra
ruins las ruinas
ruler *(for measuring)* la regla
to run correr
rush hour la hora punta
rusty oxidado(a)
rye el centeno

S

sad triste
saddle *(bike)* el sillín
  (horse) la silla de montar
safe seguro(a)
  is it safe? ¿es seguro(a)?
safe *(for valuables)* la caja fuerte
safety belt el cinturón de seguridad
safety pin el imperdible
to sail *(sport, leisure)* navegar
sailboard la tabla de windsurf
sailing *(sport)* la vela
sailing boat el velero
saint el/la santo(a)
salad la ensalada
  green salad la ensalada verde
  mixed salad la ensalada mixta
  potato salad la ensalada de patatas
  tomato salad la ensalada de tomate

salad dressing el aliño
salami el salchichón ; el salami
salary el sueldo
sale(s) las rebajas
salesman/woman el/la vendedor(a)
sales rep el/la representante
salt la sal
salt water el agua salada
salty salado(a)
same mismo(a)
sample la muestra
sand la arena
sandals las sandalias
sandwich el bocadillo ; el sándwich
  toasted sandwich el sándwich
  tostado
sanitary towels las compresas
satellite dish la antena parabólica
satellite TV la televisión por satélite
Saturday el sábado
sauce la salsa
  tomato sauce la salsa de tomate
saucepan la cacerola
saucer el platillo
sauna la sauna
sausage la salchicha
to save *(life)* salvar
  (money) ahorrar
savoury salado(a)
saw la sierra
to say decir
scales *(weighing)* el peso
to scan escanear
scan el escáner
scarf *(woollen)* la bufanda
  (headscarf) el pañuelo
scenery el paisaje
schedule el programa
school la escuela
  primary school la escuela primaria
  secondary school el instituto de
  enseñanza secundaria
scissors las tijeras
score *(of match)* la puntuación
to score a goal marcar un gol

Scot el escocés/la escocesa
Scotland Escocia
Scottish escocés/escocesa
scouring pad el estropajo
screen *(computer, TV)* la pantalla
screenwash el limpiacristales
screw el tornillo
screwdriver el destornillador
  phillips screwdriver®
  el destornillador de estrella
scuba diving el submarinismo
sculpture la escultura
sea el mar
seafood el/los marisco(s)
seam *(of dress)* la costura
to search buscar
search engine el buscador
seasick mareado(a)
seaside la playa
  at the seaside en la playa
season *(of year)* la estación
  (holiday) la temporada
  in season del tiempo
seasonal estacional
season ticket el abono
seasoning el condimento
seat *(chair)* la silla
  (in bus, train) el asiento
seatbelt el cinturón de seguridad
seaweed las algas
second segundo(a)
second *(time)* el segundo
second class de segunda clase
second-hand de segunda mano
secretary el/la secretario(a)
security guard el/la guarda de
  seguridad
sedative el sedante
to see ver
self-catering sin servicio de comidas
self-employed autónomo(a)
self-service el self-service ; el
  autoservicio
to sell vender
  do you sell...? ¿tiene...?

sell-by date la fecha de limite de venta
Sellotape® el celo
to send enviar
senior citizen el/la jubilado(a)
sensible sensato(a)
separated (couple) separado(a)
separately: to pay separately pagar por separado
September septiembre
septic tank el pozo séptico
serious (accident, etc) grave
to serve servir
service (in church) la misa
(in restaurant) el servicio
is service included? ¿está incluido el servicio?
service charge el servicio
service station la estación de servicio
serviette la servilleta
set menu el menú del día
settee el sofá
several varios(as)
to sew coser
sex el sexo
shade la sombra
into the shade a la sombra
to shake (bottle) agitar
shallow poco profundo(a)
shampoo el champú
shampoo and set lavar y marcar
to share compartir ; dividir
sharp (razor, knife) afilado(a)
to shave afeitarse
shaving cream la crema de afeitar
shawl el chal
she ella
sheep la oveja
sheet (bed) la sábana
shelf el estante
shell (seashell) la concha
(egg, nut) la cáscara
sheltered protegido(a)
shepherd el/la pastor(a)

sherry el jerez
to shine brillar
shingles el herpes zóster ; la culebrilla
ship el barco
shirt la camisa
shock el susto
(electric) la descarga
shock absorber el amortiguador
shoe el zapato
shoelaces los cordones (de los zapatos)
shoe polish el betún
shoe shop la zapatería
shop la tienda
to shop hacer las compras ; comprar
shop assistant el/la dependiente(a)
shopping las compras
to go shopping ir de compras/tiendas
shopping centre el centro comercial
shore la orilla
short corto(a)
shortage la escasez
short circuit el cortocircuito
short cut el atajo
shorts los pantalones cortos
short-sighted miope
shoulder el hombro
to shout gritar
show (theatrical) el espectáculo
to show enseñar
shower (bath) la ducha
(rain) el chubasco
to take a shower ducharse
shower cap el gorro de ducha
shower gel el gel de ducha
to shrink encoger
shut (closed) cerrado(a)
to shut cerrar
shutters (outside) las persianas
shuttle service el servicio regular de enlace
sick (ill) enfermo(a)
I feel sick tengo ganas de vomitar

side el lado
side dish la guarnición
sidelight la luz de posición
sidewalk la acera
sieve (for liquids) el colador
  (for flour, etc) el tamiz
sightseeing: to go sightseeing hacer
  turismo
sightseeing tour el recorrido
  turístico
sign la señal
to sign firmar
signature la firma
signpost la señal
silk la seda
silver la plata
similar to parecido(a) a
since desde ; puesto que
  since 1974 desde 1974
  since you're not Spanish puesto
  que no es español(a)
to sing cantar
single (unmarried) soltero(a)
  (bed, room) individual
single ticket el billete de ida
sink (in kitchen) el fregadero
sir señor
sister la hermana
sister-in-law la cuñada
to sit sentarse
  sit down, please siéntese, por favor
size (clothes) la talla
  (shoes) el número
to skate patinar
skateboard el monopatín
skates los patines
skating rink la pista de patinaje
ski el esquí
to ski esquiar
ski boots las botas de esquí
skiing el esquí
ski instructor el/la monitor(a)
  de esquí
ski jump el salto de esquí
ski lift el telesquí

ski pants los pantalones de esquí
ski pass el forfait
ski pole/stick el bastón de esquí
ski run/piste la pista de esquí
ski suit el traje de esquí
skin la piel
skirt la falda
sky el cielo
sledge el trineo
to sleep dormir
  to sleep in quedarse dormido(a)
sleeper (on train) la litera
sleeping bag el saco de dormir
sleeping car el coche cama
sleeping pill el somnífero
slice (of bread) la rebanada
  (of ham) la loncha
sliced bread el pan de molde
slide (photo) la diapositiva
to slip resbalarse
slippers las zapatillas
slow lento(a)
to slow down reducir la velocidad
slowly despacio
small pequeño(a)
smaller than más pequeño(a) que
smell el olor
  a bad smell un mal olor
  a nice smell un buen olor
smile la sonrisa
to smile sonreír
to smoke fumar
  I don't smoke no fumo
  can I smoke? ¿puedo fumar?
smoke el humo
smoke alarm la alarma contra
  incendios
smoked ahumado(a)
smokers (sign) fumadores
smooth liso(a)
snack el tentempié
  to have a snack tomar algo
snack bar la cafetería
snake la serpiente

snake bite la mordedura
de serpiente
to sneeze estornudar
to snore roncar
snorkel el esnórkel
snow la nieve
to snow nevar
 it's snowing está nevando
snow board el snowboard
snowboarding: *to go snowboarding*
 ir a hacer snowboard
snow chains las cadenas
 (para la nieve)
snow tyres los neumáticos
 antideslizantes
snowed up aislado(a) por la nieve
soap el jabón
soap powder el detergente
sober sobrio(a)
socket *(for plug)* el enchufe
socks los calcetines
soda water la soda
sofa el sofá
sofa bed el sofá-cama
soft blando
soft drink el refresco
software el software
soldier el soldado
sole *(of foot, shoe)* la suela
soluble soluble
some algunos(as)
someone alguien
something algo
sometimes a veces
son el hijo
son-in-law el yerno
song la canción
soon pronto
 as soon as possible lo antes posible
sore throat el dolor de garganta
sorry: *sorry!* ¡perdón!
 I'm sorry! ¡lo siento!
sort el tipo
 what sort? ¿qué tipo?
soup la sopa

sour amargo(a)
soured cream la nata agria
south el sur
souvenir el souvenir
spa el spa ; el balneario
space el espacio
spade la pala
Spain España
Spaniard el/la español(a)
Spanish español(a)
spanner la llave inglesa
spare parts los repuestos
spare room el cuarto de invitados
spare tyre la rueda de repuesto
spare wheel la rueda de repuesto
sparkling espumoso(a)
 sparkling water el agua con gas
 sparkling wine el vino espumoso
spark plug la bujía
to speak hablar
 do you speak English? ¿habla
 inglés?
special especial
specialist el/la especialista
speciality la especialidad
speed la velocidad
speedboat la lancha motora
speeding el exceso de velocidad
speeding ticket la multa por exceso
 de velocidad
speed limit la velocidad máxima
 to exceed the speed limit exceder
 la velocidad máxima
speedometer el velocímetro
spell: *how is it spelt?* ¿cómo se
 escribe?
to spend *(money)* gastar
spice la especia
spicy picante
spider la araña
to spill derramar
spinach las espinacas
spine la columna (vertebral)
spin-dryer la secadora-
 centrifugadora

spirits el alcohol
splinter la astilla
spoke (wheel) el radio
sponge la esponja
spoon la cuchara
sport el deporte
sports centre el polideportivo
sports shop la tienda de deportes
spot (pimple) la espinilla
sprain el esguince
spring (season) la primavera
   (metal) el muelle
square (in town) la plaza
squash (game) el squash
to squeeze apretar
   (lemon) exprimir
squid el calamar
stadium el estadio
stage el escenario
stain la mancha
stained glass la vidriera
stairs las escaleras
stale (bread) duro(a)
stalls (theatre) las butacas (de patio)
stamp (postage) el sello
to stand estar de pie
star la estrella
to start (car) poner en marcha
starter (in meal) entrante
   (in car) la puesta en marcha
station la estación
stationer's la papelería
statue la estatua
stay la estancia
   enjoy your stay! ¡que lo pase bien!
to stay (remain) quedarse
   I'm staying at the hotel... estoy
   alojado(a) en el hotel...
steak el filete
to steal robar
steamed al vapor
steel el acero
steep: is it steep? ¿hay mucha
   subida?
steeple la aguja

steering wheel el volante
step el peldaño
stepdaughter la hijastra
stepfather el padrastro
stepmother la madrastra
stepson el hijastro
stereo el estéreo
sterling (pounds) las libras esterlinas
steward (on plane) el auxiliar de
   vuelo
stewardess (on plane) la azafata
to stick (with glue) pegar
sticking plaster la tirita®
still (not fizzy) sin gas
sting la picadura
to sting picar
stitches (surgical) los puntos
stockings las medias
stomach el estómago
stomach upset el trastorno
   estomacal
stone la piedra
to stop parar
store (shop) la tienda
storey el piso
storm la tormenta
   (at sea) el temporal
story la historia
straightaway inmediatamente
straight on todo recto
strange extraño(a)
straw (for drinking) la pajita
strawberry la fresa
stream el arroyo
street la calle
street map el plano de la ciudad
strength la fuerza
stress el estrés
strike (of workers) la huelga
string la cuerda
striped a rayas
stroke (medical) la trombosis
strong fuerte
stuck: it's stuck está atascado(a)
student el/la estudiante

student discount el decuento para estudiantes

stuffed relleno(a)

stung picado(a)

stupid tonto(a)

subscription la suscripción

subtitles los subtítulos

subway *(train)* el metro *(passage)* el paso subterráneo

suddenly de repente

suede el ante

sugar el azúcar

sugar-free sin azúcar

to suggest sugerir

suit *(men's and women's)* el traje

suitcase la maleta

sum la suma

summer el verano

summer holidays las vacaciones de verano

summit la cumbre

sun el sol

to sunbathe tomar el sol

sunblock la protección solar

sunburn la quemadura del sol

Sunday el domingo

sunglasses las gafas de sol

sunny: *it's sunny* hace sol

sunrise la salida del sol

sunroof el techo solar

sunscreen el filtro solar

sunset la puesta de sol

sunshade la sombrilla

sunstroke la insolación

suntan el bronceado

suntan lotion el bronceador

supermarket el supermercado

supper la cena

supplement el suplemento

to supply suministrar

to surf hacer surf
to surf the net navegar por internet

surfboard la tabla de surf

surgery *(operation)* la operación

surname el apellido

surprise la sorpresa

surrounded by rodeado(a) de

to survive sobrevivir

to swallow tragar

to sweat sudar

sweater el jersey

sweatshirt la sudadera

sweet *(not savoury)* dulce

sweet *(dessert)* el dulce

sweetener el edulcorante ; la sacarina®

sweets los caramelos

to swell *(injury, etc)* hincharse

to swim nadar

swimming pool la piscina

swimsuit el bañador

swing *(for children)* el columpio

Swiss suizo(a)

switch el interruptor

to switch off apagar

to switch on encender

Switzerland Suiza

swollen hinchado(a)

synagogue la sinagoga

syringe la jeringuilla

T

table la mesa

tablecloth el mantel

tablespoon la cuchara de servir

table tennis el ping-pong

tablet *(pill)* la pastilla

tailor's la sastrería

to take *(medicine, etc)* tomar
how long does it take? ¿cuánto tiempo se tarda?

take-away *(food)* para llevar

to take off despegar

to take out *(of bag, etc)* sacar

talc los polvos de talco

to talk to hablar con

tall alto(a)

tampons los tampones

tangerine la mandarina

tank *(petrol)* el depósito
  (fish) la pecera
tap el grifo
tap water el agua corriente
tape *(video)* la cinta
tape measure el metro
tape recorder el casete
tart la tarta
taste el sabor
to taste probar
  can I taste it? ¿puedo probarlo?
tax el impuesto
taxi el taxi
taxi driver el/la taxista
taxi rank la parada de taxis
tea el té
  herbal tea la infusión
  lemon tea el té con limón
  strong tea el té cargado
teabag la bolsita de té
teapot la tetera
teaspoon la cucharilla
tea towel el paño de cocina
to teach enseñar
teacher el/la profesor(a)
team el equipo
tear *(in material)* el rasgón
teat *(on baby's bottle)* la tetina
teenager el/la adolescente
teeth los dientes
telegram el telegrama
telephone el teléfono
to telephone llamar por teléfono
telephone box la cabina (telefónica)
telephone call la llamada (telefónica)
telephone card la tarjeta telefónica
telephone directory la guía
  (telefónica)
telephone number el número de
  teléfono
television la televisión
to tell decir
temperature la temperatura
  to have a temperature tener fiebre
temporary provisional

tenant el/la inquilino(a)
tendon el tendón
tennis el tenis
tennis ball la pelota de tenis
tennis court la pista de tenis
tennis racket la raqueta de tenis
tent la tienda de campaña
tent peg la estaca
terminal *(airport)* la terminal
terrace la terraza
to test *(try out)* probar
testicles los testículos
tetanus el tétanos
to text mandar un mensaje de texto
text message el mensaje de texto
than que
  more than you más que tú
  more than five más de cinco
to thank agradecer
thank you gracias
  thank you very much muchas
  gracias
that ese/esa
  (more remote) aquel/aquella
  that one ése/ésa/eso
  (more remote) aquél/
  aquélla/aquello
the el/la/los/las
theatre el teatro
theft el robo
their su/sus
them ellos/ellas
  (direct) los/las
there *(over there)* allí
there is/there are hay
thermometer el termómetro
these estos/estas
  these ones éstos/éstas
they ellos/ellas
thick *(not thin)* grueso(a)
thief el ladrón/la ladrona
thigh el muslo
thin *(person)* delgado(a)
thing la cosa
  my things mis cosas

to think pensar
  (to be of opinion) creer
thirsty: *I'm thirsty* tengo sed
this este/esta/esto
  this one éste/ésta
thorn la espina
those esos/esas
  (more remote) aquellos/aquellas
  those ones ésos/ésas
  (more remote) aquéllos/aquéllas
thread el hilo
throat la garganta
throat lozenges las pastillas para
  la garganta
through por
thumb el pulgar
thunder el trueno
thunderstorm la tormenta
Thursday el jueves
thyme el tomillo
ticket *(bus, train, etc)* el billete
  (entrance fee) la entrada
  a single ticket un billete de ida
  a return ticket un billete de ida
  y vuelta
  a tourist ticket un billete turístico
  a book of tickets un abono
ticket collector el/la revisor(a)
ticket office el despacho de billetes
tide *(sea)* la marea
  low tide la marea baja
  high tide la marea alta
tidy arreglado(a)
to tidy up ordenar
tie la corbata
tight *(fitting)* ajustado(a)
tights las medias
tile *(roof)* la teja
  (floor) la baldosa
till *(cash desk)* la caja
till *(until)* hasta
  till 2 o'clock hasta las 2
time el tiempo
  (clock) la hora
  what time is it? ¿qué hora es?
timer *(on cooker)* el temporizador

timetable el horario
tin *(can)* la lata
tinfoil el papel de estaño
tin-opener el abrelatas
tip la propina
to tip dar propina
tipped *(cigarette)* con filtro
tired cansado(a)
tissues los kleenex®
to a
  to London a Londres
  to the airport al aeropuerto
toadstool el hongo venenoso
toast *(to eat)* la tostada
  (raising glass) el brindis
tobacco el tabaco
tobacconist's el estanco
today hoy
toddler el/la niño(a) pequeño(a)
toe el dedo del pie
together juntos(as)
toilet los aseos ; los servicios
  toilet for disabled los servicios para
  minusválidos
toilet brush la escobilla del wáter
toilet paper el papel higiénico
toiletries los artículos
  de baño
token *(for bus)* el vale
toll *(motorway)* el peaje
tomato el tomate
  tinned tomatoes los tomates en lata
tomato juice el zumo de tomate
tomato soup la sopa de tomate
tomorrow mañana
  tomorrow morning mañana por
  la mañana
  tomorrow afternoon mañana por
  la tarde
  tomorrow evening mañana por
  la tarde/noche
tongue la lengua
tonic water la tónica
tonight esta noche
tonsillitis la amigdalitis
too *(also)* también

too big demasiado grande
too small demasiado pequeño(a)
too hot (food) demasiado caliente
too noisy demasiado ruidoso(a)
tool la herramienta
toolkit el juego de herramientas
tooth el diente
toothache el dolor de muelas
toothbrush el cepillo de dientes
toothpaste la pasta de dientes
toothpick el palillo
top: *the top floor* el último piso
top *(of hill)* la cima
  (shirt) el top
  (t-shirt) la camiseta
  on top of... sobre...
topless: *to go topless* hacer topless
torch *(flashlight)* la linterna
torn rasgado(a)
total *(amount)* el total
to touch tocar
tough *(meat)* duro(a)
tour *(trip)* el viaje
  (of museum, etc) la visita
  guided tour la visita con guía
tour guide el/la guía turístico(a)
tour operator el/la tour operador(a)
tourist el/la turista
tourist office la oficina de turismo
tourist route la ruta turística
tourist ticket el billete turístico
to tow remolcar
towbar la barra de remolque
tow rope el cable de remolque
towel la toalla
tower la torre
town la ciudad
town centre el centro de la ciudad
town hall el ayuntamiento
town plan el plano de la ciudad
toxic tóxico(a)
toy el juguete
toy shop la juguetería
tracksuit el chándal
traditional tradicional

traffic el tráfico
traffic jam el atasco
traffic lights el semáforo
traffic warden el/la guardia
  de tráfico
trailer el remolque
train el tren
  by train en tren
  the next train el próximo tren
  the first train el primer tren
  the last train el último tren
trainers las zapatillas de deporte
tram el tranvía
tranquillizer el tranquilizante
to translate traducir
translation la traducción
to travel viajar
travel agent's la agencia de viajes
travel guide la guía de viajes
travel insurance el seguro de viaje
travel sickness el mareo
traveller's cheque el cheque de viaje
tray la bandeja
treatment el tratamiento
tree el árbol
trip la excursión
trolley *(luggage, shopping)* el carrito
trouble el apuro
  to be in trouble estar en apuros
trousers los pantalones
truck el camión
true verdadero(a)
trunk *(luggage)* el baúl
trunks *(swimming)* el bañador
truth la verdad
to try *(attempt)* probar
to try on *(clothes)* probarse
t-shirt la camiseta
Tuesday el martes
tumble-dryer la secadora
tunnel el túnel
to turn girar
to turn around girar
to turn off *(light, etc)* apagar
  (tap) cerrar

to turn on *(light, etc)* encender
 (tap) abrir
turquoise *(colour)* turquesa
tweezers las pinzas
twice dos veces
twin-bedded room la habitación
 con dos camas
twins los/las mellizos(as)
 identical twins los/las gemelos(as)
twisted torcido(a)
to type escribir a máquina
typical típico(a)
tyre el neumático
tyre pressure la presión de los
 neumáticos

U

ugly feo(a)
ulcer la úlcera
umbrella el paraguas
 (sunshade) la sombrilla
uncle el tío
uncomfortable incómodo(a)
unconscious inconsciente
under debajo de
undercooked medio crudo
underground *(metro)* el metro
underpants los calzoncillos
underpass el paso subterráneo
to understand entender
 I don't understand no entiendo
 do you understand? ¿entiende?
underwear la ropa interior
underwater debajo del agua
to undress desvestirse
unemployed desempleado(a)
United Kingdom el Reino Unido
United States Estados Unidos
university la universidad
unleaded petrol la gasolina sin
 plomo
unlikely poco probable
to unlock abrir (con llave)
to unpack *(suitcases)*
 deshacer las maletas

unpleasant desagradable
to unplug desenchufar
to unscrew destornillar
up: *to get up* levantarse
upstairs arriba
urgent urgente
urine la orina
us nosotros(as)
USA EE.UU.
to use usar
useful útil
usual habitual
usually por lo general
U-turn el cambio de sentido

V

vacancy *(in hotel)* la habitación libre
vacant libre
vacation las vacaciones
vaccination la vacuna
vacuum cleaner
 la aspiradora
vagina la vagina
valid válido(a)
valley el valle
valuable de valor
valuables los objetos de valor
value el valor
valve la válvula
van la furgoneta
vase el florero
VAT el IVA
vegan vegetariano(a) estricto(a)
 I'm vegan soy vegetariano(a)
 estricto(a)
vegetables las verduras
vegetarian vegetariano(a)
 I'm vegetarian soy vegetariano(a)
vehicle el vehículo
vein la vena
velvet el terciopelo
vending machine la máquina
 expendedora
venereal disease la enfermedad
 venérea

ventilator el ventilador
very muy
vest la camiseta
vet el/la veterinario(a)
via por
to video *(from TV)* grabar (en vídeo)
video el vídeo
video camera la videocámara
video cassette la cinta de vídeo
video game el videojuego
video recorder el vídeo
video tape la cinta de vídeo
view la vista
village el pueblo
vinegar el vinagre
vineyard la viña
viper la víbora
virus el virus
visa el visado
visit la visita
to visit visitar
visiting hours *(hospital)* las horas
 de visita
visitor el/la visitante
vitamin la vitamina
voice la voz
volcano el volcán
volleyball el voleibol
voltage el voltaje
to vomit vomitar
voucher el vale ; el bono

W

wage el sueldo
waist la cintura
waistcoat el chaleco
to wait for esperar
waiter/waitress el/la camarero(a)
waiting room la sala de espera
to wake up despertarse
Wales Gales
walk un paseo
 to go for a walk dar un paseo
to walk andar

walking boots las botas de montaña
walking stick el bastón
wall *(inside)* la pared
 (outside) el muro
wallet la cartera
to want querer
 I want quiero
 we want queremos
war la guerra
ward *(hospital)* la sala
wardrobe el armario
warehouse el almacén
warm caliente
 it's warm (weather) hace calor
to warm up *(milk, etc)* calentar
warning triangle el triángulo
 señalizador
to wash (oneself) lavar(se)
wash and blow dry lavado y secado
 a mano
washbasin el lavabo
washing machine la lavadora
washing powder el detergente
washing-up bowl el barreño
washing-up liquid el líquido
 lavavajillas
wasp la avispa
wasp sting la picadura de avispa
waste bin el cubo de la basura
to watch *(look at)* mirar
watch el reloj
watchstrap la correa de reloj
water el agua
 bottled water el agua mineral
 cold water el agua fría
 drinking water el agua potable
 hot/cold water el agua caliente/fría
 mineral water el agua mineral
 sparkling water el agua con gas
 still water el agua sin gas
waterfall la cascada
water heater el calentador de agua
watermelon la sandía
waterproof impermeable
 (watch) sumergible
to waterski hacer esquí acuático

watersports los deportes acuáticos
waterwings los manguitos
waves *(on sea)* las olas
waxing *(hair removal)* la depilación (con cera)
way *(manner)* la manera
  (route) el camino
way in *(entrance)* la entrada
way out *(exit)* la salida
we nosotros(as)
weak *(coffee, tea)* poco cargado(a)
to wear llevar
weather el tiempo
weather forecast el pronóstico del tiempo
web *(internet)* el/la Internet
website la página web
wedding la boda
wedding anniversary el aniversario de boda
wedding present el regalo de boda
wedding ring la alianza
Wednesday el miércoles
week la semana
  last week la semana pasada
  next week la semana que viene
  per week por semana
  this week esta semana
  during the week durante la semana
weekday el día laborable
weekend el fin de semana
  next weekend el próximo fin de semana
  this weekend este fin de semana
weekly semanal
weekly ticket el billete semanal
to weigh pesar
weight el peso
welcome! ¡bienvenido(a)!
well *(water)* el pozo
well bien
  he's not well no se encuentra bien
well done *(steak)* muy hecho(a)
wellington boots las botas de agua
Welsh galés/galesa
  (language) el galés

west el oeste
wet mojado(a)
  (weather) lluvioso(a)
wetsuit el traje de bucear
what? ¿qué?
wheel la rueda
wheelchair la silla de ruedas
wheel clamp el cepo
when? ¿cuándo?
where? ¿dónde?
which? ¿cuál?
  which one? ¿cuál?
  which ones? ¿cuáles?
while: *in a while* dentro de un rato
white blanco(a)
who? ¿quién?
whole entero(a)
wholemeal bread el pan integral
whose? ¿de quién?
why? ¿por qué?
wide ancho(a)
widow la viuda
widower el viudo
width el ancho
wife la mujer
wig la peluca
wild salvaje
to win ganar
wind el viento
windbreak el cortavientos
windmill el molino de viento
window la ventana
  (shop) el escaparate
  (in car, train) la ventanilla
windscreen el parabrisas
windscreen wipers los limpiaparabrisas
to windsurf hacer windsurf
windy: *it's windy* hace viento
wine el vino
  red wine el (vino) tinto
  white wine el vino blanco
  dry wine el vino seco
  rosé wine el (vino) rosado
  sparkling wine el (vino) espumoso
  house wine el vino de la casa

wine list la carta de vinos
wing el ala
wing mirror el retrovisor exterior
winter el invierno
wire el alambre
with con
    with ice con hielo
    with milk con leche
    with sugar con azúcar
without sin
    without ice sin hielo
    without milk sin leche
    without sugar sin azúcar
woman la mujer
wonderful maravilloso(a)
wood *(material)* la madera
    (forest) el bosque
wooden de madera
wool la lana
word la palabra
work el trabajo
to work *(person)* trabajar
    (machine, car) funcionar
    it doesn't work no funciona
work permit el permiso de trabajo
world el mundo
world-wide mundial
worried preocupado(a)
worse peor
worth: *it's worth...* vale...
to wrap *(parcel)* envolver
wrapping paper el papel de
    envolver
wrinkles las arrugas
wrist la muñeca
to write escribir
    please write it down escríbalo,
    por favor
writing paper el papel de escribir
wrong: *what's wrong* ¿qué pasa?
wrought iron el hierro forjado

X

X-ray la radiografía
to x-ray hacer una radiografía

Y

yacht el yate
year el año
    this year este año
    next year el año que viene
    last year el año pasado
yearly anual ; anualmente
yellow amarillo(a)
Yellow Pages las páginas amarillas
yes sí
yesterday ayer
yet: *not yet* todavía no
yoghurt el yogur
    plain yoghurt el yogur natural
yolk la yema
you *(polite singular)* usted
    (polite plural) ustedes
    (singular with friends) tú
    (plural with friends) vosotros
young joven
your *(polite)* su/sus
    (familiar) tu/tus
youth hostel el albergue juvenil

Z

zebra crossing el paso de peatones
zero el cero
zip la cremallera
zone la zona
zoo el zoo
zoom lens el zoom
zucchini el calabacín

A

a to ; at
  a la estación to the station
  a las 4 at 4 o'clock
  a 30 kilómetros 30 km away
abadejo *m* haddock
abadía *f* abbey
abajo below ; downstairs
abanico *m* fan (hand-held)
abeja *f* bee
abierto(a) open
abogado(a) *m/f* lawyer
abonado(a) *m/f* season-ticket holder
abonar to pay ; to credit
abono *m* season ticket
aborto *m* abortion
  aborto no provocado miscarriage
abrebotellas *m* bottle opener
abrelatas *m* tin-opener
abrigo *m* coat
abril *m* April
abrir to open ; to turn on (tap)
abrocharse to fasten (seatbelt, etc)
absceso *m* abscess
abuela *f* grandmother
abuelo *m* grandfather
aburrido(a) boring
acá (esp LAm) here
acabar to finish
acampar to camp
acceso *m* access
  acceso andenes to the platforms
  acceso prohibido no access
  acceso vías to the platforms
accidente *m* accident
aceite *m* oil
  aceite bronceador suntan oil
  aceite de oliva olive oil
aceituna *f* olive
  aceitunas aliñadas marinated olives
  aceitunas rellenas stuffed olives
acelerador *m* accelerator
acento *m* accent
aceptar to accept
acera *f* pavement ; sidewalk

acero *m* steel
ácido *m* acid
acompañar to accompany
aconsejar to advise
acto *m* act
  en el acto while you wait (repairs)
actor *m* actor
actriz *f* actress
acuerdo *m* agreement
  ¡de acuerdo! OK ; alright
adaptador *m* adaptor
adelantar to overtake (in car)
adelante forward
adicional extra ; additional
adiós goodbye ; bye
administración *f* management
admitir to accept ; to permit
  no se admiten... ...not permitted
adolescente *m/f* teenager
aduana *f* customs
adulto(a) *m/f* adult
advertir to warn
aerodeslizador *m* hovercraft
aerolínea *f* airline
aeropuerto *m* airport
aerosol *m* aerosol
afeitarse to shave
aficionado(a) *m/f* fan (cinema, jazz, etc)
afilado(a) sharp (razor, knife)
afta *f* thrush
agencia *f* agency
  agencia de seguros insurance
  company
  agencia de viajes travel agency
agenda *f* diary ; personal organizer
agente *m/f* agent
  agente de policía policeman/woman
agitar to shake (bottle)
agosto *m* August
agotado(a) sold out ; out of stock
agradable pleasant
agradecer to thank
agridulce sweet and sour
agua *f* water
  agua caliente/fría hot/cold water
  agua destilada distilled water

agua dulce fresh water
agua mineral mineral water
agua potable drinking water
agua salada salt water
agudo(a) sharp ; pointed
águila f eagle
aguja f needle ; hand (on watch)
  aguja hipodérmica hypodermic
  needle
agujero m hole
ahogarse to drown
ahora now
ahorrar to save (money)
ahumado(a) smoked
aire m air
  aire acondicionado air-conditioning
  al aire libre open-air ; outdoor
ajo m garlic
ala f wing
alargador m extension lead
alarma f alarm
albahaca f basil
albarán m delivery note
albaricoque m apricot
albergue m hostel
  albergue juvenil youth hostel
alcanzar to reach ; to get
alcohol m alcohol ; spirits
alcohólico(a) alcoholic
alemán(mana) German
Alemania f Germany
alergia f allergy
  alergia al polen hay fever
alérgico(a) a allergic to
aletas fpl flippers
alfarería f pottery
alfiler m pin
alfombra f carpet ; rug
alforjas fpl panniers (for bike)
algas fpl seaweed
algo something
algodón m cotton
  algodón hidrófilo cotton wool
alguien someone
alguno(a) some ; any
algunos(as) some ; a few

alicates mpl pliers
alimentación f grocer's ; food
alimento m food
aliño m dressing (for food)
allí there (over there)
almacén m store ; warehouse
  grandes almacenes department
  stores
almendra f almond
almohada f pillow
almuerzo m lunch
alojamiento m accommodation
alpargatas fpl espadrilles
alquilar to rent ; to hire
  se alquila for hire
alquiler m rent ; rental
  alquiler de coches car hire
alrededor about ; around
alto(a) high ; tall
  alta tensión high voltage
altura f altitude ; height
alubia f bean
  alubias blancas butter beans
  alubias pintas red kidney beans
amable pleasant ; kind
amapola f poppy
amargo(a) bitter ; sour
amarillo(a) yellow ; amber (traffic
  light)
ambientador m air freshener
ambos(as) both
ambulancia f ambulance
ambulatorio m health centre
América del Norte f North America
amigo(a) m/f friend
  amigo(a) por correspondencia
  penfriend
amor m love
amortiguador m shock absorber
ampolla f blister
analgésico m painkiller
análisis m analysis
  análisis de sangre blood test
ananá(s) m pineapple
ancho m width
ancho(a) wide

anchoa f anchovy *(salted)*
anchura f width
ancla f anchor
Andalucía f Andalusia
andaluz(a) Andalusian
andar to walk
andén m platform
añejo(a) mature ; vintage
anestesia f anaesthetic
  anestesia local local anaesthetic
  anestesia general general
  anaesthetic
anfiteatro m circle *(theatre)*
angina (de pecho) f angina
anillo m ring
animal m animal
  animal doméstico pet
anís m aniseed liqueur ; anisette
aniversario m anniversary
  aniversario de boda wedding
  anniversary
año m year
  Año Nuevo New Year
ante m suede
antena f aerial
  antena parabólica satellite dish
anteojos mpl (LAm) binoculars
antes (de) before
antiácido m antacid
antibiótico m antibiotic
anticonceptivo m contraceptive
anticongelante m antifreeze
anticuario m antique shop
antigüedades fpl antiques
antiguo(a) old ; ancient
antihistamínico m antihistamine
antiséptico m antiseptic
anual annual
anular to cancel
anunciar to announce ; to advertise
anuncio m advertisement ; notice
anzuelo m hook *(fishing)*
apagado(a) off *(light, etc)*
apagar to switch off ; to turn off
aparato m appliance
aparcamiento m car park

aparcar to park
apartado de Correos m PO Box
apartamento m flat ; apartment
apellido m surname
apendicitis f appendicitis
aperitivo m aperitif *(drink)* ;
  appetizer ; snack *(food)*
apertura f opening
apio m celery
aplazar to postpone
apostar por to bet on
aprender to learn
apretar to squeeze
apto(a) suitable
aquí here
  aquí tiene... here is...
araña f spider
árbitro m referee
árbol m tree
arco iris m rainbow
ardor de estómago m heartburn
arena f sand
armario m wardrobe ; cupboard
arquitecto(a) m/f architect
arquitectura f architecture
arrancar to start
arreglar to fix ; to mend
arriba upstairs ; above
  hacia arriba upward(s)
arroyo m stream
arroz m rice
arruga f wrinkle
arte m art
artesanía f crafts
artesano(a) m/f craftsman/woman
articulación f joint *(body)*
artículo m article
  artículos de ocasión bargains
  artículos de regalo gifts
  artículos de tocador/baño toiletries
artista m/f artist
artritis f arthritis
asado(a) roast
asar a la parrilla/brasa to barbecue
ascensor m lift

asegurado(a) insured
asegurar to insure
aseos *mpl* toilets
asiento *m* seat
  asiento de niños child safety seat
asistencia *f* help ; assistance
  asistencia técnica repairs
asma *m* asthma
aspiradora *f* vacuum cleaner
aspirina *f* aspirin
astilla *f* splinter
atacar to attack
atajo *m* short cut
ataque *m* fit *(seizure)*
  ataque epiléptico epileptic fit
atascado(a) jammed *(stuck)*
atasco *m* hold-up *(traffic jam)*
atención *f* attention
  atención al cliente customer service
aterrizar to land
ático *m* attic ; loft
atracadero *m* mooring
atraco *m* mugging *(person)*
atrás behind
atropellar to knock down *(car)*
ATS *m/f* nurse
atún *m* tuna fish
audífono *m* hearing aid
aumentar to increase
auricular *m* receiver *(phone)*
auriculares *mpl* headphones
auténtico(a) genuine ; real
autostop *m* hitch-hiking
autobús *m* bus
autocar *m* coach *(bus)*
automático(a) automatic
autónomo(a) self-employed
autopista *f* motorway
autor(a) *m/f* author
autoservicio *m* self-service
auxiliar de vuelo *m/f* air steward/
  stewardess
Av./Avda. abbrev. for avenida
avalancha *f* avalanche
ave *f* bird
  aves de corral poultry

avellana *f* hazelnut
avena *f* oats
avenida *f* avenue
avería *f* breakdown *(car)*
averiado(a) out of order ; broken
  down
avión *m* airplane ; aeroplane
aviso *m* notice ; warning
avispa *f* wasp
ayer yesterday
ayudar to help
ayuntamiento *m* town/city hall
azafata *f* air hostess ; stewardess
azafrán *m* saffron
azúcar *m* sugar
  azúcar glasé icing sugar
azul blue
  azul claro light blue
  azul marino dark/navy blue
  día azul cheap day for train travel
  zona azul controlled parking area

B

babero *m* baby's bib
baca *f* roof rack
bahía *f* bay *(along coast)*
bailar to dance
baile *m* dance
bajar to go down(stairs) ;
  to drop *(temperature)*
bajarse (del) to get off *(bus, etc)*
bajo(a) low ; short ; soft *(sound)*
  bajo en calorías low-fat
  más bajo lower
balcón *m* balcony
balneario *m* spa
balón *m* ball
baloncesto *m* basketball
balsa salvavidas *f* life raft
bañador *m* swimming costume/
  trunks
banana *f* banana
bañarse to go swimming ; to bathe
  ; to have a bath
banca *f* banking ; bank

banco m bank ; bench
banda f band (musical)
bandeja f tray
bandera f flag
bañista m/f bather
baño m bath ; bathroom
  con baño with bath
bar m bar
barato(a) cheap
barba f beard
barbacoa f barbecue
barbería f barber's
barbilla f chin
barca f small boat
barco m ship ; boat
  barco de vela sailing boat
barra f bar ; counter ; bread stick
  barra de labios lipstick
  barra de pan French bread
barreño (de plástico) m washing-up
  bowl
barrera f barrier ; crash barrier
barrio m district ; suburb
  barrio chino red light district
barro m mud
bastante enough ; quite
bastón m walking stick
  bastón de esquí ski pole/stick
basura f rubbish ; litter
bata f dressing gown
bate m bat (baseball, cricket)
batería f battery (in car)
batido m milkshake
batidora f blender (hand-held)
baúl m trunk (luggage)
bautizo m christening
to be ser ; estar
bebé m baby
beber to drink
bebida f drink
  bebida sin alcohol soft drink
beicon m bacon
béisbol m baseball
berenjena f aubergine
berro m watercress
berza f cabbage

besar to kiss
beso m kiss
betún m shoe polish
biberón m baby's bottle
biblioteca f library
bici f bicycle
bicicleta f bicycle
  bicicleta de montaña mountain bike
bien well
bienvenido(a) welcome
bifurcación f fork (in road)
bigote m moustache
billete m ticket
  billete de ida single ticket
  billete de ida y vuelta return ticket
billetera f wallet
bistec m steak
bisutería f costume jewellery
blanco(a) white
  dejar en blanco leave blank
  (on form)
blando(a) soft
bloc m note pad
blusa f blouse
boca f mouth
bocadillo m sandwich (made with
  French bread)
boda f wedding
bodega f wine cellar ; restaurant
bolígrafo m biro ; pen
bollo m roll ; bun
bolsa f bag ; stock exchange
bolsillo m pocket
bolsita de té f teabag
bolso m handbag
bomba f pump (bike, etc) ; bomb
bombero(a) mf fireman/woman ;
  firefighter
bomberos mpl fire brigade
bombilla f light bulb
bombona de gas f gas cylinder
bombonería f confectioner's
bombones mpl chocolates
bonito(a) pretty ; nice-looking
bono m voucher
bonobús m bus pass

borracho(a) drunk
bosque m forest ; wood
bota f boot
bote m boat ; tin ; can
  bote neumático rubber dinghy
  bote salvavidas lifeboat
botella f bottle
botón m button
bragas fpl knickers
brazo m arm
brécol m broccoli
bricolaje m do-it-yourself ; DIY
brillar to shine
brindis m toast *(raising glass)*
británico(a) British
broma f joke
bromear to joke
bronceado m suntan
bronceado(a) sun-tanned
bronceador m suntan lotion
broncearse to tan
bronquitis f bronchitis
brújula f compass
bucear to dive
bueno(a) good ; fine
  ¡buenos días! good morning!
  ¡buenas noches! good evening/night!
  ¡buenas tardes! good afternoon/
  evening!
bufanda f scarf *(woollen)*
bufé m buffet
búho m owl
bujía f spark plug
bulto m lump *(swelling)*
buñuelo m fritter ; doughnut
bunyi m bungee jumping
buscar to look for
butacas fpl stalls *(theatre)*
butano m Calor gas®
butifarra f Catalan sausage
buzón m postbox ; letterbox

C

caballeros mpl gents
caballo m horse
  montar a caballo to go riding

cabello m hair
cabeza f head
cabina f cabin
  cabina (telefónica) phone box
cable m wire ; cable
  cable de remolque tow rope
  cables de arranque jump leads
cabra f goat
cacahuete m peanut
cacao m cocoa
  cacao para los labios lip salve
cacerola f saucepan
cachemira f cashmere
cada every ; each
  cada día daily *(each day)*
  cada uno each (one)
cadera f hip
caducado(a) out-of-date
caducar to expire *(ticket, passport)*
caer(se) to fall
café m café ; coffee
  (café) cortado espresso with a
  dash of milk
  corto de café milky coffee
  (café) descafeinado decaff coffee
  café en grano coffee beans
  (café) exprés/expreso espresso
  coffee
  café con hielo iced coffee
  café con leche white coffee
  café instantáneo instant coffee
  café molido ground coffee
  café solo black coffee
cafetera f cafètiere
cafetería f snack bar ; café
caja f cashdesk ; box
  caja de ahorros savings bank
  caja de cambios gearbox
  caja de fusibles fuse box
  caja fuerte safe
cajero(a) m/f teller ; cashier
  cajero automático cash
  dispenser ; auto-teller
cajón m drawer
calabacín m courgette
calabaza f pumpkin
calamares mpl squid
calambre m cramp

calcetines *mpl* socks
calculadora *f* calculator
caldereta *f* stew *(fish, lamb)*
caldo *m* stock ; consommé
calefacción *f* heating
calendario *m* calendar
calentador *m* heater
  calentador de agua water heater
calentar to heat up *(milk, etc)*
calentura *f* cold sore
calidad *f* quality
caliente hot
calle *f* street ; fairway *(golf)*
callejón sin salida *m* cul-de-sac
calmante *m* painkiller
calvo(a) bald
calzada *f* roadway
  calzada deteriorada uneven road
  surface
calzado *m* footwear
  calzados shoe shop
calzoncillos *mpl* underpants
cama *f* bed
  dos camas twin beds
  cama individual single bed
  cama de matrimonio double bed
cámara *f* camera ; inner tube
camarera *f* waitress ; chambermaid
camarero *m* barman ; waiter
camarote *m* cabin
cambiar to change ; to exchange
  cambiarse to get changed
cambio *m* change ; exchange ; gear
caminar to walk
camino *m* path ; road ; route
  camino particular private road
camión *m* lorry
camisa *f* shirt
camisería *f* shirt shop
camiseta *f* t-shirt ; vest
camisón *m* nightdress
campana *f* bell
camping *m* campsite
campo *m* countryside ; field ; pitch
  campo de fútbol football pitch
  campo de golf golf course

caña *f* cane ; rod
  caña (de cerveza) glass of beer
  caña de pescar fishing rod
Canadá *m* Canada
canadiense Canadian
Canal de la Mancha *m* English
  Channel
canasto *m* large basket
cancelación *f* cancellation
cancelar to cancel
cáncer *m* cancer
cancha de tenis *f* tennis court
canción *f* song
candado *m* padlock
  candado de bicicleta bike lock
candela *f* candle ; fire
canela *f* cinnamon
canguro *m* kangaroo
canguro *m/f* babysitter
canoa *f* canoe
cansado(a) tired
cantante *m/f* singer
cantar to sing
cantidad *f* quantity
capilla *f* chapel
capital *f* capital *(city)*
capitán *m* captain
capó *m* bonnet ; hood *(of car)*
capucha *f* hood *(jacket)*
cara *f* face
caramelo *m* sweet ; caramel
caravana *f* caravan
carbón *m* coal
  carbón vegetal charcoal
carburador *m* carburettor
carburante *m* fuel
cárcel *f* prison
cargar to load
  cargar en cuenta to charge to
  account
cargo *m* charge
  a cargo del cliente at the
  customer's expense
Caribe *m* Caribbean
carnaval *m* carnival
carne *f* meat

carne asada roast meat
carne picada mince *(meat)*
carné de conducir *m* driving licence
carné de identidad *m* identity card
carnicería *f* butcher's
caro(a) dear ; expensive
carpintería *f* carpenter's shop
carrera *f* career ; race *(sport)*
carrete *m* film *(for camera)* ;
fishing reel
carretera *f* road
carretera de circunvalación ring
road
carril *m* lane *(on road)*
carrito *m* trolley
carta *f* letter ; playing card ; menu
carta aérea air mail letter
carta certificada registered letter
carta de vinos wine list
carta verde green card
cartel *m* poster
cartelera *f* entertainments guide
cartera *f* wallet ; briefcase
carterista *m/f* pickpocket
cartero(a) *m/f* postman/woman
cartón *m* cardboard
casa *f* house ; home ; household
casa de socorro first-aid post
casado(a) married
casarse (con) to marry
cascada *f* waterfall
cáscara *f* shell *(egg, nut)*
casco *m* helmet
casero(a) home-made
comida casera home cooking
caseta *f* beach hut ; kennel
casete *m* cassette ; tape recorder
casi almost
caso: *en caso de* in case of
caspa *f* dandruff
castaña *f* chestnut
castañuelas *fpl* castanets
castellano(a) Spanish ; Castilian
castillo *m* castle
catalán/catalana Catalonian
catálogo *m* catalogue

catedral *f* cathedral
católico(a) Catholic
causa *f* cause
a causa de because of
causar to cause
cava *m* cava ; sparkling white wine
caza *f* hunting ; game
cazar to hunt
cebo *m* bait *(for fishing)*
cebolla *f* onion
ceder to give way
ceda el paso give way
celeste light blue
celo *m* Sellotape®
celoso(a) jealous
cementerio *m* cemetery
cena *f* dinner ; supper
cenar to have dinner
cenicero *m* ashtray
centímetro *m* centimetre
céntimo *m* euro cent
centralita *f* switchboard
centro *m* centre
Centroamérica *f* Central America
cepillo *m* brush
cepillo de dientes toothbrush
cepillo del pelo hairbrush
cepillo de uñas nailbrush
cera *f* wax
cerámica *f* ceramics ; pottery
cerca (de) near ; close to
cercanías *fpl* outskirts
tren de cercanías suburban train
cerdo *m* pig ; pork
cereza *f* cherry
cerillas *fpl* matches
cero *m* zero
cerrado(a) closed
cerrado por reforma closed for
repairs
cerradura *f* lock
cerrar con llave to lock
cerro *m* hill
certificado *m* certificate
certificado(a) registered
certificar to register

cervecería f pub
cerveza f beer ; lager
cesta f basket
cestería f basketwork *(shop)*
chalé m villa
chaleco m waistcoat
  chaleco salvavidas life jacket
champán m champagne
champiñón m mushroom
champú m shampoo
chancl(et)as *fpl* flip flops
chaqueta f jacket
charcutería f delicatessen
cheque m cheque
  cheque de viaje traveller's cheque
chica f girl
chichón m lump *(on head)*
chico m boy
chico(a) small
chile m chilli
chimenea f fireplace ; chimney
chiringuito m beach bar ; stall
chocar to crash *(car)*
chocolate m chocolate ;
  hot chocolate
  chocolate puro plain chocolate
chófer m chauffeur ; driver
chorizo m hard pork sausage
chubasco m shower *(rain)*
chuleta f cutlet ; chop
chupete m dummy *(for baby)*
churrería f fritter shop or stand
churro m fritter
ciclista *m/f* cyclist
ciego(a) blind
cielo m sky ; heaven
cien hundred
CIF m tax number *(for business)*
cifra f number ; figure
cigarra f cicada
cigarrillo m cigarette
cigarro m cigar ; cigarette
cima f top ; peak
cine m cinema
cinta f tape ; ribbon

  cinta de vídeo video cassette
  cinta virgen blank tape
cintura f waist
cinturón m belt
  cinturón de seguridad safety belt
circulación f traffic
circular to drive ; to circulate
  circule por la derecha keep right
  (road sign)
ciruela f plum
  ciruela pasa f prune
cirujano(a) *m/f* surgeon
cisterna f cistern
cistitis f cystitis
cita f appointment
ciudad f city ; town
ciudadano(a) *m/f* citizen
clarete m light red wine
claro(a) light *(colour)* ; clear
clase f class ; type ; lesson
  clase preferente club/business class
  clase turista economy class
clavícula f collar bone
clavija f peg
clavo m nail *(metal)* ; clove *(spice)*
cliente *m/f* customer ; client
climatizado(a) air-conditioned
clínica f clinic ; private hospital
club nocturno m night club
cobrador m conductor *(train, bus)*
cobrar to charge ; to cash
  cobrar demasiado to overcharge
cobro m payment
cocer to cook ; to boil
coche m car ; coach *(on train)*
coche cama m sleeping car
coche comedor m dining car
coche restaurante m restaurant car
cochecito (de bebé) m pram
cocido m thick stew
cocido(a) cooked ; boiled
cocina f kitchen ; cooker ; cuisine
cocinar to cook
coco m coconut
código m code
  código de barras barcode
  código postal postcode

codo m elbow
coger to catch ; to get ;
  to pick up (phone)
cola f glue ; queue ; tail
colador m strainer ; colander
colchón m mattress
colega m/f colleague
colegio m school
colgar to hang up
coliflor f cauliflower
colina f hill
colisionar to crash
collar m necklace
color m colour
columna vertebral f spine
columpio m swing (for children)
comedor m dining room
comenzar to begin
comer to eat
comercio m trade ; business
comestibles mpl groceries
comida f food ; meal
  se sirven comidas meals served
  comidas caseras home cooking
comisaría f police station
como as ; like ; since
¿cómo? how? ; pardon?
cómodo(a) comfortable
compañero(a) m/f colleague ;
  partner
compañía f company
compartimento m compartment
completo(a) full ; no vacancies
comportarse to behave
compositor(a) m/f composer
compra f purchase
  compras shopping
comprar to buy
comprender to understand
compresa f sanitary towel
comprobar to check
con with
concha f sea-shell
concierto m concert
concurrido(a) busy ; crowded

concurso m competition ; quiz
condón m condom
conducir to drive
conductor(a) m/f driver
conectar to connect ; to plug in
conejo m rabbit
conferencia f conference
confirmación f confirmation
confirmar to confirm
confitería f cake shop
confitura f jam
congelado(a) frozen
congelador m freezer
conjunto m group (music)
conmoción cerebral f concussion
conocer to know ; to be
  acquainted with
conseguir to obtain
conserje m caretaker
conservar to keep
conservas fpl tinned foods
consigna f left-luggage office
construir to build
consulado m consulate
consultorio m doctor's surgery
consumición f consumption ; drink
consumir to eat ; to use
  consumir antes de... best before...
contacto m contact ; ignition (car)
contador m meter
contagioso(a) infectious
contaminado(a) polluted
contener to hold (to contain)
contenido m contents
contento(a) pleased
contestador automático m
  answerphone
contestar to answer ; to reply
continuación f sequel
continuar to continue
contra against
contrato m contract
control m inspection ; check
convento m convent ; monastery
copa f glass ; goblet

copa de helado mixed ice cream
tomar una copa to have a drink
copia f copy ; print *(photo)*
copiar to copy
corazón m heart
corbata f tie
corcho m cork
cordero m lamb ; mutton
cordillera f mountain range
coro m choir
correa f strap ; belt
  correa de reloj watchstrap
correcto(a) right *(correct)*
correo m mail
  correo electrónico e-mail
Correos m post office
correr to run
corrida de toros f bullfight
corriente f power ; current
  (electric, water) ; draught
  (of air)
cortacircuitos m circuit breaker
cortado m espresso coffee with
  dash of milk
cortado(a) blocked *(road)*
cortar to cut
cortaúñas m nail clippers
corte m cut
cortina f curtain
corto(a) short
cosa f thing
cosecha f harvest ; vintage *(wine)*
coser to sew
costa f coast
costar to cost
costero(a) coastal
costumbre f custom *(tradition)*
coto m reserve
  coto de caza/pesca hunting/fishing
  by licence
crédito m credit
  a crédito on credit
creer to think ; to believe
crema f cream *(lotion)*
  crema bronceadora suntan lotion
  crema de afeitar shaving cream

cremallera f zip
crisis nerviosa f nervous breakdown
cruce m junction ; crossroads
crucero m cruise
crucigrama m crossword puzzle
crudo(a) raw
cruzar to cross
c/u (cada uno) each (one)
cuaderno m exercise book
cuadro m picture ; painting
  a cuadros checked *(pattern)*
cuajada f curd
¿cuál? which?
¿cuándo? when?
¿cuánto? how much?
¿cuántos? how many?
cuarentena f quarantine
Cuaresma f Lent
cuarto m room
  cuarto de baño bathroom
  cuarto de estar living room
cubierto m cover charge
  (in restaurant) ; menu
cubierto(a) covered ; indoor
cubiertos mpl cutlery
cubo m bucket ; pail ; bin
cubrir to cover
cucaracha f cockroach
cuchara f spoon
  cuchara de servir tablespoon
cucharilla f teaspoon
cuchillo m knife
cuenta f bill ; account
cuerda f string ; rope
cuero m leather
cuerpo m body
cuidado m care
  ¡cuidado! look out!
  ten cuidado be careful!
cuidadoso(a) careful
cultivar to grow ; to farm
cumpleaños m birthday
  ¡feliz cumpleaños! happy birthday!
cuna f cradle ; cot
cuñado(a) m/f brother/sister-in-law
curva f bend ; curve
  curvas peligrosas dangerous bends

D

dados *mpl* dice
daltónico(a) colour-blind
daños *mpl* damage
dar to give
  dar de comer to feed
  dar marcha atrás to reverse
  dar propina to tip *(waiter, etc)*
  dar un paseo to go for a walk
dátil *m* date *(fruit)*
datos *mpl* data ; information
dcha. abbrev. for derecha
de of ; from
de acuerdo all right *(agreed)*
debajo (de) under ; underneath
deber to owe ; to have to
debido(a) due
decir to tell ; to say
declarar to declare
dedo *m* finger
  dedo del pie toe
defecto *m* fault ; defect
degustación *f* tasting *(wine, etc)*
dejar to let ; to leave
  dejar libre la salida keep clear
delante de in front of
delegación *f* regional office
  (government)
delgado(a) thin ; slim
delicioso(a) delicious
delito *m* crime
demasiado too much
  demasiado hecho(a) overdone
demora *f* delay
denominación de origen *f*
  guarantee of quality of food
  products
dentadura postiza *f* dentures
dentífrico *m* toothpaste
dentista *m/f* dentist
dentro (de) inside
departamento *m* compartment ;
  department
dependiente(a) *m/f* sales assistant
deporte *m* sport
depósito de gasolina *m* petrol tank

derecha *f* right(-hand side)
  a la derecha on/to the right
derecho *m* right ; law
  derechos de aduana customs duty
derecho(a) right ; straight
derramar to spill
derretir to melt
desabrochar to unfasten
desafilado(a) blunt *(knife, blade)*
desaparecer to disappear
desarrollar to develop
desatascador *m* plunger *(for sink)*
desayuno *m* breakfast
descafeinado(a) decaffeinated
descansar to rest
descanso *m* rest ; interval
descarga eléctrica *f* electric shock
descargado(a) flat *(battery)*
descolgar to take down ; to pick
  up *(phone)*
descongelar to defrost ; to de-ice
describir to describe
descubrir to discover
descuento *m* discount ; reduction
desde since ; from
desear to want
desembarcadero *m* quay
desempleado(a) unemployed
desenchufado(a) off ; disconnected
deseo *m* wish ; desire
desfile *m* parade
deshacer to undo ; to unpack
desinfectante *m* disinfectant
desmaquillador *m* make-up remover
desmayado(a) fainted
desnatado(a) skimmed
desodorante *m* deodorant
despacho *m* office
despacio slowly ; quietly
despegar to take-off
despertador *m* alarm *(clock)*
despertarse to wake up
después after ; afterward(s)
desteñir: *no destiñe* colourfast
destino *m* destination

destornillador *m* screwdriver
destornillar to unscrew
desvestirse to get undressed
desvío *m* detour ; diversion
detalle *m* detail ; nice gesture
 al detalle retail *(commercial)*
detener to arrest
detergente *m* detergent ; washing
 powder
detrás (de) behind
deuda *f* debt
devolver to give/put back
día *m* day
 día festivo public holiday
 día laborable working day ;
 weekday
 todo el día all day
diabético(a) *m/f* diabetic
diamante *m* diamond
diario(a) daily
diarrea *f* diarrhoea
dibujo *m* drawing
diccionario *m* dictionary
diciembre *m* December
diente *m* tooth
dieta *f* diet
difícil difficult
¿diga? hello *(on phone)*
dinero *m* money
 dinero en efectivo cash
Dios *m* God
diplomático(a) *m/f* diplomat
dirección *f* direction ; address
 dirección de correo electrónico
 e-mail address
 dirección particular home address
 dirección prohibida no entry
 dirección única one-way
directo(a) direct *(train, etc)*
director(a) *m/f* director ; manager
dirigir to manage
disco *m* record ; disk
 disco duro hard disk
discoteca *f* disco ; nightclub
discrecional optional
discutir to quarrel ; to argue

diseño *m* design ; drawing
disquete *m* diskette
disponible available
distancia *f* distance
distinto(a) different
distribuidor automático *m* vending
 machine
distrito *m* district
DIU *m* coil *(IUD)*
diversión *f* fun
divertido(a) funny *(amusing)*
divertirse to enjoy oneself
divisa *f* foreign currency
divorciado(a) divorced
doblado(a) folded ; dubbed *(film)*
doblar to fold
doble double
docena *f* dozen
documentos *mpl* documents
dólar *m* dollar
dolor *m* ache ; pain
 dolor de cabeza headache
 dolor de garganta sore throat
 dolor de muelas toothache
 dolor de oídos earache
doloroso(a) painful
domicilio *m* home address
domingo *m* Sunday
dominó *m* dominoes
¿dónde? where?
dormir to sleep
dormitorio *m* bedroom
dorso *m* back
 véase al dorso please turn over
dosis *f* dose ; dosage
droga *f* drug
ducha *f* shower
ducharse to take a shower
dueño(a) *m/f* owner
dulce sweet
 el agua dulce fresh water
dulce *m* dessert ; sweet
durante during
duro(a) hard ; tough

E

echar to pour ; to throw ; to post
ecológico(a) organic ; environmentally friendly
edad f age (of person)
edad mínima age limit
edificio m building
edredón (nórdico) m duvet ; quilt
edulcorante m sweetener
EE.UU. USA
efecto m effect
efectos personales belongings
eje m axle (car)
ejemplar m copy (of book)
el the
él he ; him
electricidad f electricity
electricista m/f electrician
eléctrico(a) electric(al)
elegir to choose
ella she ; her
ello it
ellos(as) they ; them
embajada f embassy
embalse m reservoir
embarazada pregnant
embarcadero m jetty ; pier
embarcarse to board
embarque m boarding
embrague m clutch (in car)
emisión f broadcasting
emitido por issued by
emocionante exciting
empachado(a) upset (stomach)
empezar to begin
empleo m employment ; use
empresa f firm ; company
empujar to push
empuje push
en in ; into ; on
encaje m lace (fabric)
encantado(a) pleased to meet you!
encargado(a) m/f person in charge
encargar to order in advance
encendedor m (cigarette) lighter

encender to switch on ; to light
encender las luces switch on headlights
encendido(a) on (light, TV, engine)
enchufar to plug in
enchufe m plug ; point ; socket
encima de onto ; on top of
encontrar to find
encontrarse con to meet (by chance)
enero m January
enfadado(a) angry
enfermedad f disease
enfermera(o) m/f nurse
enfermería f infirmary ; first-aid post
enfermo(a) ill
enfrente (de) opposite
¡enhorabuena! congratulations!
enjuagar to rinse
enjuague bucal m mouthwash
enlace m connection (train, etc)
ensalada f salad
enseñar to show ; to teach
entender to understand
entero(a) whole
entierro m funeral
entrada f entrance ; admission
entrada libre admission free
entrada por delante enter at the front
entrar to go in ; to get in ; to enter
entre among ; between
entreacto m interval
entregar to deliver
entremeses mpl hors d'œuvres
entrevista f interview
envase m container ; packaging
enviar to send
envío m shipment
envolver to wrap
epiléptico(a) epileptic
equipaje m luggage ; baggage
equipaje de mano hand-luggage
equipo m team ; equipment
equitación f horseriding
equivocación f mistake ; misunderstanding

error *m* mistake
es he/she/it is
escala *f* stopover
escalar to climb *(mountains)*
escalera *f* stairs ; ladder
  escalera de incendios fire escape
  escalera (de mano) ladder
  escalera mecánica escalator
escaleras *fpl* stairs
escalón *m* step *(stair)*
escapar to escape
escaparate *m* shop window
escenario *m* stage *(theatre)*
escoba *f* broom *(brush)*
escocés(cesa) Scottish
Escocia *f* Scotland
escoger to choose
esconder to hide
escribir to write
escrito: *por escrito* in writing
escuchar to listen to
escuela *f* school
escultura *f* sculpture
escurrir to wring
ese/esa that
esguince *m* sprain
esmalte *m* varnish
esos/esas those
espacio *m* space
espalda *f* back *(of body)*
España *f* Spain
español(a) Spanish
espantoso(a) awful
esparadrapo *m* sticking plaster
especia *f* spice
especialidad *f* speciality
especialista *m/f* specialist
espectáculo *m* entertainment ; show
espejo *m* mirror
  espejo retrovisor rear-view mirror
esperar to wait (for) ; to hope
  espere su turno please wait your
  turn
espina *f* fish bone ; thorn
  espina dorsal spine
espinacas *fpl* spinach

espinilla *f* spot *(pimple)*
esponja *f* sponge
esposa *f* wife
esposo *m* husband
espuma *f* foam ; mousse *(for hair)*
  espuma de afeitar shaving foam
espumoso(a) frothy ; sparkling
esq. *abbrev.* for esquina
esquí *m* skiing ; ski
  esquí acuático water-skiing
  esquí de fondo cross-country skiing
esquiar to ski
esquina *f* street corner
está you *(formal)*/he/she/it is
estación *f* railway station ; season
  estación de autobuses bus/coach
  station
  estación de servicio petrol/service
  station
estacionamiento *m* parking space
estacionar to park
estadio *m* stadium
Estados Unidos *mpl* United States
estanco *m* tobacconist's
estante *m* shelf
estar to be
estatua *f* statue
este *m* east
éste/esta this
estéreo *m* stereo
estómago *m* stomach
estornudar to sneeze
estos/éstas these
estragón *m* tarragon
estrecho(a) narrow
estrella *f* star
estreñimiento *m* constipation
estreno *m* premiere ; new release
estropeado(a) out of order
estudiante *m/f* student
etiqueta *f* label ; ticket ; tag
  de etiqueta formal dress
euro *m* euro
eurocheque *m* Eurocheque
Europa *f* Europe
evidente obvious

evitar to avoid
examen *m* examination
excelente excellent
excepcional rare *(unique)*
excepto except
exceso *m* excess
excursión *f* tour ; excursion
éxito *m* success
expedido(a) issued
experto(a) expert
explicar to explain
exportación *f* export
exportar to export
exposición *f* exhibition
expreso *m* express train
exprimir to squeeze
extintor *m* fire extinguisher
extranjero(a) *m/f* foreigner
  en el extranjero abroad

F

FC/f.c. *abbrev.* for ferrocarril
fabada *f* pork and bean stew
fábrica *f* factory
fácil easy
factura *f* receipt ; bill ; account
  factura detallada itemized bill
facturación *f* check-in
falda *f* skirt
falso(a) fake
falta *f* foul *(football)* ; lack
familia *f* family
famoso(a) famous
farmacia *f* chemist's ; pharmacy
  farmacia de guardia duty chemist
faro *m* headlamp ; lighthouse
  faro antiniebla fog-lamp
farola *f* lamppost
faros *mpl* headlights
favor *m* favour
  por favor please
favorito(a) favourite
fax *m* fax
febrero *m* February
fecha *f* date

fecha de adquisición date of purchase
fecha de caducidad expiry date
fecha de expedición date of issue
fecha de nacimiento date of birth
feliz happy
  ¡Feliz Año Nuevo! Happy New Year!
femenino(a) feminine
feo(a) ugly
feria *f* trade fair ; funfair
ferrocarril *m* railway
festivos *mpl* public holidays
fiambre *m* cold meat
fianza *f* bail bond ; deposit
fibra sintética *f* man-made fibre
ficha *f* token ; counter *(in games)*
fichero *m* file *(computer)*
fiebre *f* fever
fiesta *f* party ; public holiday
fila *f* row ; line *(row, queue)*
filete *m* fillet ; steak
filial *f* branch
filtro *m* filter
  filtro de aceite oil filter
  filtro solar sunscreen
fin *m* end
  fin de semana weekend
finalizar to end ; to finish
finca *f* farm ; country house
fino fine ; thin
fino *m* light, dry, very pale sherry
firma *f* signature
firmar to sign
  firme aquí sign here
flojo(a) weak *(coffee, tea)*
flor *f* flower
florero *m* vase
floristería *f* florist's shop
foca *f* seal
foco *m* spotlight ; headlamp
folleto *m* leaflet ; brochure
fonda *f* inn ; small restaurant
fondo *m* bottom *(of pool, etc)*
fontanero *m* plumber
forfait *m* lift pass *(skiing)*
formulario *m* form

fósforo m match
foto f picture ; photo
fotocopia f photocopy
fotocopiar to photocopy
fotografía f photograph
fotógrafo(a) m/f photographer
fractura f fracture
frágil fragile
francés(cesa) French
Francia f France
frecuente frequent
fregadero m sink (in kitchen)
fregona f mop (for floor)
freír to fry
frenar to brake
freno m brake
frente a opposite
frente f forehead
fresa f strawberry
fresco(a) fresh ; crisp ; cool
frigorífico m fridge
frío(a) cold
frito(a) fried
frontera f border ; frontier
frotar to rub
fruta f fruit
  fruta del tiempo fruit in season
frutería f fruit shop
frutos secos mpl nuts (to eat)
fuego m fire
fuente f fountain
fuera outdoors ; out
fuerte strong ; loud
fuga f leak (of gas, liquid)
fumadores mpl smokers
fumar to smoke
  prohibido fumar no smoking
función f show
funcionar to work ; to function
  no funciona out of order
funcionario(a) m/f civil servant
funda f case ; crown (for tooth) ;
  pillowcase
  funda de gafas glasses case
  funda nórdica duvet cover

fusible m fuse
fútbol m football
futbolista m/f football player

G

gafas fpl glasses
  gafas de sol sunglasses
galería f gallery
  galería de arte art gallery
galés(lesa) Welsh
Gales m Wales
gallego(a) Galician
galleta f biscuit
ganar to earn ; to win (sports, etc)
garaje m garage
garantía f guarantee
garganta f throat
gas m gas
  con gas fizzy
  gas butano Calor gas®
  sin gas non-fizzy ; still
gasa f gauze ; nappy
gaseosa f lemonade
gasoil m diesel fuel
gasóleo m diesel oil
gasolina f petrol
  gasolina sin plomo unleaded petrol
  gasolina súper 4-star petrol
gasolinera f petrol station
gastado(a) worn
gastar to spend (money)
gastos mpl expenses
gastritis f gastritis
gato m cat ; jack (for car)
gaviota f seagull
gendarme m/f policeman/woman
  (Lat. Am.)
gendarmería f police (Lat. Am.)
gemelo(a) m/f identical twin
género m type ; material
generoso(a) generous
gente f people
gerente m/f manager/manageress
ginebra f gin
girar to turn around

globo *m* **balloon**
glorieta *f* **roundabout**
golfo de Vizcaya *m* **Bay of Biscay**
goma *f* **rubber ; eraser**
gomita *f* **rubber band**
gordo(a) **fat**
gorra *f* **cap** *(hat)*
gorro *m* **hat**
gotera *f* **leak**
gótico(a) **Gothic**
grabar en vídeo **to video** *(from TV)*
gracias **thank you**
grada *f* **tier**
gramo *m* **gram(me)**
Gran Bretaña *f* **Great Britain**
grande **large ; big ; tall**
grandes almacenes *mpl* **department store**
granja *f* **farm**
granjero(a) *m/f* **farmer**
grasiento(a) **greasy**
gratinado(a) **au gratin ; grilled**
gratinar **to grill**
gratis **free** *(costing nothing)*
grave **serious** *(accident, etc)*
grifo *m* **tap**
gripe *f* **flu**
gris **grey**
gritar **to shout**
grosella negra *f* **blackcurrant**
grosella roja *f* **redcurrant**
grúa *f* **crane ; breakdown van**
grueso(a) **thick** *(not thin)*
grupo *m* **group ; band** *(rock)*
  grupo sanguíneo **blood group**
guacamole *m* **avocado dip**
guantes *mpl* **gloves**
  guantes de goma **rubber gloves**
guapo(a) **handsome ; attractive**
guardacostas *m/f* **coastguard**
guardar **to put away ; to keep**
guardarropa *m* **cloakroom**
guardería *f* **nursery**
  guardia infantil **nursery school**
guardia *f* **guard**

de guardia **on duty**
Guardia Civil **Civil Guard**
guarnición *f* **garnish**
guerra *f* **war**
guía *m/f* **courier ; guide**
Guía del ocio *f* **What's on**
guía (telefónica) *f* **phone directory**
guiar **to guide**
guindilla *f* **chilli pepper**
guiso *m* **stew ; casserole**
guitarra *f* **guitar**
gusano *m* **maggot ; worm**
gustar **to like ; to enjoy**

H

haba *f* **broad bean**
habano *m* **Havana cigar**
habitación *f* **room**
  habitación doble **double room**
  habitación individual **single room**
hablar (con) **to speak/talk to**
  se habla inglés **English spoken**
hacer **to do ; to make**
  hacer autostop **to hitchhike**
  hacer cola **to queue**
  hacer daño **to hurt ; to damage**
  hacer footing **to jog**
  hacer las maletas **to pack** *(case)*
  hacer punto **to knit**
  hacer surf **to surf**
  hacer topless **to go topless**
  hacer transbordo de **to change** *(bus/train)*
  hacer turismo **to sightsee**
hacia **toward(s)**
  hacia adelante **forwards**
  hacia atrás **backwards**
hamburguesa *f* **hamburger**
harina *f* **flour**
hasta **until ; till**
hay **there is/there are**
hecho(a) **finished ; done**
  hecho a mano **handmade**
  hecho(a) de... **made of...**
helada *f* **frost**
heladería *f* **ice-cream parlour**

helado *m* ice cream
helicóptero *m* helicopter
hemorragia *f* haemorrhage
hemorroides *fpl* haemorrhoids
hepatitis *f* hepatitis
herida *f* wound ; injury
herido(a) injured
herir to hurt
hermano(a) *m/f* brother/sister
hermoso(a) beautiful
hernia *f* hernia
herramienta *f* tool
hervido(a) boiled
hervidor de agua *m* kettle
hervir to boil
hidrofoil *m* hydrofoil
hidropedal *m* pedal boat/pedalo
hielo *m* ice
  con hielo with ice
hierba *f* grass ; herb
hierbabuena *f* mint
hierro *m* iron
  hierro forjado wrought iron
hígado *m* liver
higo *m* fig
  higos chumbos prickly pears
hijo(a) *m/f* son/daughter
hilo *m* thread ; linen
hincha *m/f* fan (football, etc)
hinchado(a) swollen
hipermercado *m* hypermarket
hípica *f* showjumping
hipódromo *m* racecourse (horses)
histórico(a) historic
hogar *m* home ; household
hoja *f* sheet ; leaf
  hoja de registro registration form
  hoja de afeitar razor blade
hola hello ; hi!
hombre *m* man
hombro *m* shoulder
hora *f* hour ; appointment
  hora punta rush hour
  horas de visita visiting hours
horario *m* timetable
horchata de chufa *f* refreshing tiger
  nut drink

hormiga *f* ant
horno *m* oven
  al horno baked ; roasted
  (horno) microondas microwave
horquilla *f* hairgrip
hospital *m* hospital
hostal *m* small hotel ; hostel
hotel *m* hotel
hoy today
huelga *f* strike (of workers)
hueso *m* bone
huésped *m/f* guest
huevo *m* egg
  huevo de Pascua Easter egg
  huevos de corral free-range eggs
  huevos duros hard-boiled eggs
  huevos escalfados poached eggs
  huevos revueltos scrambled eggs
humo *m* smoke

I

ida *f* outward journey
  de ida y vuelta return (ticket)
idioma *m* language
iglesia *f* church
igual equal
imán *m* magnet
impar odd (number)
imperdible *m* safety pin
impermeable *m* raincoat ;
  waterproof
importante important
importar to matter ; to import
importe total *m* total (amount)
imprescindible essential
impreso *m* form
  impreso de solicitud application
  form
  impresos printed matter
impuesto *m* tax
incendio *m* fire
incluido(a) included
incómodo(a) uncomfortable
inconsciente unconscious
indicaciones *fpl* directions

índice *m* index
indigestión *f* indigestion
individual individual ; single
infarto *m* heart attack
infección *f* infection
inferior inferior ; lower
inflamación *f* inflammation
información *f* information
informe *m* report *(medical, police)*
infracción *f* offence
  infracción de tráfico traffic offence
ingeniero(a) *m/f* engineer
Inglaterra *f* England
inglés(lesa) English
ingredientes *mpl* ingredients
inhalador *m* inhaler *(for medication)*
inmediatamente immediately
inmunización *f* immunisation
inquilino(a) *m/f* tenant
insecto *m* insect
insolación *f* sunstroke
instituto *m* institute ; secondary
  school
instrucciones *fpl* directions ;
  instructions
instructor(a) *m/f* instructor
instrumento *m* tool
insulina *f* insulin
interesante interesting
interior inside
intermitente *m* indicator *(in car)*
internacional international
Internet *m or f* internet
intérprete *m/f* interpreter
interruptor *m* switch
intoxicación por alimentos *f* food
  poisoning
introducir to introduce ; to insert
  introduzca monedas insert coins
inundación *f* flood
invierno *m* winter
invitación *f* invitation
invitado(a) *m/f* guest
invitar to invite
inyección *f* injection

ir to go
  ir a buscar to fetch
  ir de compras/tiendas to go
  shopping
  ir en bicicleta to cycle
  irse a casa to go home
  irse de to leave *(a place)*
Irlanda *f* Ireland
Irlanda del Norte *f* Northern Ireland
irlandés(desa) Irish
isla *f* island
Italia *f* Italy
italiano(a) Italian
itinerario *m* route ; schedule
ITV *m* MOT
IVA *m* VAT
izq./izqda. *abbrev. for* izquierda
izquierda *f* left
izquierdo(a) left

J

jabón *m* soap
jamás never
jamón *m* ham
  jamón serrano cured ham
  jamón (de) York boiled ham
Japón *m* Japan
japonés/japonesa *m/f* Japanese
jaqueca *f* migraine
jardín *m* garden
jarra *f* jug ; mug
jefe(a) *m/f* chief ; head ; boss
jerez *m* sherry
jerga *f* slang
jeringuilla *f* syringe
joven young
joya *f* jewel
  joyas jewellery
joyería *f* jeweller's
jubilado(a) *m/f* retired person
jubilarse to retire
judías *fpl* beans
judío(a) Jew
juego *m* game
jueves *m* Thursday

juez(a) *m/f* judge
jugador(a) *m/f* player
jugar to play ; to gamble
julio *m* July
jugo *m* juice
juguete *m* toy
juguetería *f* toy shop
junio *m* June
junto(a) together
  junto a next to
juventud *f* youth

K

kilo *m* kilo(gram)
kilometraje *m* mileage
  kilometraje ilimitado unlimited
  mileage
kilómetro *m* kilometre
kiosko (de prensa) *m* newsstand
kiwi *m* kiwi fruit

L

la the ; her ; it ; you *(formal)*
labio *m* lip
laborable working *(day)*
  laborables weekdays
laca *f* hair spray
lado *m* side
  al lado de beside
ladrar to bark
ladrillo *m* brick
ladrón(ona) *m/f* thief
lago *m* lake
lámpara *f* lamp
lana *f* wool
lancha *f* launch
  lancha motora motor launch
lápiz *m* pencil
  lápiz de ojos eyeliner
largo(a) long
  largo recorrido long-distance *(train, etc)*
lata *f* can *(container)* ; tin
latón *m* brass
lavable washable

lavabo *m* lavatory ; washbasin
lavado de coches *m* car wash
lavado(a) washed
  lavado en seco dry-cleaning
  lavado y marcado shampoo and set
lavadora *f* washing machine
lavanda *f* lavender
lavandería *f* laundry ; launderette
lavavajillas *m* dishwasher
lavar to wash
  lavarse to wash oneself
laxante *m* laxative
leche *f* milk
  leche desnatada skimmed milk
  leche de soja soya milk
  leche de vaca cow's milk
  leche entera wholemilk
  leche hidratante moisturizer
  leche semidesnatada semi-skimmed
  milk
lechuga *f* lettuce
lector de CD *m* CD player
lectura de labios *f* lip-reading
leer to read
legumbres *fpl* pulses
lejía *f* bleach
lejos far
lencería *f* lingerie
lengua *f* language ; tongue
lente *f* lens
  lentes de contacto contact lenses
lentejas *fpl* lentils
lentillas *fpl* contact lenses
lento(a) slow
león *m* lion
lesbiana *f* lesbian
letra *f* letter *(of alphabet)*
levantar to lift
levantarse to get up ; to rise
ley *f* law
libra *f* pound *(currency, weight)*
  libra esterlina pound sterling
libre free/vacant
  libre de impuestos tax-free
  dejen el paso libre keep clear
librería *f* bookshop
libro *m* book

licencia f permit ; licence
licenciarse to graduate
licor m liqueur
  licores spirits
lidia f bullfight
ligero(a) light (not heavy)
lima f file (for nails) ; lime
límite m limit ; boundary
  límite de velocidad speed limit
limón m lemon
limonada f lemonade
limpiar to clean
limpieza en seco f dry-cleaning
limpio(a) clean
línea f line
lino m linen
linterna f torch ; flashlight
liquidación f sales
líquido m liquid
  líquido de frenos brake fluid
liso(a) plain ; smooth
lista f list
  lista de correos poste restante
  lista de precios price list
listo(a) ready
  listo(a) para comer ready-cooked
litera f berth ; couchette ; sleeper
litoral m coast
litro m litre
llaga f ulcer (mouth)
llamada f call
  llamada a cobro revertido reverse
  charge call
llamar to call ; to ring ; to knock
  (on door)
llano(a) flat
llanta f tyre
llave f key ; tap ; spanner
  llave de contacto ignition key
  llaves del coche car keys
  llave inglesa spanner
  llave tarjeta card key
llavero m keyring
Lleg. abbrev. for llegadas
llegada f arrival
  llegadas (Lleg.) arrivals

llegar to arrive ; to come
llenar to fill ; to fill in
lleno(a) full (up)
  lleno, por favor fill it up, please
llevar to bring ; to wear ; to carry
  para llevar to take away
llorar to cry (weep)
lluvia f rain
lobo m wolf
local m premises ; bar
localidad f place
  localidades tickets (theatre)
loción f lotion
loncha f slice (ham, etc)
Londres m London
longitud f length
lotería f lottery
luces fpl lights
luchar to fight
lugar m place
  lugar de expedición issued in
  lugar de nacimiento place of birth
  lugar fresco cool place
lujo m luxury
luna f moon
  luna de miel honeymoon
lunes m Monday
lupa f magnifying glass
luz f light
  luz de freno brake light
  luz de posición sidelight

M

macedonia f fruit salad
madera f wood
madrastra f stepmother
madre f mother
maduro(a) ripe ; mature
maíz m maize ; corn
mal/malo(a) bad (weather, news)
maleta f case ; suitcase
maletero m boot (car)
Mallorca f Majorca
malo(a) bad
mañana tomorrow

mañana f morning
mancha f stain ; mark
mandar to send
  mandar por fax to fax
mandíbula f jaw
mando a distancia m remote control
manera f way ; manner
manga f sleeve
manguera f hosepipe
manillar m handlebars
mano f hand
  de segunda mano secondhand
manopla f mitten
  manopla de horno oven glove
manso(a) tame (animal)
manta f blanket
mantel m tablecloth
mantener to maintain ; to keep
mantequería f dairy products
  (Lat. Am.)
mantequilla f butter
  mantequilla de cacahuete peanut
  butter
mantita f picnic rug
manzana f apple ; block (of houses)
manzanilla f camomile tea ; dry
  sherry
mapa m map
  mapa de carreteras road map
maquillaje m make-up
máquina f machine
  máquina de afeitar razor
  máquina de fotos camera
mar m sea
marca f brand ; make
marcapasos m pacemaker
marcar to dial
  marcar un gol to score a goal
marcha f gear
  marcha atrás reverse gear
marco m picture frame
marea f tide
  marea alta/baja high/low tide
mareado(a) sick (car, sea) ; dizzy
margarina f margarine
marido m husband

marioneta f puppet
mariposa f butterfly
marisco m seafood ; shellfish
marisquería f seafood restaurant
mármol m marble
marrón brown
marroquí Moroccan
marroquinería f leather goods
martes m Tuesday
martillo m hammer
marzo m March
más more ; plus
  más que more than
  más tarde later
masa f pastry (dough)
masculino(a) male
matar to kill
matrícula f any kind of vehicle
  number plate
matrimonio m marriage
máximo m maximum
mayo m May
mayonesa f mayonnaise
mayor bigger ; biggest
  la mayor parte de most of
  mayor que bigger than
  mayores de 18 años over-18s
mayúscula f capital letter
mazapán m marzipan
mazo m mallet
mecánico m mechanic
mechero m lighter
medianoche f midnight
medias fpl tights ; stockings
medicina f medicine ; drug
médico(a) m/f doctor
medida f measurement ; size
medio m the middle
medio(a) half
  media hora half an hour
  media pensión half board
  medio hecho(a) medium rare
mediodía:las doce del
  mediodía midday ; noon
medir to measure
Mediterráneo m Mediterranean

medusa f jellyfish
mejicano(a) m/f Mexican
Méjico m Mexico
mejilla f cheek
mejor best ; better
  mejor que better than
mejorana f marjoram
melocotón m peach
melón m melon
menaje m kitchen utensils
  menaje de hogar household goods
mendigo(a) m/f beggar
menestra f vegetable stew
meningitis f meningitis
menor smaller/smallest ; least
Menorca f Minorca
menos minus ; less ; except
  menos que less than
mensaje m message
mensual monthly
menta f mint ; peppermint
mentira f lie *(untruth)*
menú m menu
  menú del día set menu
mercado m market
mercancías fpl goods
mercería f haberdasher's
merendero m open-air snack bar ;
  picnic area
merienda f afternoon snack ; picnic
mermelada f jam
  mermelada de naranja orange
  marmalade
mes m month
mesa f table
mesón m traditional restaurant
metal m metal
metro m metre ; underground ; tape
  measure
México m Mexico
mezclar to mix
mi my
mí me
miel f honey
mientras while
miércoles m Wednesday

miga f crumb
migraña f migraine
mil thousand
mil millones billion
milímetro m millimetre
millón m million
mínimo m minimum
minusválido(a) m/f disabled person
minuto m minute
miope short-sighted
mirar to look at ; to watch
misa f mass *(in church)*
mismo(a) same
mitad f half
mixto(a) mixed
mochila f backpack ; rucksack
  mochila portabebés baby sling
moda f fashion
moderno(a) modern
modo m way ; manner
  modo de empleo instructions for use
mojado(a) wet
mole m black chilli sauce
molestar to disturb
molestia f nuisance ; discomfort
molido(a) ground *(coffee beans, etc)*
molino m mill
  molino de viento windmill
monasterio m monastery
moneda f currency ; coin
  introduzca monedas insert coins
monedero m purse
monitor(a) de esquí m/f ski
  instructor
montaña f mountain
montañismo m mountaineering
montar to ride
  montar a caballo to horse ride
montilla m a sherry-type wine
monumento m monument
moqueta f fitted carpet
mora f mulberry ; blackberry
morado(a) purple
mordedura f bite
morder to bite

moratón m bruise
morir to die
mosca f fly
mosquitera f mosquito net
mostrador m counter ; desk
mostrar to show
moto f (motor)bike ; moped
  moto acuática jet ski
motocicleta f motorbike
motor m engine ; motor
mozo m luggage porter
mucho a lot ; much
mucho(a) a lot (of) ; much
muchos(as) many
muela f tooth
muelle m quay ; pier
muerto(a) dead
muestra f exhibition ; sample
mujer f woman ; wife
multa f fine (to be paid)
mundo m world
muñeca f wrist ; doll
muro m wall
músculo m muscle
museo m museum ; art gallery
música f music
muy very
  muy hecho(a) well done (steak)

N

nacer to be born
nacimiento m birth
nación f nation
nacional national ; domestic (flight)
nacionalidad f nationality
nada nothing
  de nada don't mention it
  nada más nothing else
nadador(a) m/f swimmer
nadar to swim
nadie nobody
naipes mpl playing cards
naranja f orange
naranjada f orangeade

nariz f nose
nata f cream
  nata agria soured cream
  nata líquida single cream
natación f swimming
natural natural ; fresh ; plain
naturista m/f naturist
navaja f pocketknife ; penknife
Navidad f Christmas
neblina f mist
necesario(a) necessary
necesitar to need ; to require
nectarina f nectarine
negarse to refuse
negativo m negative (photo)
negocios mpl business
negro(a) black
neumático m tyre
  neumáticos antideslizantes snow
  tyres
nevar to snow
nevera f refrigerator
  nevera portátil cool-box
nido m nest
niebla f fog
nieto(a) m/f grandson/daughter
nieve f snow
niña f girl ; baby girl
niñera f nanny
ningún/ninguno(a) none
niño m boy ; baby ; child
  niños children (infants)
nivel m level ; standard
Nº abbrev. for número
noche f night
  esta noche tonight
Nochebuena f Christmas Eve
Nochevieja f New Year's Eve
nocivo(a) harmful
nombre m name
  nombre de pila first name
norte m north
Norteamérica f America ; USA
norteamericano(a) American
nosotros(as) we
notaría f solicitor's office

notario(a) *m/f* **notary ; solicitor**
noticias *fpl* **news**
novela *f* **novel**
novia *f* **girlfriend ; fiancée ; bride**
noviembre *m* **November**
novio *m* **boyfriend ; fiancé ;
  bridegroom**
nube *f* **cloud**
nublado(a) **cloudy**
nudo *m* **knot**
nuestro(a) **our ; ours**
Nueva Zelanda *f* **New Zealand**
nuevo(a) **new**
nuez *f* **walnut**
número *m* **number ; size ; issue**
  número par **even** *(number)*
nunca **never**

O

o **or**
  o... o... **either... or...**
obispo *m* **bishop**
objetivo *m* **lens** *(on camera)*
objeto *m* **object**
  objetos de valor **valuables**
obligatorio(a) **compulsory**
obra *f* **work ; play** *(theatre)*
  obra maestra **masterpiece**
  obras **road works**
observar **to watch**
obstruido(a) **blocked** *(pipe)*
obtener **to get** *(to obtain)*
océano *m* **ocean**
ocio *m* **spare time**
octubre *m* **October**
ocupado **engaged**
oeste *m* **west**
oferta *f* **special offer**
oficina *f* **office**
  oficina de correos **Post Office**
oficio *m* **church service ; profession**
ofrecer **to offer**
oído *m* **ear**
oír **to hear**
ojo *m* **eye**

¡ojo! **look out!**
ola *f* **wave** *(on sea)*
olivo *m* **olive tree**
olor *m* **smell**
oloroso *m* **cream sherry**
olvidar **to forget**
onda *f* **wave**
ópera *f* **opera**
operación *f* **operation**
operador(a) *m/f* **operator**
oportunidades *fpl* **bargains**
orden *f* **command**
orden *m* **order**
ordenador *m* **computer**
  ordenador portátil **laptop**
oreja *f* **ear**
organizar **to arrange ; to organize**
orilla *f* **shore**
orina *f* **urine**
oro *m* **gold**
oscuro(a) **dark ; dim**
oso *m* **bear** *(animal)*
ostra *f* **oyster**
otoño *m* **autumn ; fall**
otro(a) **other ; another**
  otra vez **again**
oxígeno *m* **oxygen**

P

paciente *m/f* **patient** *(in hospital)*
padrastro *m* **stepfather**
padre *m* **father**
  padres **parents**
paella *f* **paella** *(rice dish)*
pagado(a) **paid**
pagar **to pay for ; to pay**
  pagar al contado **to pay cash**
  pagar por separado **to pay
  separately**
pagaré *m* **IOU**
página *f* **page**
  página web **website**
  páginas amarillas *fpl* **Yellow Pages**
pago *m* **payment**

pago por adelantado payment in advance
pague en caja please pay at cash desk

país *m* country
paisaje *m* landscape ; countryside
pájaro *m* bird
pajita *f* straw (for drinking)
palabra *f* word
palacio *m* palace
palco *m* box (in theatre)
pálido(a) pale
palillo *m* toothpick
palo *m* stick ; mast
  palo de golf golf club
paloma *f* pigeon ; dove
pan *m* bread ; loaf of bread
  pan de centeno rye bread
  pan de molde sliced bread
  pan integral wholemeal bread
  pan tostado toast
panadería *f* bakery
pañal *m* nappy
panecillo *m* bread roll
paño *m* flannel ; cloth
pantalla *f* screen
pantalones *mpl* trousers
  pantalones cortos shorts
pantys *mpl* tights
pañuelo *m* handkerchief ; scarf
  pañuelo de papel tissue
papa *m* pope
papel *m* paper
  papeles del coche log book (car)
  papel higiénico toilet paper
papelería *f* stationer's
paquete *m* packet ; parcel
par even (number)
par *m* pair
para for ; towards
parabrisas *m* windscreen
parachoques *m* bumper (car)
parada *f* stop
parado(a) unemployed
parador *m* state-run hotel

parafina *f* paraffin
paraguas *m* umbrella
parar to stop
parecido(a) a similar to
pared *f* wall (inside)
pareja *f* couple (2 people)
parque *m* park
  parque de atracciones funfair
  parque nacional national park
parquímetro *m* parking meter
parrilla *f* grill ; barbecue
  a la parrilla grilled
particular private
partida *f* game ; departure
  partida de nacimiento birth certificate
partido *m* match (sport) ; party (political)
partir to depart
pasa *f* raisin ; currant
pasado(a) stale (bread) ; rotten
pasaje *m* ticket ; fare ; alleyway
pasajero(a) *m/f* passenger
pasaporte *m* passport
pasar to happen
pasatiempo *m* hobby ; pastime
Pascua *f* Easter
  ¡Felices Pascuas! Happy Easter!
paseo *m* walk ; avenue ; promenade
pasillo *m* corridor ; aisle
paso *m* step ; pace
  paso a nivel level crossing
  paso de ganado cattle crossing
  paso de peatones pedestrian crossing
  paso inferior subway
  paso subterráneo subway
pasta *f* pastry ; pasta
  pasta de dientes toothpaste
pastel *m* cake ; pie
  pasteles pastries
pastelería *f* cakes and pastries ; cake shop
pastilla *f* tablet ; pill
  pastilla de jabón bar of soap

pastor(a) *m/f* shepherd ; minister

patata *f* potato
  patatas fritas french fries ; crisps

patinaje *m* skating

patinar to skate

patines *mpl* skates
  patines en línea rollerblades

pato *m* duck

pavo *m* turkey

paz *f* peace

p. ej. *abbrev. for* por ejemplo

peaje *m* toll

peatón/peatona *m/f* pedestrian

peces *mpl* fish

pecho *m* chest ; breast

pechuga *f* breast *(poultry)*

pedir to ask for ; to order
  pedir prestado to borrow

pegamento *m* gum ; glue

pegar to stick (on) ; to hit

peine *m* comb

pelar to peel *(fruit)*

película *f* film

peligro *m* danger
  peligro de incendio fire hazard

peligroso(a) dangerous

pelo *m* hair

pelota *f* ball
  pelota vasca Basque ball game
  pelota de golf golf ball
  pelota de tenis tennis ball

peluca *f* wig

peluquería *f* hairdresser's

pendientes *mpl* earrings

pene *m* penis

penicilina *f* penicillin

pensar to think

pensión *f* guesthouse
  media pensión half board
  pensión completa full board

pensionista *m/f* senior citizen

peor worse ; worst

pequeño(a) little ; small ; tiny

pera *f* pear

percha *f* coat hanger

perder to lose ; to miss *(train, etc)*

perdido(a) missing *(lost)*

perdiz *f* partridge

perdón *m* pardon ; sorry

perdonar to forgive

perejil *m* parsley

perezoso(a) lazy

perfecto(a) perfect

perforar: *no perforar* do not pierce

perfumería *f* perfume shop

periódico *m* newspaper

periodista *m/f* journalist

perla *f* pearl

permiso *m* permission ; pass ;
  permit ; licence
  permiso de caza hunting permit
  permiso de residencia residence
  permit
  permiso de trabajo work permit

permitido(a) permitted ; allowed

permitir to allow ; to let

pero but

perro *m* dog

persiana *f* blind *(for window)*

persona *f* person

personal *m* staff

pesado(a) heavy ; boring

pesar to weigh

pesca *f* fishing

pescadería *f* fishmonger's

pescado *m* fish

pescador(a) *m/f* fisherman/woman

pescar to fish

peso *m* weight ; scales

petirrojo *m* robin

pez *m* fish

picado(a) chopped ; minced ; rough
  (sea) ; stung *(by insect)*

picadura *f* insect bite ; sting

picante peppery ; hot ; spicy

picar to itch ; to sting

pie *m* foot

piedra *f* stone

piel f fur ; skin ; leather

pierna f leg

pieza f part ; room
  piezas del coche car parts

pijama m pyjamas

pila f battery (radio, etc)

píldora f pill

pileta f sink ; (LAm) washbasin

pimienta f pepper (spice)
  a la pimienta au poivre

pimiento m pepper (vegetable)

piña f pineapple

pinacoteca f art gallery

pinchar to have a puncture

pinchazo m puncture

pinchos mpl savoury titbits
  pinchos morunos kebabs

pintar to paint

pintura f paint ; painting

pinza f clothes peg
  pinzas tweezers

pipa f pipe (smoker's)

pipirrana f salad with tomato,
  pepper, onion, egg and fish

Pirineos mpl Pyrenees

piruleta f lollipop

pisar to step on ; to tread on
  no pisar el césped keep off grass

piscina f swimming pool

piso m floor ; storey ; flat
  piso deslizante slippery road

pista f track ; court

pistacho m pistachio

pisto m sautéed vegetables

pistola f gun

placa f licence plate

plancha f iron (for clothes)
  a la plancha grilled

planchar to iron

plano m plan ; town map

planta f plant ; floor ; sole (of foot)
  planta baja ground floor

plata f silver ; (LAm) money

plátano m banana ; plane tree

platea f stalls (theatre)

platería f jeweller's

platillo m saucer

platinos mpl points (in car)

plato m plate ; dish (food) ; course
  plato del día dish of the day
  plato principal main course

playa f beach ; seaside

plaza f square (in town)
  plaza de toros bull ring
  plazas libres vacancies

plazo m period ; expiry date

plomo m lead (metal)

pluma f feather

pobre poor

poco(a) little
  poco hecho(a) rare (steak)
  un poco de a bit of
  pocos(as) (a) few

poder to be able

podólogo(a) m/f chiropodist

podrido(a) rotten (fruit, etc)

policía f police
  Policía Nacional national police
  Policía Municipal/Local local police

policía m/f policeman/woman

polideportivo m leisure centre

póliza f policy ; certificate
  póliza de seguros insurance policy

pollería f poultry shop

pollo m chicken

polo m ice lolly

poltrona f armchair

polvo m powder ; dust
  polvos de talco talcum powder

pomada f ointment

pomelo m grapefruit

ponche m punch

poner to put
  poner en marcha to start (car)
  ponerse en contacto
  to contact

por by ; per ; through ; about
  por adelantado in advance
  por correo by mail

por ejemplo for example
por favor please
porción *f* portion
porque because
portaequipajes *m* luggage rack
portero *m* caretaker ; doorman
portugués/portguesa Portuguese
posible possible
posología *f* dosage
postal *f* postcard
postigos *mpl* shutters
postre *m* dessert ; pudding
potable drinkable
potaje *m* stew ; thick soup
pote *m* stew
potito *m* baby food
pozo *m* well *(water)*
pozo séptico septic tank
prado *m* meadow
precio *m* price ; cost
precioso(a) lovely
precipicio *m* cliff ; precipice
preciso(a) precise ; necessary
preferir to prefer
prefijo *m* dialling code
pregunta *f* question
preguntar to ask
premio *m* prize
prensa *f* press
preocupado(a) worried
preparado(a) cooked
preparar to prepare ; to cook
presa *f* dam
prescribir to prescribe
presentar to introduce
preservativo *m* condom
presión *f* pressure
presión arterial blood pressure
prestar to lend
primavera *f* spring *(season)*
primer/o(a) first
primeros auxilios mpl first aid
primo(a) *m/f* cousin
princesa *f* princess

principal main
príncipe *m* prince
principiante *m/f* beginner
prioridad (de paso) *f* right of way
prismáticos *mpl* binoculars
privado(a) private
probador *m* changing room
probar to try ; to taste
probarse to try on *(clothes)*
problema *m* problem
procedente de... coming from...
productos *mpl* produce ; products
productos lácteos dairy products
profesión *f* profession ; job
profesor(a) *m/f* teacher
profundo(a) deep
programa *m* programme
programa de ordenador computer
program
prohibido(a) prohibited/no...
prohibido bañarse no bathing
prohibido el paso no entry
prometer to promise
prometido(a) engaged
(to be married)
pronóstico *m* forecast
pronóstico del tiempo weather
forecast
pronto soon
pronunciar to pronounce
propiedad *f* property
propietario(a) *m/f* owner
propina *f* tip
propio(a) own
protegido(a) sheltered
provisional temporary
próximo(a) next
público *m* audience
público(a) public
puchero *m* cooking pot ; stew
pueblo *m* village ; country
puente *m* bridge
puerro *m* leek
puerta *f* door ; gate

cierren la puerta close the door
puerta de embarque boarding gate
puerta principal front door
puerto *m* port
puerto de montaña moutain pass
puesta de sol *f* sunset
puesta en marcha *f* starter *(of car)*
puesto que since
pulgar *m* thumb
pulgas *fpl* fleas
pulmón *m* lung
pulpo *m* octopus
pulsera *f* bracelet
punto *m* stitch
punto muerto neutral *(car)*
puntuación *f* score *(of match)*
puré *m* purée
puro *m* cigar
puro(a) pure

Q

que than ; that ; which
¿qué? what? ; which?
¿qué tal? how are you?
quedar to remain ; to be left
quedar bien to fit *(clothes)*
queja *f* complaint
quemado(a) burnt
quemadura *f* burn
quemadura del sol sunburn
quemar to burn
querer to want ; to love
querer decir to mean
querido(a) dear *(on letter)*
queroseno *m* paraffin
queso *m* cheese
¿quién? who?
quincena *f* fortnight
quinientos(as) five hundred
quiosco *m* kiosk
quiste *m* cyst
quitaesmalte *m* nail polish remover
quitamanchas *m* stain remover

quitar to remove
quizá(s) perhaps

R

rabia *f* rabies
ración *f* portion
raciones snacks ; tapas
radiador *m* radiator
radio *f* radio
radio *m* spoke *(wheel)*
radiocasete *m* cassette player
radiografía *f* X-ray
rallador *m* grater
rama *f* branch *(of tree)*
ramo *m* bunch *(of flowers)*
rápido *m* express train
rápido(a) quick ; fast
raqueta *f* racket
rasgar to tear ; to rip
rastrillo *m* rake
rastro *m* flea market
rata *f* rat
ratero *m* pickpocket
rato *m* a while
ratón *m* mouse
razón *f* reason
real royal
rebajas *fpl* sale(s)
recalentar to overheat
recambio *m* spare ; refill
recargar to recharge *(battery, etc)*
recepción *f* reception
recepcionista *m/f* receptionist
receta *f* prescription ; recipe
recibir to receive
recibo *m* receipt
recientemente recently
reclamación *f* claim ; complaint
reclamar to claim
recoger to collect
recogida *f* collection
recogida de equipajes baggage
reclaim

recomendar to recommend
reconocer to recognize
recordar to remember
recorrido *m* journey ; route
  de largo recorrido long-distance
recuerdo *m* souvenir
recuperarse to recover *(from illness)*
red *f* net
redondo(a) round *(shape)*
reducción *f* reduction
reducir to reduce
reembolsar to reimburse ; to refund
reembolso *m* refund
refresco *m* refreshment ; drink
refugio *m* shelter ; moutain hut
regadera *f* watering can
regalo *m* gift ; present
régimen *m* diet
región *f* district ; area ; region
registrarse to register *(at hotel)*
regla *f* period *(menstruation)* ; ruler
  (for measuring)
reina *f* queen
Reino Unido *m* United Kingdom
reintegro *m* withdrawal *(from bank
  account)*
reírse to laugh
rejilla *f* rack *(luggage)*
relámpago *m* lightning
rellenar to fill in
reloj *m* clock ; watch
remar to row *(boat)*
remitente *m/f* sender
remolcar to tow
remolque *m* tow rope ; trailer
RENFE *f* Spanish National Railways
reparación *f* repair
reparar to repair
repetir to repeat
repollo *m* cabbage
representante *m/f* sales rep
repuestos *mpl* spare parts
resaca *f* hangover

resbaladizo(a) slippery
resbalarse to slip
rescatar to rescue
reserva *f* booking(s) ; reservation
reservado(a) reserved
reservar to reserve ; to book
resfriado *m* cold *(illness)*
residente *m/f* resident
resistente a resistant to
  resistente al agua waterproof
  resistente al calor resistant to heat
respirar to breathe
responder to answer ; to reply
responsabilidad *f* responsibility
respuesta *f* answer
restaurante *m* restaurant
resto *m* the rest
retrasado(a) delayed
retraso *m* delay
  sin retraso on schedule
retrato *m* portrait
retrovisor exterior *m* wing mirror
reumatismo *m* rheumatism
reunión *f* meeting
revelar to develop *(photos)*
revisar to check
revisión *f* car service ; inspection
revisor(a) *m/f* ticket collector
revista *f* magazine
rey *m* king
rezar to pray
riada *f* flash flood
rico(a) rich *(person)*
rincón *m* corner
riñón *m* kidney
riñonera *f* bumbag
río *m* river
robar to steal
robo *m* robbery ; theft
robot (de concina) *m* food
  processor
rodaballo *m* turbot
rodeado(a) de surrounded by
rodilla *f* knee

rodillo m rolling pin
rojo(a) red
románico(a) Romanesque
romántico(a) romantic
romería f procession
romper to break ; to tear
ron m rum
roncar to snore
ropa f clothes
  ropa de cama bedclothes
  ropa interior underwear
ropero m wardrobe
rosa f rose
rosa pink
rosado m rosé
roto(a) broken
rotonda f roundabout (traffic)
rotulador m felt-tip pen
rubeola f rubella ; German measles
rubio(a) blond ; fair haired
rueda f wheel
  rueda de repuesto spare tyre
  rueda pinchada flat tyre
ruido m noise
ruinas fpl ruins
ruta f route
  ruta turística tourist route

S

S.A. abbrev. for Sociedad Anónima
sábado m Saturday
sábana f sheet (bed)
saber to know (facts) ; to know how
sabor m taste ; flavour
sacacorchos m corkscrew
sacar to take out (of bag, etc)
sacarina f saccharin
saco m sack
  saco de dormir sleeping bag
sagrado(a) holy
sal f salt
  sin sal unsalted
sala f hall ; hospital ward

sala de conciertos concert hall
  sala de embarque departure lounge
  sala de espera waiting room
salado(a) savoury ; salty
salario m wage
salchicha f sausage
saldo m balance (of account)
saldos mpl sales
salida f exit/departure
  salida de incendios fire exit
  salida del sol sunrise
salir to go out ; to come out
salmón m salmon
  salmón ahumado smoked salmon
salsa f gravy ; sauce ; dressing
saltar to jump
salteado(a) sauté ; sautéed
salud f health
  ¡salud! cheers!
salvar to save (life)
salvaslip m panty liner
salvavidas m lifebelt
salvia f sage (herb)
sandalias fpl sandals
sandía f watermelon
sangrar to bleed
sangría f sangria (red wine and fruit punch)
santo(a) saint ; holy ; saint's day
sarampión m measles
sarpullido m skin rash
sartén f frying pan
sastrería f tailor's
secado a mano m blow-dry
secador (de pelo) m hairdryer
secadora f dryer (spin, tumble)
secar to dry
seco(a) dry ; dried (fruit, beans)
secretario(a) m/f secretary
seda f silk
  seda dental dental floss
seguida: en seguida straight away
seguido(a) continuous
  todo seguido straight on

seguir to continue ; to follow
según according to
segundo *m* second *(time)*
segundo(a) second
  de segunda mano secondhand
seguramente probably
seguridad *f* reliability ; safety ;
  security
seguro *m* insurance
  seguro del coche car insurance
  seguro de vida life insurance
  seguro médico medical insurance
seguro(a) safe ; certain
sello *m* stamp *(postage)*
semáforo *m* traffic lights
semana *f* week
  Semana Santa Holy Week ; Easter
semanal weekly
semilla *f* seed ; pip
señal *f* sign ; signal ; road sign
sencillo(a) simple ; single *(ticket)*
señor *m* gentleman
  Señor (Sr.) M. ; Sir
señora *f* lady
  Señora (Sra.) Mrs ; Ms ; Madam
señoras ladies
señorita *f* Miss
  Señorita (Srta.)... Miss...
sentarse to sit
sentir to feel
separado(a) separated
septentrional northern
septiembre *m* September
sequía *f* drought
ser to be
seropositivo(a) HIV positive
serpiente *f* snake
servicio *m* service ; service charge
  área de servicios service area
  servicio incluido service included
  servicios toilets
  servicios de urgencia emergency
  services
servilleta *f* serviette ; napkin
servir to serve

sesión *f* performance ; screening
  sesión de noche late night
  performance
  sesión de tarde eve performance
  sesión numerada seats bookable in
  advance
sesos *mpl* brains
seta *f* mushroom
sexo *m* sex ; gender
si if
sí yes
sida *m* AIDS
sidra *f* cider
siempre always
siento: *lo siento* I'm sorry
sierra *f* mountain range ; saw
siga follow
  siga adelante carry on
  siga recto keep straight on
siglo *m* century
siguiente following ; next
silencio *m* silence
silla *f* chair ; seat
  silla de paseo pushchair
  silla de ruedas wheelchair
sillón *m* armchair
simpático(a) nice ; kind
sin without
  sin plomo unleaded
síntoma *m* symptom
sírvase vd. mismo serve/help
  yourself
sistema *m* system
sitio *m* place ; space ; position
slip *m* pants ; briefs
sobre on ; upon ; about ; on top of
sobre *m* envelope
  sobre acolchado padded envelope
sobrecarga *f* surcharge
sobrecargar to overload
sobredosis *f* overdose
sobrino(a) *m/f* nephew/niece
sobrio(a) sober
sociedad *f* society
  Sociedad Anónima Ltd ; plc

socio(a) m/f **member ; partner**

socorrista m/f **lifeguard**

¡socorro! **help!**

soja f **soya**

sol m **sun ; sunshine**

solamente **only**

soldado m/f **soldier**

solicitar **to request**

solitario m **patience** (cardgame)

solo(a) **alone ; lonely**

sólo **only**

solomillo m **sirloin**

soltero(a) m/f **bachelor/spinster**

soltero(a) **single** (unmarried)

sombra f **shade ; shadow**
   sombra de ojos **eye shadow**

sombrero m **hat**

sombrilla f **sunshade ; parasol**

somnífero m **sleeping pill**

sonido m **sound**

sonreír **to smile**

sonrisa f **smile**

sopa f **soup**

sordo(a) **deaf**

sorpresa f **surprise**

sótano m **basement**

soya/soja f **soya**

Sr. abbrev. for señor

Sra. abbrev. for señora

Srta. abbrev. for señorita

stop m **stop** (sign)

su **his/her/its/their/your**

suavizante m **hair conditioner ; fabric softener**

submarinismo m **scuba diving**

subterráneo(a) **underground**

subtítulo m **subtitle**

sucio(a) **dirty**

sucursal f **branch** (of bank, etc)

sudadera f **sweatshirt**

sudar **to sweat**

suegro(a) m/f **father/mother-in-law**

suela f **sole** (of foot, shoe)

sueldo m **wage**

suelo m **soil ; ground ; floor**

suelto m **loose change** (money)

sueño m **dream**

suerte f **luck**
   ¡(buena) suerte! **good luck!**

Suiza f **Switzerland**

suizo(a) **Swiss**

sujetador m **bra**

superior **higher**

supermercado m **supermarket**

supositorio m **suppository**

sur m **south**

surfing m **surfing**

surtidor m **petrol pump**

sus **his/her/their/your**

T

tabaco m **tobacco ; cigarettes**

tabla f **board**
   tabla de cortar **chopping board**
   tabla de planchar **ironing board**
   tabla de surf **surf board**

tablao (flamenco) m **Flamenco show**

tableta f **tablet ; bar** (chocolate)

taco m **stuffed tortilla**

tacón m **heel** (shoe)

taladradora f **drill** (tool)

talco m **talc**

TALGO m **Intercity express train**

talla f **size**

tallarines mpl **noodles ; tagliatelle**

taller m **garage** (for repairs)

talón m **heel ; counterfoil ; stub**
   talón bancario **cheque**

talonario m **cheque book**

también **as well ; also ; too**

tampoco **neither**

tampones mpl **tampons**

tapa f **lid**

tapas fpl **appetizers ; snacks**

tapón m **cap** (of bottle etc)

taquilla f **ticket office**

tarde f evening ; afternoon
  de la tarde pm
tarde late
tarifa f price ; rate
  tarifa baja cheap rate
  tarifa máxima peak rate
tarjeta f card
  tarjeta de crédito credit card
  tarjeta de embarque boarding pass
  tarjeta de visita business card
  tarjeta telefónica phonecard
tarro m jar ; pot
tarta f cake ; tart
tasca f bar ; cheap restaurant
taxista m/f taxi driver
taza f cup
tazón m bowl (for soup, etc)
té m tea
teatro m theatre
techo m ceiling
  techo solar sunroof
tejado m roof
tela f material ; fabric
  tela impermeable groundsheet
telaraña f web (spider)
teleférico m cablecar
telefonear to phone
telefonista m/f telephonist
teléfono m phone
  (teléfono) móvil mobile (phone)
  teléfono público payphone
telegrama m telegram
telesilla m ski lift ; chairlift
telesquí m ski lift
televisión f television
televisor m television set
télex m telex
temperatura f temperature
templo m temple
temporada f season
  temporada alta high season
temporal m storm
temporizador m timer (on cooker)
temprano(a) early
tendedero m clothes line

tenedor m fork (for eating)
tener to have
  tener fiebre to have a temperature
  tener miedo de to be afraid of
  tener morriña to be homesick
  tener 'overbooking' to be
  overbooked
  tener que to have to
  tener razón to be right
  tener suerte to be lucky
tentempié m snack
tequila m tequila
tercero(a) third
terciopelo m velvet
termo m flask (thermos)
termómetro m thermometer
ternera f veal
terraza f terrace ; balcony
terremoto m earthquake
terreno m land
terrorista m/f terrorist
testículos mpl testicles
tetera f teapot
tetina f teat (on baby's bottle)
ti you (sing. with friends)
tía f aunt
tiempo m time ; weather
tienda f store ; shop ; tent
  tienda de ropa clothes shop
tierra f earth
tijeras fpl scissors
timbre m doorbell ; official stamp
tímido(a) shy
timón m rudder
tinta f ink
tinte m dye
  tinte de pelo hair dye
tinto m red wine
tintorería f dry-cleaner's
tío m uncle
típico(a) typical
tipo m sort
  tipo de cambio exchange rate
tique m ticket

tirador m handle
tirar to throw (away) ; to pull
  para tirar disposable
tire pull
tirita® f (sticking) plaster
toalla f towel
tobillo m ankle
tocar to touch ; to play (instrument)
  no tocar do not touch
tocino m bacon ; fat
todo(a) all
  todo everything
  todo el mundo everyone
  todo incluido all inclusive
tomar to take ; to have (food/drink)
  tomar el sol to sunbathe
tomate m tomato
tomillo m thyme
tónica f tonic water
tono m tone
  tono de marcar dialling tone
tonto(a) stupid
toquen: *no toquen* do not touch
torcedura f sprain
torero m bullfighter
tormenta f thunderstorm
tornillo m screw
toro m bull
torre f tower
torta f cake
tortilla f omelette
tos f cough
toser to cough
tostada f toast
trabajar to work (person)
trabajo m work
tradicional traditional
traducción f translation
traducir to translate
traer to fetch ; to bring
tráfico m traffic
tragar to swallow
traje m suit ; outfit
  traje de baño swimsuit

traje de bucear wetsuit
traje de etiqueta evening dress
(man's)
traje de noche evening dress
(woman's)
trampolín m diving board
tranquilo(a) calm ; quiet
tranquilizante m tranquilliser
transbordador m car ferry
transbordo m transfer
tranvía m tram ; short-distance train
trapo m cloth (for cleaning, etc)
tras after ; behind
trastorno estomacal m stomach
  upset
tratar con cuidado handle with care
travesía f crossing
tren m train
triángulo señalizador m warning
  triangle
triste sad
trozo m piece
trucha f trout
trueno m thunder
trufa f truffle
tú you (singular with friends)
tu your (singular with friends)
tubería f pipe (drain, etc)
tubo de escape m exhaust pipe
tumbarse to lie down
tumbona f deckchair
túnel m tunnel
turista m/f tourist
turístico(a) tourist
turno m turn
  espere su turno wait your turn
turrón m nougat
TVE abbrev. for **Televisión Española**

U

Vd(s). abbrev for **usted(es)**
úlcera f ulcer (stomach)
últimamente lately

último(a) last
ultracongelador m deep freeze
ultramarinos m grocery shop
un(a) a/an
uña f nail (finger, toe)
ungüento m ointment
únicamente only
unidad f unit
Unión Europea f European Union
universidad f university
unos(as) some
urgencias fpl casualty department
urgente urgent ; express
usar to use
uso m use ; custom
  uso externo/tópico for external use
  only
usted you (polite singular)
ustedes you (polite plural)
útil useful
utilizar to use
uva f grape
  uvas verdes/negras green/black
  grapes
UVI/UCI f intensive care unit

V

vaca f cow
vacaciones fpl holiday
  vacaciones de verano summer
  holidays
vacío(a) empty
vacuna f vaccination
vagina f vagina
vagón m railway carriage
vale OK
vale... it's worth...
vale m token ; voucher
válido(a) valid (ticket, licence, etc)
valle m valley
valor m value
válvula f valve
vapor m steam

al vapor steamed
vaqueros mpl jeans
variado(a) assorted ; mixed
varios(as) several
vasco(a) Basque
vaso m glass (for drinking)
Vd(s). abbrev. for usted(es)
veces fpl times
vecino(a) m/f neighbour
vegetariano(a) m/f vegetarian
vehículo m vehicle
vela f candle ; sail ; sailing
velocidad f speed
  límite de velocidad speed limit
  velocidad máxima speed limit
velocímetro m speedometer
vena f vein
venda f bandage
vendedor(a) m/f salesman/woman
vender to sell
  se vende for sale
veneno m poison
venenoso(a) poisonous
venir to come
venta f sale ; country inn
ventana f window
ventanilla f window (in car, train)
ventilador m fan (electric)
ver to see ; to watch
verano m summer
verdad f truth
  ¿de verdad? really?
verdadero(a) true ; genuine
verde green
verdulería f greengrocer's
verduras fpl vegetables
vereda f footpath (in the country)
verificar to check
versión f version
  versión original original version
vespa® f motor scooter
vestido m dress
vestir de etiqueta formal dress
vestirse to get dressed

veterinario(a) *m/f* **vet**
vez *f* **time**
vía *f* **track ; rails ; platform**
  por vía oral/bucal **orally**
viajar to **travel**
viaje *m* **journey ; trip**
  viaje de negocios **business trip**
  viaje organizado **package tour**
viajero *m* **traveller**
víbora *f* **adder ; viper**
vida *f* **life**
vídeo *m* **video ; video recorder**
videocámara *f* **camcorder**
videojuego *m* **video game**
vidriera *f* **stained-glass window**
vidrio *m* **glass** *(substance)*
vieira *f* **scallop**
viejo(a) **old**
viento *m* **wind**
viernes *m* **Friday**
  Viernes Santo **Good Friday**
viña *f* **vineyard**
vinagre *m* **vinegar**
vinagreta *f* **vinaigrette** *(dressing)*
vino *m* **wine**
  vino blanco **white wine**
  vino rosado **rosé wine**
  vino seco **dry wine**
  vino tinto **red wine**
violación *f* **rape**
violar to **rape**
violeta *f* **violet** *(flower)*
virus *m* **virus**
  virus del sida, VIH **HIV**
visa *f* **visa**
visita *f* **visit**
visitar to **visit**
víspera *f* **eve**
vista *f* **view**
viudo(a) *m/f* **widow/widower**
vivir to **live**
V.O. (versión original) **undubbed version (of film)**
volante *m* **steering wheel**

volar to **fly**
volcán *m* **volcano**
voleibol *m* **volleyball**
voltaje *m* **voltage**
volumen *m* **volume**
volver to **come/go back ; to return**
vomitar to **vomit**
vosotros **you** *(plural with friends)*
voz *f* **voice**
vuelo *m* **flight**
vuelta *f* **turn ; return ; change** *(money)*
vuestro(a) **your** *(plural with friends)*

W

Walkman® *m* **Walkman®**
wáter *m* **lavatory ; toilet**
whisky *m* **whisky**
windsurf *m* **windsurfing**

Y

y **and**
yate *m* **yacht**
yerno *m* **son-in-law**
yo **I ; me**
yogur *m* **yoghurt**
  yogur natural **plain yoghurt**

Z

zanahoria *f* **carrot**
zapatería *f* **shoe shop**
zapatillas *fpl* **slippers**
  zapatillas de deporte **trainers**
zapato *m* **shoe**
zarzuela *f* **Spanish light opera ; casserole**
zona *f* **zone**
  zona azul **controlled parking area**
  zona de descanso **layby**
  zona restringida **restricted area**
zorro *m* **fox**
zumo *m* **juice**

Grammar

NOUNS

Unlike English, Spanish nouns have a gender: they are either *masculine* (**el**) or *feminine* (**la**). Therefore words for *the* and *a(n)* must agree with the noun they accompany – whether *masculine*, *feminine* or *plural*:

	masc.	fem.	plural
the	**el gato**	**la plaza**	**los gatos, las plazas**
a, an	**un gato**	**una plaza**	**unos gatos, unas plazas**

The ending of the noun will usually indicate whether it is *masculine* or *feminine*:

-**o** or -**or** are generally *masculine*
-**a**, -**dad**, -**ión**, -**tud**, -**umbre** are generally *feminine*

NOTE: *feminine* nouns beginning with a stressed **a**- or **ha**- take the *masculine* article **el**, though the noun is still *feminine*.

PLURALS

The articles **el** and **la** become **los** and **las** in the plural. Nouns ending with a vowel become plural by adding -**s**:

> **el gato → los gatos**
> **la plaza → las plazas**
> **la calle → las calles**

Where the noun ends in a consonant, -**es** is added:

> **el color → los colores**
> **la ciudad → las ciudades**

Nouns ending in -**z** change their ending to -**ces** in the plural:

> **el lápiz → los lápices**
> **la voz → las voces**

ADJECTIVES

Adjectives normally follow the noun they describe in Spanish, e.g. **la manzana roja** (the red apple)

Some common exceptions which go before the noun are:

buen good	**gran** great
ningún no, not any	**mucho** much, many
poco little, few	**primer** first
tanto so much, so many	**último** last

e.g. **el último tren** (the last train)

Spanish adjectives also reflect the gender of the noun they describe. To make an adjective *feminine*, the *masculine* -**o** ending is changed to -**a** ; and the endings -**án**, -**ón**, -**or**, -**és** change to -**ana**, -**ona**, -**ora**, -**esa**:

masc.	**el libro rojo**	*fem.* **la manzana roja**
	(the red book)	(the red apple)
masc.	**el hombre hablador**	*fem.* **la mujer habladora**
	(the talkative man)	(the talkative woman)

To make an adjective plural an **-s** is added to the singular form if it ends in a vowel. If the adjective ends in a consonant, **-es** is added:

masc.	**los libros rojos**	*fem.* **las manzanas rojas**
	(the red books)	(the red apples)
masc.	**los hombres habladores**	
	(the talkative men)	
fem.	**las mujeres habladoras**	
	(the talkative women)	

MY, YOUR, HIS, HER

These words also depend on the gender and number of the noun they accompany and not on the sex of the 'owner'.

	with masc. *sing. noun*	*with fem.* *sing. noun*	*with plural* *nouns*
my	**mi**	**mi**	**mis**
your (*familiar sing.*)	**tu**	**tu**	**tus**
your (*polite sing.*)	**su**	**su**	**sus**
his/her/its	**su**	**su**	**sus**
our	**nuestro**	**nuestra**	**nuestros/** **nuestras**
your (*familiar pl.*)	**vuestro**	**vuestra**	**vuestros/** **vuestras**
their	**su**	**su**	**sus**
your (*polite pl.*)	**su**	**su**	**sus**

There is no distinction between **his** and **her** in Spanish: **su billete** can mean either **his** or **her ticket**.

PRONOUNS

subject		*object*	
I	**yo**	**me**	**me**
you (*familiar sing.*)	**tú**	**you**	**te**
you (*polite sing.*)	**usted (Vd.)**	**you**	**le**
he/it	**él**	**him/it**	**le, lo**
she/it	**ella**	**her/it**	**le, la**
we	**nosotros**	**us**	**nos**
you (*familiar pl.*)	**vosotros**	**you**	**os**
you (*polite pl.*)	**ustedes (Vds.)**	**you**	**les**
they (*masc.*)	**ellos**	**them**	**les, los**
they (*fem.*)	**ellas**	**them**	**les, las**

Subject pronouns (**I**, **you**, **he**, etc.) are generally omitted in Spanish, since the verb ending distinguishes the subject:

hablo	I speak
hablamos	we speak

However, they are used for emphasis or to avoid confusion:

> yo voy a Mallorca y él va a Alicante
> <u>I</u> am going to Mallorca and <u>he</u> is going to Alicante

Object pronouns are placed before the verb in Spanish:

la veo	I see <u>her</u>
los conocemos	we know <u>them</u>

However, in commands or requests they follow the verb:

¡ayúdame!	help <u>me</u>!
¡escúchale!	listen to <u>him</u>

except when they are expressed in the negative:

¡no me ayudes!	don't help <u>me</u>
¡no le escuches!	don't listen to <u>him</u>

The object pronouns shown above can be used to mean to me, to us, etc., but to him/to her is **le** and to them is **les**. If **le** and **les** occur in combinations with **lo/la/las/los** then **le/les** change to **se**, e.g. **se lo doy** (I give it to him).

VERBS

There are three main patterns of endings for Spanish verbs – those ending -**ar**, -**er** and -**ir** in the dictionary.

	cantar	**to sing**
	canto	I sing
	cantas	you sing
(*usted*)	canta	(s)he sings/you sing
	cantamos	we sing
	cantáis	you sing
(*ustedes*)	cantan	they sing/you sing
	vivir	**to live**
	vivo	I live
	vives	you live
(*usted*)	vive	(s)he lives/you live
	vivimos	we live
	vivís	you live
(*ustedes*)	viven	they live/you live
	comer	**to eat**
	como	I eat
	comes	you eat
(*usted*)	come	(s)he eats/you eat
	comemos	we eat
	coméis	you eat
(*ustedes*)	comen	they eat/you eat

Like French, in Spanish there are two ways of addressing people: the polite form (for people you don't know well or who are older) and the familiar form (for friends, family and children). The polite you is **usted** in the singular, and **ustedes** in the plural. You can see from above that **usted** uses the same verb ending as for he and she; **ustedes** the same ending as for they. Often the words **usted** and **ustedes** are omitted, but the verb ending itself indicates that you are using the polite form. The informal words for you are **tú** (singular) and **vosotros** (plural).

THE VERB 'TO BE'

There are two different Spanish verbs for **to be** – **ser** and **estar**.

Ser is used to describe a permanent state:

soy inglés	I am English
es una playa	it is a beach

Estar is used to describe a temporary state or where something is located:

¿cómo está?	how are you?
¿dónde está la playa?	where is the beach?

	ser	to be
	soy	I am
	eres	you are
(usted)	es	(s)he is/you are
	somos	we are
	sois	you are
(ustedes)	son	they are/you are

	estar	to be
	estoy	I am
	estás	you are
(usted)	está	(s)he is/you are
	estamos	we are
	estáis	you are
(ustedes)	están	they are/you are

Other common irregular verbs include:

	tener	to have
	tengo	I have
	tienes	you have
(usted)	tiene	(s)he has/you have
	tenemos	we have
	tenéis	you have
(ustedes)	tienen	they have/you have

	ir	to go
	voy	I go
	vas	you go
(usted)	va	(s)he goes/you go
	vamos	we go
	vais	you go
(ustedes)	van	they go/you go

	poder	to be able
	puedo	I can
	puedes	you can
(usted)	puede	(s)he can/you can
	podemos	we can
	podéis	you can
(ustedes)	pueden	they can/you can

	querer	to want
	quiero	I want
	quieres	you want
(usted)	quiere	(s)he wants/you want
	queremos	we want
	queréis	you want
(ustedes)	quieren	they want/you want

	hacer	to do
	hago	I do
	haces	you do
(usted)	hace	(s)he does/you do
	hacemos	we do
	hacéis	you do
(ustedes)	hacen	they do/you do

	venir	to come
	vengo	I come
	vienes	you come
(usted)	viene	(s)he comes/you come
	venimos	we come
	venís	you come
(ustedes)	vienen	they come/you come

PAST TENSE

To form the past tense, for example: I gave/I have given,
I finished/I have finished, combine the present tense of the verb **haber** –
to have with the past participle of the verb (**cantado, comido, vivido**):

	haber	to have
	he	I have
	has	you have
(usted)	ha	(s)he has/you have
	hemos	we have
	habéis	you have
(ustedes)	han	they have/you have
e.g.	he cantado	I sang/I have sung
	ha comido	he ate/he has eaten
	hemos vivido	we lived/we have lived

To form a negative **no** is placed before all of the verb:

	no he cantado	I haven't sung
e.g.	no ha comido	he hasn't eaten
	no hemos vivido	we haven't lived